MW00997219

Psi Factor

Psi Factor

CHRONICLES OF THE PARANORMAL

ŁIJ

EDITED BY
Dan Aykroyd

WITH *Tommi Lewis*

ANDREWS AND McMEEL
A Universal Press Syndicate Company
Kansas City

PSI FACTOR: CHRONICLES OF THE PARANORMAL

© 1997 by Paranormal Productions, Inc. All rights reserved. Printed in the United States of America. No part of this book may be used or reproduced in any manner whatsoever without written permission except in the context of reviews. For information, write to: Andrews and McMeel, a Universal Press Syndicate Company, 4520 Main Street, Kansas City, Missouri 64111.

ISBN: 0-8362-2588-0

EDITED by Dan Aykroyd
WITH Tommi Lewis
DESIGN by Steven Stewart
COVER DESIGN by Tim Lynch

ACKNOWLEDGMENTS
To Erin Gebroe for assistance in script adaptation. To Jane Gillam for copyediting. To James Nadler, Atlantis Films, executive producer of PSI FACTOR: CHRONICLES OF THE PARANORMAL. Also to Bob Cook, Mary Beth McAdaragh, Andi Sporkin, and Todd Beck at Eyemark Entertainment. To Martha Mansfield at Atlantis Films. To Ruth Drizen Dohs. And Jake Morrissey, editor at Andrews and McMeel.

All photos in this book are taken directly from the PSI FACTOR television program except: pp. 12, 126, 126 Brooke Palmer; 34, 68, 154 George Kraychyk; and 170 Michael Courtney.

Library of Congress Cataloging-in-Publication data is on file with the Library of Congress.

PSI FACTOR: web site address
www. psifactor.com

CONTENTS

Like my great-grandfather, grandfather, and father before me, I have always been fascinated by the paranormal. Likewise, mankind has always been intrigued by ghosts, magic, and demonology; and these kinds of subjects figure prominently in our myths. People simply want to know more.

This is clearly one reason I was so eager to host the television series **Psi Factor: Chronicles of the Paranormal,** on which this book is based. Each chapter contains adapted scripts from the first fifteen episodes in the series. The stories have their own unique variation on the many facets of paranormal experiences.

It's important to remember that these stories are far from tall tales. They are, instead, dramas inspired by the investigations from one of the world's premier paranormal organizations, the Office of Scientific Investigation and Research (O.S.I.R.). The O.S.I.R. is the only investigative body of its kind that takes an objective look at anomalous events with a mandate to either prove a hoax, look for natural causes for paranormal events or analyze their unexplained aspects—if there are any.

It is my hope in presenting these stories that readers will not only be entertained but may come to understand more about the things that mystify us all. These real cases challenge our current comprehension of time, nature and life. Some stories may shock you; some may make you think and also debunk hoaxes where they exist.

DAN AYKROYD

HOST, PSI FACTOR: CHRONICLES OF THE PARANORMAL

ABOUT THE EDITOR

Actor and comedian Dan Aykroyd's great-grandfather was a dentist who followed the work of the British Society for Psychical Research. As a young boy, Aykroyd began a lifelong study of the paranormal. He was instrumental in convincing the Office of Scientific Investigation and Research (O.S.I.R.) to open up its case files to the public. In the fall of 1996, Aykroyd returned to television after seventeen years to host **Psi Factor: Chronicles of the Paranormal,** *a weekly dramatic anthology series inspired by the investigations of the O.S.I.R.*

CONNOR DOYLE
(PORTRAYED BY PAUL MILLER)

A former Navy commander, case manager Doyle is a born leader. He often feels torn between his role as an objective scientist and his desire to help people caught up in strange and frightening events.

CURTIS ROLLINS
(PORTRAYED BY MAURICE DEAN WINT)

Curtis Rollins is a behavioral scientist who spent several years with the FBI. The case manager brings intense dedication to solving cases. He believes there should be an answer to every mystery and puts his job above all of life's other priorities.

LINDSAY DONNER
(PORTRAYED BY NANCY ANN SAKOVICH)

She's got a double master's in psychology and biology and is the newest member of the O.S.I.R. team. Donner is smart, zealous, and continually questions the O.S.I.R.'s secretive practices.

ANTON HENDRICKS
(PORTRAYED BY COLIN FOX)

A psychiatrist, Hendricks mixes a rigorously intellectual approach to cases with heartfelt concern for the paranormal phenomena witnesses. He often gives a spiritual or even a philosophical spin to the events the team encounters.

PETER AXON
(PORTRAYED BY BARCLAY HOPE)

The O.S.I.R.'s investigations have altered how physicist/statistician Axon sees the world. Once a true skeptic, outspoken, sometimes abrasive, Axon now challenges conventional wisdom and the easy explanation.

RAY DONAHUE
(PORTRAYED BY PETER MACNEIL)

A onetime Chicago homicide police officer, team criminologist Donahue does not talk much about his mysterious past. On cases, he clears the path for the team with his knowledge of police procedures, mercenary tactics and crowd and riot control.

NATASHA CONSTANTINE
(PORTRAYED BY LISA LACROIX)

She's a former journalist who holds a master's degree in anthropology. Constantine is tough, driven, ambitious, and interested in exploring explanations beyond the purely scientific.

FRANK ELSINGER
(PORTRAYED BY NIGEL BENNET)

All case managers report to Elsinger, the O.S.I.R. Director of Operations. Soft-spoken and authoritative, Elsinger often has another agenda going that he cannot reveal to the team in the field.

DR. CLAIRE LINDA DAVISON
(PORTRAYED BY SOO GARAY)

A crack pathologist by training, Davison brings a critical eye to investigations.

L. Q. COOPER
(PORTRAYED BY PETER BLAIS)

The O.S.I.R.'s lead zoologist, he passionately studies any life form he encounters. His keen enthusiasms are sometimes lost on others, especially Axon.

SANDRA MILES
(PORTRAYED BY LINDSAY COLLINS)

A world-renowned forensic chemist, Miles attacks her work with insight and a wry sense of humor.

MARIAN SMITHWICK
(PORTRAYED BY ELIZABETH SHEPHERD)

One of the founders of the O.S.I.R., she helped draft the organization's rules and procedures when she joined in the mid-'60s. She is a warm but effective team leader.

DR. ALEXANDRA CORLISS
(PORTRAYED BY TAMARA GORSKI)

A team psychologist, Corliss is in her late twenties. For now, she has put her personal life on hold while she explores the unknown with the O.S.I.R.

ONE   C R Y P T O Z O O L O G Y

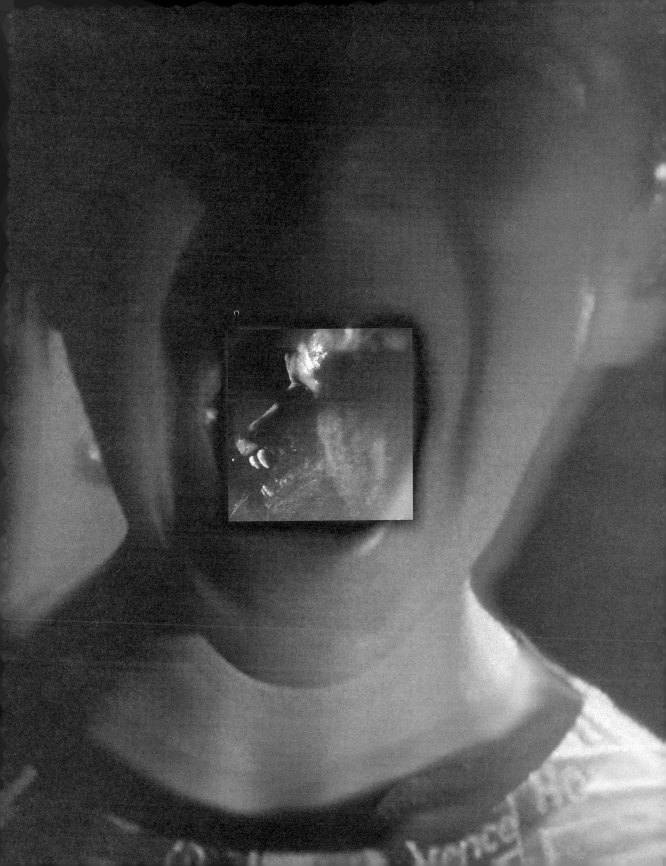

The Wolf Man, An American Werewolf in London and The Howling are horror films known to millions. What you may not know is that they were inspired in part by the documented cases of human lycanthropes, or werewolves, that were extensively witnessed and investigated in Saint Claude and Poligny, France, during the 1500s. These ancient accounts and the myths they originated remain an indelible part of our interest in the supernatural. Is it actually possible for a man to take on the physical attributes of a wolf? **DAN AYKROYD**

The HUNTER

TIME & PLACE *Late at night at a farm in Dexter County, Indiana.**

An old pickup truck stops near a toolshed, and George Collins gets out, whistling a tuneless tune. He begins to unload tools and put them in the shed when a ragged breathing comes over the pasture from a distance. George hears something and turns to listen. "Damn coyotes," he says, grabbing a flashlight and shotgun.

George moves into the field, shooing away what he assumes are coyotes. Then he stops. His face drains of color. Several cows lie in a bloody heap, their throats slashed and stomachs disemboweled.

Then George hears movement on the edge of the pasture. He looks up to see the shape of what appears to be a wild beast, illuminated by the full moon. Almost humanlike, it flashes into the woods.

TIME & PLACE *Later that day, several farmers and sheriff's deputies move through the forest in pairs.*

SHERIFF HARRISON REED walks through the woods with George Collins. "Ten head of cattle lost in three days, five last month alone," George says. "You try and run a farm with those figures."

*Names, places, and dates in this book have been changed to protect individuals' privacy.

"I know, George. We'll deal with it. It's probably just a mean pack of coyotes," Reed says.

"For the last time, Sheriff. It wasn't no coyotes, you got that? How do you explain three cows cut down with their stomachs ripped out in two seconds? One creature alone did it."

The farmers are still searching through the woods when Deputy Sheppard warns Ray Velez, a local farmhand, not to stray too far from the group. Everybody should be in pairs, but Ray wants a shot at finding and killing whatever they're after. As he hunts through the trees, aiming his rifle ahead, he hears a noise behind him. He whirls to see something as it barrels down on him.

Sheriff Reed, George and the others continue their search when suddenly Sheppard comes tearing in from out of the forest. "Sheriff! He's ... It got him! Oh sweet Lord, it got him!" Sheppard yells, pointing the search group toward Ray's body. The search group runs forward and, strangely, Sheppard hangs back watching the others' reactions.

Later, Sheriff Reed explains to O.S.I.R. case manager Connor Doyle what happened. "We went out looking for whatever was killing George Collins' livestock," he begins. "I thought it was just some bold coyotes, or even some kids pulling a sick joke on the old man. Until Velez was killed. Something ripped poor Ray to shreds not 100 yards away from one of my deputies."

"I SAW IT MYSELF. A HUGE, HAIRY MAN, SOMETIMES RUNNING ON ALL FOURS, WITH GLOWING EYES."

"Did you find anything out there, any evidence?" Doyle asks.

"We laid down traps all over the woods but never caught a thing."

O.S.I.R. investigators interview George Collins. "Something is killing my livestock," he says, "and it isn't some regular-type animal. It's a werewolf. I saw it myself. A huge, hairy man, sometimes running on all fours, with glowing eyes. Maybe you should talk to Galen. He was around that night. Always wandering around my land. Maybe he saw something."

Dexter County coroner Jackson Volstead discusses the autopsy results: "The damage to Mr. Velez's body matches the singular bite and claw marks we found on the mutilated livestock. The victim's throat was slashed first so as to silence him as quickly as possible. This was followed by swift disembowelment. He died from shock and blood loss. I can't conclusively determine what could have caused this kind of mutilation."

The next day, O.S.I.R. physicist/statistician Peter Axon and L. Q. Cooper, O.S.I.R.'s zoologist, walk into the pasture where George Collins first found his dead livestock. They see a decomposing cow surrounded by flies.

Approaching the animal, Cooper pulls out a pair of rubber surgeon's gloves and puts them on before handing a pair to Axon. "These incision marks are extraordinarily jagged," Cooper says. "Jugular severed just below the neck." Cooper reaches into the stomach of the cow and feels around. "Remarkable," he says. "This animal has no heart. It's missing."

"ACCORDING TO OUR information, he's apparently a drifter, no fixed address," Doyle says as they reach a wide alley between two warehouses. Several drifters stand around oil drums, warming themselves with the fires.

The O.S.I.R. operatives fan out in twos and threes to talk with them. A few start to move away as Doyle and O.S.I.R. psychobiologist Lindsay Donner approach. Then Doyle sees a dark, heavyset figure in a dirty overcoat turning the corner and entering the alley.

"Are you Galen?" Doyle asks as the other drifters back into the shadows.

"I'm really very busy right now. It's a bad time, actually," Galen says.

"Please. It'll only take a minute," Donner says.

"For you, pretty lady, five minutes," Galen says.

"There have been some livestock killings out on the Collins farm. Do you know anything about it?" Donner asks.

"LAB REPORTS SAY THE WOLF AND HUMAN PRINTS ARE AUTHENTIC," DOYLE SAYS. "IF IT'S A HOAX, IT'S A DAMN GOOD ONE."

"The locals say that they've seen you there wandering through the woods," Doyle says.

"We aren't going to charge you with any crime. We just want to know if you saw anything unusual," Donner says.

"Just fresh air. Trees. Birds. The smell of real food. That's all. It's public land. I have rights."

"A man named Ray Velez was murdered out there last week," Doyle explains. "If you remember anything we should know, you can contact us through Sheriff Reed."

"I'M THINKING ABOUT the autopsy report," Cooper says. "All the cattle we found were missing their hearts, but Velez, the man who died ... Our pathologist said his vitals were left intact. Whatever attacked him was out to kill, but it didn't want a trophy."

"You think it was a different killer?" Axon asks.

"The method and claw marks match, but I think the reasoning behind Velez's murder might be divergent," Axon says.

"Animals attack for two reasons," Cooper says. "One, for food. Two, to protect their territory. I think whatever this thing is, people came too close for comfort, and it felt threatened."

Just then, an investigator calls them over to fresh single-file animal tracks in the mud. "Unmistakable. You can tell by the paw-pad formation," Cooper says. *"Canis lupus—wolf."*

Cooper and Axon follow the trail of wolf prints through the woods. Slowly the prints become those of a barefoot human. Doyle speaks into his recorder: "Case log update. We have completed the initial phase of our investigation. All evidence points to a violent, unpredictable life form of tremendous strength and power."

In the mobile lab, the main screen shows the altered footprints Cooper and Axon found.

"Psychological assessments of the witnesses reveal strong paranoia; this community is frightened and angry," O.S.I.R. psychiatrist Hendricks says.

"Lab reports say the wolf and human prints are authentic," Doyle adds. "If it is a hoax, it's a damn good one."

"Our psychological profile shows that this could be the work of a psychotic individual suffering from a clinical psychological disorder known as lycanthropy, when the subject believes he is able to become a wolf," Hendricks says.

"I don't see how the claw and bite marks could possibly be man-made," Cooper says, confused.

"There is also an epidermal condition known as hypertrichosis, when someone has hair coming out of every pore in their skin," Hendricks says.

"I don't know if hypertrichosis explains some psycho ripping the hearts out of half a dozen cattle and murdering a farmhand," Cooper says.

About an hour before sundown, Axon and Cooper, equipped with night-vision goggles and thermal cameras, move toward the woods. They hide in some underbrush overlooking the pasture.

George Collins and Sheriff Reed join Donner and Doyle nearby. "You sure you know what you're doing? There's a lot of people out here waiting for something real deadly to wander by," Reed says. "Just you take care of this nice lady," Reed warns Doyle. He heads off.

"Nice guy," Doyle notes.

That night, Sheriff Reed drives his jeep along the dark county road. Seeing something, he slows to a halt and gets out, noticing the freshly killed carcass of a mutilated cow. Reed bends down to look closer.

Reed walks back to his jeep and gets in the driver's side, leaving his door open. He calls for the dispatcher on the radio, but his voice trails off as he senses the presence of something.

"Oh, Lord," Reed says as a creature leaps upon him with lightning speed. The creature rips Sheriff Reed to pieces, and his bloodied body falls onto the road.

In the mobile lab, Doyle hears the dispatcher trying to reach Sheriff Reed over the radio. Worried, Doyle leaves to look for Reed, whom he finds mutilated in the road.

■TIME & PLACE■■ *A couple of hours later, Doyle, Donner, Cooper, Axon and Hendricks meet for a round table.*

" C O O P E R ,   Y O U R   R E P O R T   mentioned the possibility of this creature reacting to an invasion of its territory," Doyle says.

"Possibly," Cooper says, "but the kills have been expanding in location.

"And part of this doesn't make sense. Wolves hunt in packs. This creature seems to hunt alone," Cooper says.

"But kills like a wolf," Donner says. "All kills, both human and animal, occurred during the height of a lunar cycle, which corresponds to ancient werewolf legends."

"Two days left of full moon," Axon notes.

"It pulled that cow from a neighboring farm and left it on the road for someone to find," Donner adds. "It laid a trap."

That evening, Doyle moves through the lab as investigators man consoles and view scanning monitors. Donner and Axon are at a scanning post on the edge of the woods.

"To tell you the truth," Donner tells Axon, "I don't like having to carry weapons. They make me nervous."

"They're just there as a precaution. Doyle's being extra-cautious," Axon says.

Donner suddenly points to a tracking scanner. The flashing light on the screen blinks, accompanied by an increasingly fast beeping. Axon and Donner turn to see a dark shape in the underbrush. Then it's gone.

THE CREATURE CLOSES IN ON DONNER AGAIN. SHE RECOGNIZES A LONGING IN ITS EYES, A HUMANITY.

Doyle notes movement too and alerts Axon and Donner through the comlink. Doyle's monitor shows an image of the creature as it indistinctly flashes through the field. It runs low to the ground and incredibly fast toward a group of livestock.

Nearby, a wolf's howl pierces the night. Donner tries to pick up the figure on her night-vision goggles again. "It's moving too fast. I can't lock on to it," she says.

Axon turns as the creature claws at his face. Falling back, he clutches his head. The creature knocks over Donner, who loses her night-vision goggles. As she gets to her feet, trying to keep calm, she looks out into the dim night. "Peter," Donner whispers, slowly reaching for her gun.

The creature closes in on Donner again. It looks at her for a moment. She recognizes a longing in its eyes, a humanity. Then snarling, it leaps. Donner swiftly raises her gun, firing repeatedly at the creature, which howls in pain as the bullets find their mark. It rapidly shuffles off toward the woods.

The investigators leave the lab to search in the forest.

Axon sits up groggily, his forehead bleeding profusely. He smiles grimly as he gets to his feet. Nearby, the creature's hairy hands claw across the field. Increasingly weak, it breathes more raggedly. Then it slumps, finally dead. Slowly, its wolflike hands become human.

A formation of O.S.I.R. operatives in night-vision goggles moves through the field in a sweep formation, and one yells that he's found the animal. Doyle and Donner run over.

On the ground lies Galen, the drifter. Bullet holes cover his chest, and blood bathes his face and neck.

Doyle gives a final case log entry: "An autopsy on a transient known only as Galen reveals that the bullets in his body matched Donner's gun. As well, partially digested livestock organs were found inside his stomach. How Galen transformed into a beastlike creature remains a mystery. All livestock killings in this county have stopped since the end of this case."

Epilogue

It would appear from the documented circumstances in this case that the transient Galen did in fact assume the physical characteristics of a wolf with murderous effect. Moreover, this does not seem to be an isolated event. There have been multiple reports of this type from around the world. And the physiological process of transformation from Homo sapiens *to* Canis lupus *remains a mystery.*

D A N   A Y K R O Y D

A harmless recluse dies in a small rural community. A strange chain of occurrences follows that terrorizes the residents. Could there be a connection between the events? This was the question that ultimately confronted the O.S.I.R. in one of its most challenging and frightening cases.

DAN AYKROYD

Reptilian REVENGE

TIME & PLACE *The middle of the day at a dilapidated stone farmhouse in Blind River, Wisconsin.*

As Tyler approaches the farmhouse with Mr. Donizetti's groceries, he calls out, but nobody answers. The tall, skinny delivery boy gently pushes the front door open and walks inside.

Setting the groceries on the kitchen counter, Tyler hears an intense rattling sound coming from the basement. Puzzled, he heads down the dark stairway. The noise intensifies. It sounds like a windstorm rattling a hundred windows.

In the basement at the end of a dimly lit hallway is a door, which Tyler tries to open. It's jammed but gives a few inches when Tyler pushes on it. Tyler peers through the crack and sees two legs sprawled out behind the door. With his shoulder, he shoves the door open and finds the 80-year-old Mr. Donizetti on the floor, clenching a pistol and bathed in blood. Horrified but still confounded by the sound, he looks up, sees something terrifying and takes off in a heated run.

TIME & PLACE *Later that day at the farmhouse, young Tyler waits outside while two police officers investigate inside.*

WITH REVOLVERS DRAWN Sheriff Karen

Newman, 40, and 28-year-old Deputy Carl Hall move cautiously down the stairs toward the room. "Let's be careful," Newman says softly.

Hall nods and pushes open the door to the room. Newman kneels down next to Mr. Donizetti's body, checking for a pulse. "He's cold, been here for a while," she says, standing and looking around the room. It's a large room lit with blue-and-green-gelled heat lamps. Dozens of mesh, glass and plastic cages sit on shelves; some are tipped over on the floor; some are empty.

"What was the old coot keeping down here?" Hall asks.

"Whatever they were, they're not here now," Newman says.

TIME & PLACE   *A few hours later at the sherriff's office.*

DEPUTY HALL ESCORTS Conrad Paul Reyes, 30-ish,

out of his cell. "We're not going to see you in here anytime soon, Reyes?" Hall asks.

Reyes, suffering from a nasty hangover, grunts a response. "Sign here and you're on your way," Hall says, sliding a form in front of him. "And, Conrad," Hall says, "next time someone looks at you funny in a bar, just walk away."

Minutes later, Newman walks up to the dispatch desk, holding a manila envelope. "That wasn't Conrad Paul Reyes I just saw stumbling out of here, was it?" she asks Hall.

"Sleeping off a D&D, poor fool. Now he's got a doozie of a hangover. What's in the envelope?" Hall asks.

"The preliminary on Donizetti," Newman says. "Suicide from a single shot to the head."

"So that's settled, but what about the delivery kid's story?"

"He must have been hallucinating or something. Or maybe the trauma of seeing the old man there on the floor ..." Newman stops mid-sentence, holding her hand up for silence. Hall watches as she moves to an air-vent grate high on the wall. They hear a rattling sound. Something is moving in the vent.

Annoyed, Newman grabs a wire hanger, stands on a chair and pries off the grate.

Dozens of snakes are staring back at her through the opened vent. "Oh, God, oh, God," she says, choking back a yell. Rattlesnakes, vipers, pythons and cobras spill out onto the floor. On Newman's cue, she and Hall run for the back door. Behind them, the snakes take over the police station.

TIME & PLACE   *Later that day in the O.S.I.R. mobile lab, case manager Connor Doyle, criminologist Ray Donahue, zoologist L. Q. Cooper, psychiatrist Dr. Anton Hendricks, physicist/statistician Peter Axon, and psychobiologist Lindsay Donner view a video of the snakes discovered at the police station.*

CASE MANAGER DOYLE speaks into a recorder.

"File #99101. Concern for the safety of the Blind River citizens encouraged the County Sheriff's Department to contact the O.S.I.R. for assistance to deal with complaint of a purported snake migration phenomenon." Doyle pauses the video and turns to the team.

"This footage is inexplicable," Cooper says.

"Man, I feel for those officers," Axon says.

"Not a big fan of the mysterious slithering serpent, are we, Peter?" Donner chides.

"I don't like snakes, no," Axon answers.

"Cooper," Doyle says, "any plausible explanations for the phenomenon come to mind?"

"A family of snakes migrating is common enough, depending on the particular habitat and time of year, of course," Cooper answers. "But the variety of species described, traveling together as a unified group, defies categorization."

"Donner, you and Anton proceed with preliminary interviews," Doyle orders. "See what the subjects are saying and if they all saw the same thing. And Peter, oversee the on-site inspection and circumstantial assessment."

"Great. I can't wait," Axon says.

TIME & PLACE   *Back at the sheriff's office, a handful of scared citizens gathers.*

" Y O U   F O U N D   T H O S E   snakes yet?" demands one resident.

"Yeah, Sheriff, what are you doing about it?" pleads another.

"Settle down. We have no concrete evidence the snakes are still here. They've probably moved on," Newman answers, in a vain attempt to maintain calm.

"Give me a break, Newman. You're as scared as the rest of us. Someone's going to get killed!"

Meanwhile, the O.S.I.R. investigators replay videotaped interviews in the mobile lab, searching for an explanation.

"I don't know why I went inside," the delivery boy says, shaking. "I mean, I knew Mr. Donizetti was a little weird, but he never leaves his house, and I just wanted to make sure the old guy was okay. When I went down to that room and saw him on the floor with all those snakes freaking out and banging on the walls of their cages, I was never more scared in my life."

Deputy Hall describes his experience with equal terror: "Sheriff Newman pried off the air-vent grate," he explains, "and out they came. They were everywhere, and how Newmie kept her cool is still beyond me. She grabbed me and we ran out back. Actually, I ran and jumped on a shed where we keep the lawn mower while Newmie just kept running. Then it was the strangest thing. The snakes came out of the station, moving in a group as if they were being led along. Then they turned and headed through the parking lot and disappeared into the field. All moving together."

Video footage also shows interviews with witnesses on the street: "We were walking back from a movie when all of a sudden those snakes came down the sidewalk, straight at us," one witness says. "I mean, there must have been at least a hundred of them. Then they just went past us, through my legs even. And the next thing I know, they're gone. Not a scratch. It was a miracle to be sure."

The O.S.I.R. investigators return to Mr. Donizetti's house to speak with neighbor Carlene Jansen, who's lived next door for 10 years. Jansen knew about the snake collection, she says, but didn't realize how dangerous it was. "A lot of folks are saying that the snakes are some ghostly manifestations of him. I will tell you one thing, though. He loved those snakes and cared for them as if they were his own children." Inside Mr. Donizetti's house, zoologist Cooper examines the homemade cages. "They wouldn't keep a hamster inside, much less a king cobra," he says, picking up a cobra's shedded skin among evidence of 18 different snake species from around the world.

"How did the delivery boy find Donizetti?" Donahue asks.

"Lying back this way with the gun still in his hand," answers physicist Peter Axon.

Donahue sighs, looking puzzled. "It's just that in twelve years in homicide," he says, "I never saw a suicide victim found with the gun still in his hand."

Later in the day in the O.S.I.R. mobile lab, a roundtable is in progress. A map of Blind River is projected on a screen.

"MY ASSESSMENTS CONFIRM that

some phenomenon is responsible for creating extreme phobic-related behaviors in the townspeople," Hendricks says.

"How is it manifesting itself?" Doyle asks.

"High-anxiety levels, increased blood pressure. Unfortunately, I found no direct correlation between my findings and the described phenomenon."

"Environmental assessment, Peter?" Doyle asks.

"No hazardous materials or toxic gases. All chemical and geophysical analyses came up negative as to explain why a massive group of snakes would be witnessed," Axon reports.

"DON'T MOVE A MUSCLE," COOPER WARNS. "EVERYONE FREEZE! THEY'RE ALL AROUND US!"

"And Donizetti's place?" Doyle asks.

"No contributing factors found. It's clean, except for one thing," Axon says. "He had poisonous snakes as pets."

"Cooper, what've you got?" Doyle asks.

Cooper brings up some video footage of a variety of snakes. "Here are some of the different species I've been able to determine thus far," Cooper says. "I have evidence of king cobras cohabiting with rattlers. Not only are cobras snake eaters, but they are extremely territorial."

"Yet, witnesses have reported these species traveling together?" Doyle asks.

"Precisely. In extremely rare cases I've come across unrelated species gathering together to escape an immediate threat, like a forest fire. But, as a rule, it's completely contrary to their instincts," Cooper explains.

"Remarkable there've been no reported injuries to the public from the snakes to date," says Donner.

"Physically hurt, no," offers Hendricks. "But psychologically the people of Blind River are pretty shaken up."

"Initiate counseling sessions," Doyle orders. "And Code Red is still in effect. Proceed with environmental monitoring and surveillance."

Behind the sheriff's office the next day, Donahue, Cooper, Axon and Donner move through the trees, armed with environmental-scanning equipment as well as motion-detecting sensors.

"MOVE SLOW AND easy," Cooper says. "Snakes are deaf to airborne sounds. They respond to movement and vibrations." Cooper leads the way, sweeping at the grass with a long stick.

"I don't like this," Axon says, nervously.

"Don't worry. Chances are slim of us encountering snakes, or any other reptiles for that matter at this time of day," Cooper says.

Donahue stops suddenly off to the side. He stares intensely at his beeping motion-detecting sensor, then peers up into the thick foliage. The others have all stopped in their tracks, looking in the same direction. "Movement detected. Coming fast, coming right at us," Donahue says.

Axon backs away and stumbles. The beeping increases in volume and frequency, then stops suddenly. "What's happening?" Axon asks. Behind Axon, a snake lowers from a tree branch, settling inches from his head. The snake flicks its tongue. Axon turns to find himself face to face with the reptile.

"Don't move a muscle!" Cooper warns. "Everyone freeze! They're all around us."

Axon slides away from the snakes, but they continue to slither toward him and the rest of the investigators. Miraculously, the snakes pass by them.

TIME & PLACE Later that night at the O.S.I.R. mobile lab unit, investigators feed a mouse to a diamondback rattler they've caught.

COOPER HAS INSERTED a tracking device in the mouse so the investigators can monitor the snake's movements. They free the snake, and it eagerly rejoins its mates.

After studying the grounds of a citizen's home where the snakes had been, the investigators brainstorm in the mobile lab unit.

"Mr. Edmunds said he'd experienced a break-in the night before we found the snakes gathered below his house," Cooper says.

"And we discovered several other break-ins that correlate with the dates and times of several of the reported snake sightings," says Lindsay Donner.

"But every time I go to predict their next movement," Cooper says, "the snakes change their pattern."

Doyle asks for an update on Mr. Donizetti's death. "Why he committed suicide remains a mystery," Donner says, "since he left no note."

Just then, Donahue walks in, announcing that the autopsy shows that Mr. Donizetti suffocated before enduring the gunshot. Mr. Donizetti was murdered. Doyle orders a couple of operators to see if anyone unusual visited Blind River at the time of the murder and if that person could be linked to the break-ins.

From the monitoring device inside the diamondback rattler, investigators inside the mobile lab detect the snakes moving in the northeast area of town. Someone shouts for help. "Let's move in, near the Quik-Bite Cafe. They appear to be chasing someone," investigator Wilkinson says.

As the investigators prepare to leave, **REPTILIAN** R E V E N G E
the door of the Quik-Bite Cafe crashes open,
and a disheveled-looking man bursts in asking where the bathroom is. The short-order cook points downstairs as the people eating turn their heads, alarmed. The cook leans over the counter to look out the front door. Dozens of snakes are forcing themselves against the door, squeezing it open a crack so they can slither through. The patrons are now screaming.

The disheveled man runs downstairs to the men's bathroom, but it's locked. He desperately bangs on the door. The snakes slide down the stairs. The man panics. He bangs on another locked door. He backs into the hallway's dead end. A snake rushes him and strikes. He tumbles to the ground, the snake firmly clamped to his leg. Dozens of snakes attack him as the investigators pull up outside—too late.

Clad in protective chaps and overalls, the investigators move cautiously down the stairs, unsure of what they will find.

"It's too quiet," Donahue whispers. "I don't like it."

"Still no sign of snakes, but wait a minute." Cooper sees a man's foot at the end of the hall. "Someone's here! Stand by!"

They see a man lying on his back, dead. His arms and legs are covered in bites. His face, frozen in terror.

"He's been bitten," Cooper says, "but I can't tell how many times."

Donahue rushes over. "We've got a match to the other set of fingerprints we found on the Smith and Wesson shells at Donizetti's house. It's coming through right now." An officer comes downstairs with a printout photo. Doyle grabs it.

"Conrad Paul Reyes. Age 34. History of misdemeanors, three convictions. Current address"—Doyle looks up—"the Blind River morgue." The man in the picture and the dead body on the floor match; they are the same man.

Several weeks later, Doyle gives a log update: "Mr. Donizetti's murderer, Conrad Paul Reyes, suffered more than 300 snake bites, not to mention that several of his bones were crushed and shattered. It appears that the old man's death resulted from a robbery gone bad. We have been monitoring Blind River, but have found no trace of the snakes, nor were there any further sightings."

Epilogue

Over the next several weeks, the residents reported dozens of rare snakes found dead from unknown causes in the woods surrounding the Blind River region. Perhaps the old man's etheric life energy or some type of non-corporeal psi interactive force manipulated the many different snakes he cared for to hunt down and kill his murderer. Then there's another speculation open to us. It might not be a scientific one, but it seems to describe perfectly the very heart of what occurred: Donizetti's snakes were acting out of love and revenge.

DAN AYKROYD

The family home—ideally a place where parents create a sanctuary from the uncertainties and turmoil of the world outside. Jeremy Stansky, a happy, healthy 8-year-old boy, had every reason to expect that his home was a safe refuge from danger and strife. His mother, Debbie, and father, Kevin, believed that their own diligent efforts had made this family home the loving, comfortable haven their child deserved. Yet despite Jeremy's expectations, under cover of darkness, a mysterious intruder entered their refuge, violated its tranquillity and created a nightmare. A nightmare the O.S.I.R. was brought in to dispel.   **DAN AYKROYD**

The PRESENCE

TIME & PLACE   *The middle of the night in the Stanskys' home in Seattle, Washington.*

Jeremy Stansky's eyes are open, but his face is blank. The 8-year-old boy sleepwalks downstairs, through the hallway. He passes a cage, in which two gerbils are hyperventilating. Jeremy stops at the kitchen, staring ahead. Dirty dishes litter the counter. Jeremy stands swaying when suddenly his eyes widen.

In the master bedroom, Debbie Stansky, 38, sleeps alone. A cacophonous crashing from downstairs wakes the attractive woman, who bolts awake with a gasp. Pulling on her robe, Debbie hurries downstairs. Jeremy stands transfixed at the kitchen entrance. As she approaches him, Jeremy wakes up. Debbie looks past him, startled to see the floor strewn with broken dishes.

"Jeremy! For crying out loud," she yells, but her expression softens as she sees Jeremy's face.

"Mom, it's here again," Jeremy says.

She puts her arm around him. "No one's here but you and me, kiddo. You were sleep-walking again."

"It's back, Mom. It's back. In the kitchen, I swear!"

"Okay, honey. I'll clean this up after we get you back to bed. Come on."

Before they reach the top of the stairs, they hear another loud crash from the kitchen. Debbie wheels around, instinctively clutching Jeremy.

TIME & PLACE *Later that night, Kevin Stansky, 39, walks in the front door with his suitcase, returning from a business trip.*

DEBBIE GREETS HIM, and he goes upstairs to unpack.

"As soon as I told Sally Burchill what's been happening, she got right on the phone to this man," Debbie explains. "He's part of some special psychic hotline."

"Unquiet spirits in your home? Dial 1-800-FLAKES," Kevin says, skeptical.

"Kevin, you haven't been here. I don't know what's happening, but whatever it is, it's scaring the hell out of me."

Just then, Jeremy appears at their bedroom door holding Mr. Grimshaw, his teddy bear. "Daddy, I'm scared," he says.

"I know, son. Everything's all right." He turns to his wife. "Debbie, I think we should start by asking someone who knows what they're doing." They hear another loud crash downstairs. Jeremy cries out, hugging his father.

TIME & PLACE *The next morning O.S.I.R. case manager Connor Doyle speaks into a headset while two technicians conduct tests with a variety of equipment in the Stansky home.*

"FILE #92109, 0930 hours. Connor Doyle. On-

site inspection, assessment and preliminary interviews under way. Final objective is to locate and identify the phenomenon."

The investigators study videotaped footage of psychic Desmond Mohns. "I could tell by her emotions she had encountered an active malevolence," Mohns begins. "It surrounded her aura. When I visited her home, I could distinctly feel this evil presence. It was a vengeful spirit. I even had a plan to dispel it ... until you people showed up."

The tape switches to the Stanskys. "All I know is something is going on in our house," Kevin says. "And it isn't some kind of 'vengeful spirit.' I can't figure it out, so I called a friend who works at the University of Washington. He connected me with your organization."

"No, I don't want to believe in all that stuff the psychic said, but who knows," Debbie says. "Lately, I'd almost believe in ghosts or poltergeists if that's what it takes to get rid of it. I'm frightened. My little boy is frightened, terrified. He refuses to go to sleep in our house."

Jeremy explains his experience: "I hadn't seen it in a while, but now it came back. It looked right at me. It wanted to get me, but Mommy saved me. I'm scared."

Jeremy sits at a small desk in the corner of his room petting Ripple, the family cat. O.S.I.R. psychologist Dr. Alexandra Corliss sits on the edge of the bed.

"Is that your cat, Jeremy?" Corliss asks.

"This is Ripple. He's everyone's cat."

"Jeremy, your mom tells me you said 'It's back' the other night. What did you mean?"

"I don't remember," Jeremy says.

"Are you sure?"

"All right. It was Mr. Grimshaw. Are you happy now?"

"Who is Mr. Grimshaw, Jeremy?"

Jeremy picks up his teddy bear. "Grimshaw the bear," he says. "Don't you know anything? He did it. All of it."

In the back yard, Corliss asks Kevin and Debbie when the sleepwalking started. "Two months ago, maybe?" Kevin guesses.

"Something like that. I talked to a doctor. She said I shouldn't be too concerned and hopefully it's just a phase," Debbie says.

"Dr. Corliss, do you really think Jeremy could be responsible for the damage?" Kevin asks.

"I've heard that children can sometimes generate poltergeists," Debbie says. "You know, talk with spirits."

"We can't reach any conclusions until we have all the data in," Corliss says. "I'll have a better idea when I regress Jeremy using hypnosis."

TIME & PLACE   Corliss draws the curtains in the living room, asking Jeremy if he can hear her.

"YES," JEREMY RESPONDS.

"I want you to understand that you're perfectly safe. Nothing can hurt you. Jeremy, you're in the house. Are you alone?" Corliss asks.

"No. It's here."

"I want you to go back to the last time you saw it. Where are you?"

"In the kitchen. It's night," Jeremy says, his breathing speeding up.

"What do you see?"

"I hear it. Breathing."

"Breathing how?"

Jeremy mimics Darth Vader-like breathing. Corliss looks at Doyle. Jeremy is now verging toward panic.

"And I see its eyes. Red eyes. Glowing at me. Red eyes!" Jeremy says.

"Jeremy, who is looking at you?" Corliss asks.

"The monster! He's going to get me!"

"He's getting hysterical," Corliss tells Doyle. "We'll try again later. Jeremy, come back now." Jeremy gasps, and his eyes flutter open.

Later, the full O.S.I.R. team gathers in the mobile lab for a roundtable session.

"Family psychodynamics are fairly normal given the circumstances. Mr. Stansky's work forces him to travel, which may result in some unspecified anxiety in Jeremy," Corliss says.

"Did the hypnosis reveal anything about the incident?" Doyle asks.

"Only that his imagination is quite vivid, or he really saw something outlandish that night," Corliss says. "His age makes it difficult to gauge his perceptions. He's still learning how to separate the real from the imagined."

"Peter, bring us up to speed on your analysis," Doyle says.

"We ran full environmental scans on the house and surrounding area. Baseline results are all well within the normal range. No toxic gases, no contaminants in the food or water, no abnormal concentrations of energy fields," physicist/statistician Axon reports.

In the house, Jeremy tentatively moves down the basement stairs. "Ripple? Here, kitty!"

Jeremy is being watched by someone, or something, in the rafters. Debbie calls down the basement stairs to Jeremy. "Jeremy! Come upstairs and wash up!"

"What about Ripple? I can't find him," Jeremy says. Before Jeremy turns to go, he looks back. Finally, he leaves, still being watched by ... something.

After dinner, O.S.I.R. investigators rig up sophisticated audio and video equipment. Two technicians hook a pajama-clad Kevin up to a biophysical monitoring system. Jeremy, scared, hovers nearby.

In the mobile lab, Doyle, Axon and the technicians view a bank of monitors with various views of the house. One monitor features the sleeping Jeremy. Superimposed on his image are scrolling biostatistics. Jeremy starts to twitch.

"Hold on. Biostats rising in sector seven," Axon says.

Jeremy then moves into the hallway. Sleep-walking, he starts downstairs, moving toward the kitchen. Over his shoulder, he stops in the doorway. As he stares into the dark kitchen, a deep whooshing sound intensifies. Fear floods his face.

"IF JEREMY EVEN SEES AN AD ON TV FOR A HORROR FILM, IT MEANS WEEKS OF SLEEPLESS NIGHTS."

Out of the darkness, a barely discernible amorphous shape appears, its two red eyes glowing. The whooshing sound reaches a terrifying pitch, and Jeremy's face registers panic. The dark shape begins to take the shape of a monster.

"The kid's biostats are going through the roof," Axon says.

The surveillance monitor shows Jeremy's figure still lying in bed, twitching frantically. He then awakens with a jolt and bolts upright.

TIME & PLACE *Outside the Stansky house the next morning, Kevin Stansky runs across the front lawn to Doyle.*

"MY KID IS a mess, Mr. Doyle," Kevin says. "He won't eat, and he looks exhausted. He's shaking in fear, talking about monsters. I think he's about ready to snap."

"I understand he's in some emotional distress. We learned that much from our assessments. Mr. Stansky, is there anything that could've precipitated his condition? Anything we could have missed?"

"I don't know. He's just going through a very tough phase. If he even sees an ad on TV for a horror film, it means weeks of sleepless nights."

"I understand. I have noticed that Jeremy's behavior has become erratic since we arrived," Doyle says. "He could be in need of some stability."

"Mr. Doyle, we need a break, time away from here. We need to calm Jeremy down."

"We could move you out temporarily and try a different approach to monitoring the house. We'll move you out tonight."

The following week, two O.S.I.R. technicians monitor a bank of video screens showing various parts of the house. Doyle, Axon and Corliss approach the mobile unit. An O.S.I.R. security operative stands watch.

"Peter? Your take on the situation?" Doyle asks.

"It's been a week and, as of yet, no observable phenomenon has been detected."

"Agreed," Doyle says, "but let's not discount the accuracy of each individual's story during DEP testing. Let's return the Stanskys to their home and maintain environmental surveillance."

The house is dark and empty as Doyle and Axon enter, flicking on a light. They step back, motioning the Stanskys to proceed into the house. Jeremy, pale, comes in, clutching Mr. Grimshaw. Doyle briskly flips on lights. Axon pauses in the downstairs hallway as he passes the thermostat. He frowns, reaching to adjust it.

SUDDENLY, FROM DOWNSTAIRS COMES A LOUD CRASH. "SOMETHING KNOCKED THE CAMERA OVER," AN O.S.I.R. TECHNICIAN SAYS.

"Someone altered the environment. Temperature differential at minus 15 degrees," Axon says into his headset.

Doyle sees the door to the basement stairs half open, leading down into darkness. As he turns to leave, he stops, looking around again, then moving to the door. Someone, or something, is watching.

Meanwhile, in another part of the house, Debbie moves quietly through the hall toward Jeremy's room. Concerned, she gently opens the door to find Jeremy moaning and twitching in his sleep. She gently pulls up the blanket covering Jeremy, who is clutching a small handmade cross. He clutches Mr. Grimshaw, the teddy bear, in the other hand.

Downstairs in the kitchen, Corliss talks to Kevin. "You know how it is," Kevin says. "Once you let your imagination get the better of you ..."

"If we had any reason to believe your family was in danger, you wouldn't be here. We'll be monitoring you constantly from the mobile unit," Corliss assures him.

Kevin slides a frozen dessert into the microwave. The heat from the furnace in the basement comes on through the vent with a low whoosh. Colorful plastic strands tied to the vent shoot into the air. Corliss turns to look at the vent.

"Just the heat coming on," Kevin says.

Kevin switches on the microwave. Corliss glances at it, noticing the two red lights—the colon between digits—on the microwave's control panel light up. She swivels to look back at the heating vent.

An hour later in the mobile lab, the team watches the tape of Jeremy's hypnosis session. He demonstrates the Darth Vader-like breathing of the "intruder."

"A N D   N O W   I see its eyes. Red eyes. Glowing at me. Red eyes!" Jeremy says on the tape, which Corliss stops.

"It's only a theory, at this point, but it certainly points toward a rational explanation for the boy's story," she says.

"A composite memory," Doyle says, nodding.

"I'll run more tests to confirm it, but hypothetically he saw something while in a sleepwalking state. This half-imagined image got mixed up with two other sense-impressions associated with the kitchen—the sound from the heat vent and the red lights on the microwave," Corliss says.

"And we have our 'demon,' but the question remains: What did the actual damage?" Doyle wonders.

The team keeps vigil. Suddenly, a technician sees something change on a seismic accelerometer. They focus in on the monitor showing the kitchen, but nothing is moving now.

Back in the master bedroom, Debbie hangs up her robe. She gets into bed beside Kevin when Jeremy lets out a piercing scream. Debbie and Kevin rush into Jeremy's room. "What's wrong, sweetie?" Debbie asks.

"The monster! It's here! I saw it!"

"It was a dream, Jeremy. That's all," Kevin says.

Then, from downstairs comes a loud crash. On monitor three in the mobile lab, the image suddenly goes wonky. It shows the kitchen sideways, from floor level. "Something knocked the camera over. Additional vibrations coming from the kitchen," a technician says.

Meanwhile, something huge slides down the basement stairs into the darkness. The technician swiftly rewinds the tape, punching in a key code. A dark shadow floods the monitor screen.

Corliss stands at Doyle's shoulder. They look at each other, surprised, and Doyle runs to the house. He hurries inside, followed by several security operatives carrying flashlights and environmental monitoring equipment.

Kevin looks down from the top of the stairs, his family clustered fearfully behind him. "What is it?" he asks.

Doyle and his team thunder down the basement stairs. Doyle swiftly moves his flashlight around. "Up there!" yells an operative.

Doyle swivels to look. The operative is pointing at the ceiling, where his light illuminates a 24-foot python hanging massively across the wooden beams.

Later that night, Doyle speaks into his recorder: "Final case log entry. Our monster is a giant green python, *Python molurus bivittatus.* Originally kept as a pet by a couple on the next block. When they moved out and abandoned it, the snake must have found its way into the local sewer system. The reptile gained access to the Stansky home through a basement drain. Our initial setup activity then frightened it off. In addition, the low thermostat while the family vacated the house temporarily made it too cold an environment to inhabit. The whereabouts of the family cat remains unknown."

Corliss sits with Jeremy upstairs in his room. "... And then your imagination did the rest, convincing you there was some sort of monster in the house. There was something there, but it wasn't a monster. There's nothing to be afraid of now," she explains.

Jeremy remains silent, still disturbed.

Epilogue

The intruder that violated the Stansky home was neither a malevolent poltergeist, nor a grotesque monster, nor a mysterious undiscovered force of nature. It was just a very ordinary and very earthbound reptile. After the python was removed to the local zoo, the Stansky family experienced no further nocturnal visitations, and they resumed their normal lives undisturbed. Jeremy's sleepwalking phase eventually passed. Though the explanation secured by the O.S.I.R. was ultimately a simple one, nevertheless a family's sanctuary had been violated. Simple reason or not, the Stanskys feel a great debt to the O.S.I.R. for restoring their home as the shelter and refuge it is supposed to be.

DAN AYKROYD

TWO   HAUNTING APPARITIONS

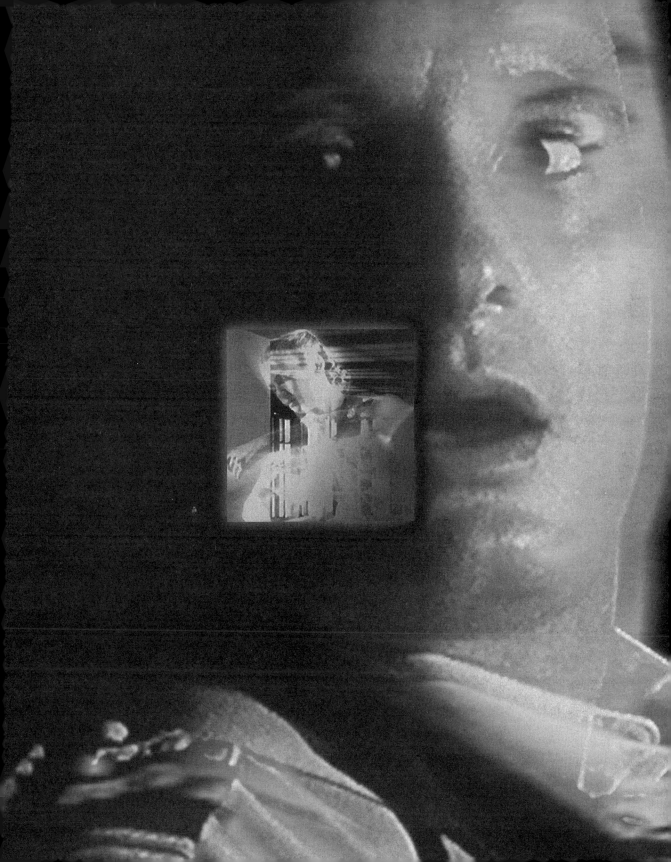

Ghosts and apparitions have been written about throughout the evolution of story-telling. Human experience provides a factual basis for this. Now research indicates most hauntings are harmless. In many sightings, ghosts are seen by only one person, the phantom's kindred spirit among the living. Catherine Cartwright misses her deceased husband, Robert, her kindred spirit among the dead. Is Catherine's love for her husband so strong that it invites him to reach out from beyond the grave? Or is her need so desperate that she has created these disturbing experiences herself?

DAN AYKROYD

G h o s t l y V O I C E S

TIME & PLACE *Nighttime at a large, secluded, classic Georgian home on well-manicured grounds in Warburton County, Massachusetts.*

Catherine Cartwright, 80, lies in bed. Her physician, Dr. Willard Marlow, removes a pressure cuff from her arm.

"Everything's back to normal, Katy, but I'd like to prescribe a light sedative," Marlow says.

"I don't take drugs, Willard. I'm not the wilting lily you seem to think I am. Besides, Jeffrey will be home soon."

"All right, but if you won't accept my medical help, take some advice. If you think you're seeing those things again, take that camcorder I gave you and ..."

"You still don't believe me, do you? I'll prove it to you. Now, good night."

Marlow leaves, and Catherine falls asleep. Suddenly, a door slams down the corridor, awakening Catherine. A methodical rapping moves down the corridor, closing on her room. Catherine sinks deeper into her bed, terrified.

A wind rises in the corridor. A light snaps on outside Catherine's room and flickers. A chair moves down the corridor past the door. Moaning sounds begin.

Rolling back her covers, Catherine turns to her bedside table where a picture of her husband, Robert, is draped with black crepe. She picks up the camcorder and starts recording. In the corridor, wind fans at her face and distorted opera music plays. The hall lights blink on and off. The furniture wobbles. The wind picks up. A vase flies off a table and crashes into the wall.

"Who's there?" Catherine calls.

As Catherine turns the corner, a blast of light blinds her. She drops the camera and raises her hands as the wind blows her back. As she lowers her fingers to peek out, the wind increases. She's knocked over by the wind. She fights to raise her head once again. As a clap of thunder breaks over her, Catherine ducks her head, becoming motionless.

Three days later, Jeffrey Cartwright, 43, is working at his desk when Catherine walks in.

"Everything okay, Mom? You really worried me the other day."

"I'm actually more worried about you working so hard, just like your father. You really shouldn't stay up so late."

"Don't worry. I'll be turning in soon," Jeffrey says. "Good night."

Later that night, Jeffrey sleeps at his desk when the door to the study swings open. A wind rustles his papers, and a low roll of thunder wakes him. Jeffrey ventures into the garden. At the bottom of a staircase, he sees Catherine sprawled on the ground, barely conscious, but clutching the camcorder. Panicking, Jeffrey lifts his mother and carries her back to the house.

AT THE BOTTOM OF A STAIRCASE, HE SEES CATHERINE SPRAWLED ON THE GROUND, BARELY CONSCIOUS, CLUTCHING THE CAMCORDER.

TIME & PLACE *The next week, at Dr. Marlow's office, he is discussing Catherine Cartwright with an O.S.I.R. case manager, Curtis Rollins.*

"JEFFREY WAS HOME at the time but he didn't see or hear anything," Dr. Marlow says. "I discussed with him the possibility of placing Katy somewhere where she could get more attention, but then she gave me this. She asked me not to show it to anybody else until I got a professional opinion."

Marlow plays a tape from Catherine's video on the night of her haunting. The video continues as Catherine enters the upstairs corridor. Rollins freezes the tape.

"After I saw this," Dr. Marlow says, "I wasn't sure that committing her was the right course of action."

"I want to investigate this further. How is Mrs. Cartwright's condition now?" Rollins asks.

"She continues to report these sightings and, in her weakened state, they're exhausting her. She very nearly died last week."

"And you're saying no one else has seen this tape?" Rollins asks. Dr. Marlow nods yes. "Let's keep it that way."

Later that day, at the Cartwright mansion, Dr. Marlow brings Rollins to meet Catherine. "What's your diagnosis of me ... am I going crazy?" she asks. She takes Rollins down the hallway, pointing at various "haunted" items. "And that's the chair that moved. And this painting, that's the one that keeps falling. I suppose while we're here, I should show you Robert's study. Of course it hasn't been touched," Catherine says.

"These are lovely antiques," Rollins says.

"Robert loved beautiful things and especially his Oriental carpets," Catherine says. "You know, I wonder when was the last time we had these rugs cleaned ..."

"With your permission we'd like to try to determine the nature of this phenomenon," Rollins says to Catherine. "And we'd like to do it undercover."

TIME & PLACE *The Cartwright mansion, the next day. Four O.S.I.R. operatives, including Rollins, are disguised as carpet cleaners.*

J E F F R E Y   S T A N D S   I N the foyer talking to one of the carpet-cleaning crew members: "Take special care of the Persian Kilims in the sitting room."

Meanwhile an operative examines the furniture and walls with his hazmat kit, disguised as a toolbox. Ray Donahue, O.S.I.R. criminologist, makes his way to the area where Jeffrey found Catherine.

O.S.I.R. psychobiologist Lindsay Donner and Donahue interview Catherine privately. "Of course I'm scared," Catherine says. "Sometimes I don't know if it's all in my head, but then with Willard's video camera, it's hard to disagree with that kind of evidence. And Jeffrey doesn't believe me. He says he does but I know he doesn't."

Later on, outside, Donner and Donahue are talking to an officer next to his police cruiser.

"Jeffrey Cartwright?" the cop repeats. "He's a nice-enough guy. Living up there with his mom, taking care of his old lady. Couple a times over the past month, I've responded to distress calls from the house, but they asked us to keep it quiet."

"Keep what quiet?" Donahue asks.

"Well, you know, the stories. Ghosts. Junk like that. We found nothing except a lonely old lady."

Nearby, Thomas Rigetti, a grizzled local, trims a hedge. Donner introduces herself as a landscape architect and asks him about his job. "Once a month they hire me to come up and fix up the gardens," Rigetti says.

"Think they'd mind if we looked around a bit, just for research purposes?" Donner asks.

"I don't care, but Mrs. Cartwright might. The old lady's going bonkers. She keeps wandering out here in the middle of the night."

Later that evening in the O.S.I.R. mobile lab, Rollins reports. "Psychological and physiological assessment of Mrs. Cartwright has been completed," Rollins says. "Results were normal. All baseline environmental results were within normal ranges."

That same evening, back at the Cartwright mansion.

JEFFREY TUCKS HIS mother into bed and leaves her room. Soon, the mysterious wind picks up. Objects jerk and move by themselves and lights flicker as if a presence is moving toward Catherine's bedroom.

"Katy," a voice calls out as Catherine's door swings open.

"Jeffrey? Is that you? Robert? Could it be?" Catherine wonders.

"Katy, I need you," the distorted voice intones.

Catherine moves down the corridor, where the sconce lights come on down the hallway. She comes to a closed door at the end of the corridor. Catherine opens it and steps into the darkened room. Inside Robert's study, a blue light hits her full force. Reminders of her life with Robert are revealed as the strange light plays over them. Catherine follows it, noticing the photographs. A window snaps open. Catherine edges toward the window.

"Join me, Katy," the voice continues.

Transfixed, Catherine climbs onto the window seat, reaching into the wind. She rises up on one foot, lets go of the window casing and reaches out. Before she can step out of the window, a figure grabs her from behind, pulling her back into the study.

Catherine collapses into Jeffrey's arms.

"WHAT IF THIS ISN'T A POLTERGEIST OR SOMETHING, BUT A SPIRIT, ROBERT'S SPIRIT?"

"Why did you stop me, Jeffrey? Your father was calling to me. Didn't you hear it?" Catherine asks.

"Mom, it was your imagination. Please try and get some rest."

The next morning in the mobile lab, Donner, Rollins and Donahue watch the playback of the incident.

"THE AUDIO IS garbled, but she identifies the voice as Robert. Were they very close?" Rollins asks.

"Extremely," Donner says. "Catherine and Robert Cartwright both attended church regularly, indicating a well-established belief in the probability of an afterlife."

"Let's review her preliminary interview," Rollins says.

"And you know, it was the funniest thing, these things all began on the anniversary of the day he proposed to me!" Catherine says on the tape. "Now how could anyone else know that? I'm the last one to take stock in such things, but I've always had an open mind, and, as I was just saying to Robert the other—I mean Jeffrey, as I was saying to Jeffrey—what if this isn't a poltergeist or something, but a spirit, Robert's spirit?"

Donahue freezes the tape. "Jeffrey Cartwright is booked on the morning flight to New York for a two-day business trip," he says.

"As soon as he's gone, let's set up complete on-site environmental monitoring and surveillance," Rollins says.

TIME & PLACE   *The next morning at the Cartwright mansion. The O.S.I.R. operatives are still undercover.*

DONAHUE MOUNTS A

thermograph camera on the wall. Both he and a nearby operative are dressed as carpet cleaners. The operative vacuums the hall carpet, keeping watch as Donahue works.

Nearby, Rollins examines a thin filament with Donner.

"Analysis is back on the fiber optics that were found during circumstantial assessment,"

Donner says. "Well over spec. Whoever ordered these renovations was planning for the 21st century, and they spent a bundle doing it."

WHEN CATHERINE OPENS HER BEDROOM DOOR, SHE'S IMMEDIATELY LIT BY A BLUE AURA AND HIT BY A GUST OF WIND.

"Have the lab look into who designed this hardware and what company installed it," Rollins orders.

That evening, Rollins visits Catherine. She is wired with bio-monitoring equipment to track her physiological state and vital signs.

"Dr. Rollins, I know you come highly recommended by Dr. Marlow, but is all this really necessary?" Catherine asks.

"It is, Mrs. Cartwright. My team has found some odd electrical installations in your house. Fiber optics. State-of-the-art conduits," Rollins says.

"What are you saying?" Catherine asks, cutting him off.

"What if this phenomenon is not Robert?" Rollins asks.

"I feel his presence," Catherine says.

"Then help us prove what it really is. Let us continue our work."

Investigators watch the monitors in the mobile lab. An image from camera twelve reveals the gardens and the house, while another monitor shows a shimmering figure on the second floor. Rollins sits at the console with Donner and Donahue.

"Laser scan detecting movement in the southwest quadrant," Rollins says. "I'm going in. Morgan and Silva, meet me in sector seven."

Catherine lies in bed gazing at a picture of her and Robert. She looks up as though disturbed by something.

Donner and Donahue watch the surveillance monitors in the mobile lab.

"Something seems to be moving through the walls of the structure. How's Catherine doing?" Donahue asks through the comlink.

"She seems fine. Vital signs are still within normal range," Donner says.

"I'm still tracking unidentified movement in the southwest sector," Donahue says.

A sound outside Catherine's door steals her attention from the photograph.

"Robert ...," Catherine says, moving toward the door. Donner moves from the video image of Catherine's room to Catherine's biostat readouts.

"Vitals beginning to rise. Pulse 120 over 60," Donner says.

When Catherine opens her bedroom door, she's immediately lit by a bright blue aura and hit by a gust of wind.

"Katy, you must follow me. Here, Catherine, touch me," the voice says.

Catherine reaches out, blinded by the increasing light of the aura; her foot edges off the top stair. Below her, a figure in black wearing night-vision goggles dashes up the stairs, catching Catherine and pulling her back onto the landing.

The intensity of the light increases, and the wind whips up along the corridor. Catherine stares at the figure. He sits her down on the floor, shielding her from the wind. It's Rollins.

"We're getting strong thermal readings from your location," Donner says through the headset.

"How many figures on the scan?" Rollins asks.

"Three."

"Someone's moving fast behind you," Donahue warns.

Rollins spins around, but nobody is there. The wind has increased, and the eerie light of the aura streams from the stairwell as Rollins turns and heads down the corridor.

"It just moved right past you, heading southeast," Donahue says.

Rollins feels his way along the wall. He taps hard and a panel opens, revealing some dials and buttons.

"I'm shutting it down," Rollins says into the comlink.

As he hits a few buttons, the wind stops. Rollins yanks out a cable. The aura slowly fades, and the corridor goes black. Two investigators appear at Rollins' side.

"Our target's moving outside. Security's on the way to intercept," Donahue says.

In the gardens, a man dashes past a hedge, where Donahue and two security operatives confront him. He runs in the opposite direction, but Donahue neatly subdues him, bringing him to the ground. Moments later, Rollins and Donner approach as the operatives bring the figure forward. Catherine, wearing a shawl against the night cold, arrives.

"Thomas? It was you ...?" Catherine asks.

"Local law enforcement is on its way," Donahue says.

"Contact Jeffrey Cartwright. Tell him his mother needs him right away," Rollins says.

▮ TIME & PLACE ▮   *Later that night, Jeffrey returns home to the Cartwright mansion.*

J E F F R E Y   H E A D S   T H R O U G H   the foyer to the
stairs where he flips on the lights and starts upstairs. Something moves behind him, and he

turns around. A chair slides across the corridor, and a wind starts to blow. Jeffrey shakes his head, annoyed, and moves down the corridor. He pushes aside the same panel Rollins found earlier, hitting a couple of buttons. The effects die as quickly as they began. He turns around to see a figure standing opposite him.

"Welcome home, Mr. Cartwright," Rollins says.

"Who the hell are you?" Jeffrey asks.

Catherine and two cops emerge from the room behind Rollins. One of them is the cop from the interview.

"Jeffrey Cartwright, you are under arrest for larceny by scheme and aggravated assault. Anything you say can and will be used against you in a court of law ..."

Catherine looks at Jeffrey, crestfallen. Later, Rollins, Donahue, Donner and Catherine review Catherine Cartwright's original video footage on her TV.

"So right from the start you had your suspicions?" Catherine asks.

"When Dr. Marlow first showed me your tape, I noticed how the camcorder responded to the light show," Rollins says.

"MRS. CARTWRIGHT, I FEEL ROBERT, WHEREVER HIS SPIRIT IS, FEELS THE SAME AS YOU DO."

"The aperture compensated to a halogen light source of 400 watts or brighter. We just needed to investigate to be certain it was a hoax," adds Donahue.

"Mrs. Cartwright, I'm sorry for the way it turned out," Donahue says.

"And all for what? Money. And I thought it might be Robert. I'm just an old fool," Catherine says, disappointed.

"No, Mrs. Cartwright," Donner says, "I think maybe Robert, wherever his spirit is, feels the same as you do."

As Donner takes Catherine's hand, Catherine smiles sadly and turns to Robert's photo on the nightstand. Rollins gives a final log entry: "Investigation reveals that Jeffrey Cartwright had rigged the house with state-of-the-art special effects. Lasers, remote-controlled furniture, wind machines were all controlled by one Thomas Rigetti, Jeffrey Cartwright's accomplice. As sole heir to the family fortune, Cartwright admitted that he intended to have his mother committed. He has been charged with malicious mischief and criminal intent."

Epilogue

The strange occurrences at the Cartwright mansion had nothing in fact to do with the love Catherine held for her deceased husband, Robert. They were a cruel and malicious hoax engineered by her heartless and greedy son. Perhaps it is not the ghosts of loved ones we should be apprehensive about, but rather the darker motives of the living human heart. **DAN AYKROYD**

Specters—fully audible and visual apparitions of human figures that seem to materialize out of thin air and just as quickly vanish. Research indicates they may be the residual traces of souls reluctant to move on permanently through the veil that separates this world from the next. The O.S.I.R. is frequently called upon to document occurrences of this nature. Some cases are truly exceptional, as in Clara's friend.

DAN AYKROYD

C l a r a ' s   F R I E N D

Late afternoon at the Preston home, a beautiful three-story Victorian in Lethbridge, Alberta.

"**H**oney, go get your sister. I need some help setting the table," Belinda Preston tells her 6-year-old daughter, Marnie, who goes upstairs for Clara.

As Marnie approaches Clara's bedroom, she hears giggling. Confused, she peers through the open door and sees Clara, 11, sitting on the edge of her bed, leaning close to a figure seated in a chair opposite her.

Clara looks at the figure and giggles. Marnie rolls her eyes and leaves. As Marnie arrives at the bottom of the stairs, Belinda hands her some wine glasses.

"Clara's with a friend," Marnie says.

"What friend?" Belinda asks, heading upstairs. She stops in the doorway and sees Clara talking to the figure. Her husband, Dennis, moves beside her.

"Mom, Dad, I want you to meet Bobbie." The figure slowly stands and turns around. Barbara Corbett, 16, is striking and exotic, wearing a dress from the 1930s, tied up with a belt. She smiles mysteriously.

42

Belinda asks her if she's in Clara's class. Barbara looks at Clara, who appears to listen.

"Awww. Bobbie says it was nice to see you finally, but she has to go," Clara says. Barbara smiles again before rushing toward the window. Instead of crashing into it, she fuses through the solid glass and disappears.

That evening, Belinda hustles Marnie and Clara out the door, passing them an overnight bag. Tammy Estarhaus, 40, leads the two girls to her car.

"Sorry to have to cancel dinner. Are you sure this is no problem?" Belinda asks Tammy.

"No. I'll call you in the morning," Tammy says.

TIME & PLACE *The next morning, O.S.I.R. psycho-biologist Lindsay Donner, psychiatrist Dr. Anton Hendricks and case manager Curtis Rollins stand in the front yard.*

ROLLINS SPEAKS INTO a recorder: "Initial case log. File #847117. Confirming arrival to residence occupied by the Preston family. Team is investigating complaint of an alleged haunting. In process of obtaining blueprints for the house. Preliminary interviews under way."

Investigators talk to Marnie Preston first. "Over the last couple weeks, I'd seen her around, with Clara, I mean," Marnie says. "And except for the weird clothes the 'ghost' wore, it was neat. Clara doesn't have a lot of friends, you know. She keeps to herself."

Family friend Tammy Estarhaus gives her take on the situation: "When George and I showed up for dinner that night, Belinda and Dennis were in an absolute panic. You'd think they'd seen the devil himself. I guess I understand their concern, if you believe their story. Marnie doesn't seem too concerned about it all, but Clara, she's so sad. And she's such a sweet kid."

Donner interviews Clara Preston in the Esterhaus recreation room. "Her name's Bobbie and she's not just a friend. She's my best friend. I don't know what the big deal is. We just talk and stuff," Clara says.

"What's Bobbie's last name, Clara?"

"I don't know. Never asked, I guess."

"Did you meet her at school?" Donner asks.

"No. She just showed up one day in our back yard. It was the same day I got a 98 on my English exam. She was real impressed. Three weeks ago yesterday."

Donner notes that that was September 9 and asks Clara what they talk about.

"Just the usual stuff. She's not from around here, you know. She's just different. And you want to know the coolest thing?"

"What's that?"

"We don't have to talk out loud. I can hear her thoughts, and she can hear mine."

An hour later, Rollins, Donner and Hendricks watch a tape of the interview in the mobile lab. "Clara and Bobbie only seem able to meet at the Preston residence," Donner says. "Clara's really anxious to come home and see her friend again, but her parents won't let her until we clear this thing up."

Rollins and Donner discuss the case at the Preston house. "Spoke to the neighbors. They reported seeing nothing out of the ordinary," Donner says. "Although Mrs. Kepler, who lives next door to the north, recalls seeing Clara talking to another girl in the back yard early last week. She wouldn't have given it another thought, but what stuck out was the way the other girl was dressed."

"What was she wearing?" Rollins asks.

"Apparently, a dress Mrs. Kepler says she would have worn as a teenager. It was straight out of the '30s," Donner says.

"Let me guess," Rollins says. "You tie it up with a bow." Donner follows his gaze toward Bobbie, wearing the very dress they are describing. They stop. Donner adjusts the video camera attached to her headset. Rollins speaks into his comlink: "Attention, team. We have a guest in the front hall."

Bobbie watches the investigators. She looks tired, but her smile hasn't lost its previous allure. An investigator begins snapping photographs furiously.

Bobbie looks behind her to see investigators observing her from the other end of the hall. She looks back at Rollins. Then she runs up the stairs and dissolves through a stained glass door.

TIME & PLACE *After Bobbie's appearance, investigators move to the mobile lab, where Rollins gives a file update.*

"FILE UPDATE. DAY three, 1300 hours. We are conducting environmental assessments of the home. To date, all baseline results are well within normal ranges. Rollins, out."

Rollins leads a roundtable as a blueprint of the house is displayed on the main screen. He passes out enlarged photos taken in the hallway.

"She was right there," Hendricks says. "We all witnessed the girl, but she's not visible in any of the still photographs or the video footage."

"During the next phase of the investigation, we'll activate infrared, thermal-imaging, magnetic-field monitoring," Rollins says. "The physiological assessment of the Preston family showed no aberrations that could account for the apparent apparition," he continues. "What happened during regressive hypnosis?"

Hendricks plays an audiotape playback machine.

"Clara, you're speaking with your friend, Bobbie."

"Yes. In my head."

"But neither of you is moving your lips."

"No. It's so cool."

"Show me what she sounds like. What is she saying right now?"

At this point, Hendricks increases the volume of the tape recording. Clara's voice changes slightly, becoming Bobbie. "What I'd give for a Blue Bonnet Cherry Cola."

"What's that?" Clara asks in her own voice.

"If you come with me, Clara, I could show you. Come with me back to my place where we can be friends forever."

Hendricks pauses the tape, opening a file. "Now I'm embarrassed to admit I know this but Blue Bonnet Cherry Cola hasn't been manufactured since 1943," he says.

"Who is Bobbie," Rollins asks, "and where does she want to take Clara?"

The next morning, Rollins gives another file update: "Day four, 0900 hours. Since our arrival, team members have had firsthand contact with the phenomenon on six separate occasions. Round-the-clock environmental and audio/video surveillance has been established at the Preston residence."

At Tammy's home, Hendricks attaches biophysical monitoring systems on Clara and Marnie. Donner looks on.

"Since we haven't been able to record Bobbie by conventional methods, like photographs or video, we will be monitoring everyone's vital signs, like your heart rate or brain-wave activity," Hendricks says. "That way, we will be able to tell if any of you is having an encounter with the phenomenon."

Back in the mobile lab, Donner, Hendricks and three investigators note the various camera angles of the Preston home. Rollins buttons up his shirt, covering the electrodes attached to his chest, and leaves for the Prestons.

As Rollins moves along the upstairs hallway, Hendricks notes his heart rate and stress sensors rising rapidly. A surveillance monitor shows Rollins frozen in the middle of the hall, staring straight ahead. Yet the hall appears empty.

Rollins stares at Bobbie. With her eyes closed, she slowly moves her head to and fro as if listening to a slow waltz. Another investigator edges closer, holding a portable contact dosimeter toward Bobbie, who seems oblivious to their presence.

From the mobile lab, Donner watches Rollins and the investigator do their strange dance around the bedroom. Hendricks monitors the investigators' biostat readouts.

"We're not seeing what they're seeing," Donner tells Hendricks.

Inside, the investigator watches the needle stay steady as she passes the instrument inches from Bobbie. Rollins notes this. Bobbie suddenly moves away and begins waltzing around Rollins. He stands still as Bobbie passes right through him.

Donner and Hendricks see Rollins shudder on the surveillance monitor. "Curtis, what just happened?" Hendricks asks.

"CLARA, HAVE YOU MET MS. CORBETT BEFORE?" DONNER ASKS. "SHE LOOKS FAMILIAR, BUT, NO, I DON'T THINK SO," CLARA ANSWERS.

Rollins and the investigator look and find that Bobbie is gone.

Later, Rollins speaks into his recorder: "Case log update. Historical and background checks revealed a living descendant of a previous owner of the Preston home, one Dawn Hinton, twenty-five. Archival research presently under way."

Dawn moves over by the bench swing, where a large box containing photo albums and scrapbooks sits. "It's all pretty much how I remember it, except the renovations, of course," Dawn says. "Man, the hours I spent in that tree. It was like a giant storybook with an infinite number of possibilities. One day, it was a ship; another, a castle."

"How often did you come and visit your great-grandmother?" Donner asks.

"Every summer till I was ten, I guess. Yeah, that was the year Nanna had to sell the house and move to Parkhill."

"Nanna was your great-grandmother. My research says her name was Barbara Winston," Donner says.

"Yeah, while she was married. But everyone called her Bobbie."

"Thanks. It's a great help. Just one more question. When did Bobbie, your great-grandmother, pass away?"

"Oh, she's still alive, but she suffered a stroke. She's been in a coma for about three weeks now."

TIME & PLACE *The next day, Donner, Hendricks and Clara make their way down a busy hallway of Mackenzie General Hospital.*

"THERE'S SOMEONE I want you to meet," Donner tells Clara.

They come to a room, walk inside and see Dawn Hinton and her baby daughter standing beside 80-year-old Barbara Corbett, who is hooked up to intravenous and various monitoring devices.

"Clara, have you ever met Ms. Corbett before?" Donner asks.

"She looks kind of familiar, but no, I don't think so."

Donner picks up the chart at the end of the bed. It shows the admitting day as September 9, 1630 hours. The name at the top reads Barbara Corbett.

"When did Barbara revert back to her maiden name?" Donner asks Dawn.

"Only recently. She was so depressed after Great-grandpa died; it's like she wanted to go back in time."

Dawn reaches into her diaper bag, pulls out a worn diary and hands it to Donner. "I was digging around the garage and found Great-grandma Bobbie's diary."

Clara moves over. "Her name is Bobbie?"

Back in the mobile lab, a 16mm home movie plays on the screen. On it, young Barbara swings on the new bench swing in the back yard. She wears the same dress and belt she has appeared in before.

"This is home movie footage taken of sixteen-year-old Barbara Corbett. Silver nitrate tests confirm that this film was developed in 1931," Donner explains.

"Well, that's the same girl I saw in the hallway," Rollins says.

"The home movie was apparently filmed on the afternoon of her sixteenth birthday. I cross-referenced this with Barbara's entry on that date in her diary," Donner says, starting to read from it. "'Today was the happiest day of my life. I turned sixteen ... finally! But the best part was I met the most wonderful boy. Douglas Winston. He has invited me to the show this Saturday. I don't think I'm ever going to be able to sleep again.'"

"Since Barbara is still alive, albeit in a comatose state, it appears we are dealing with an out-of-body experience," Rollins says. "Bobbie could be a form of involuntary subatomic transmission."

"Or a psi-based haunt. Focused psychokinetic astral projection in the form of, as Barbara's diary put it, the happiest day of her life."

"I propose an experiment whereby we move the Prestons back into their house and ask Clara to convince Bobbie to return to her corporeal state," Donner says.

The team worries about the potential risk to Barbara Corbett and psychological upheaval to Clara. But as neither Barbara nor Clara is thriving in their situation, Rollins makes the difficult decision to proceed with Donner's experiment.

Later that day, Dennis, Belinda, Marnie and an excited Clara follow Donner into the house. Investigators monitor their biostats from the mobile lab.

The next day, Donner walks with Clara. "It's been hours. Where is she?" Clara asks.

"Don't worry, Clara," Donner says. "We've all seen your friend over the past several days. She hasn't gone anywhere ... I hope."

That night, Donner sleeps in a chair at the end of Clara's bed when Clara sits up, hearing a giggle. Donner wakes, watching young Barbara not 3 feet from her, engrossed in an apparent deep conversation with Clara. "They appear to be talking, but I can't hear them," Donner tells Rollins through the comlink.

"Go to a level 5. Try and communicate with the apparition," Rollins says.

Donner leans forward. "Barbara? Barbara Corbett?"

Young Barbara doesn't respond. Clara looks over, slightly annoyed. "Bobbie's telling me about Doug, a guy she's met."

"What's she saying?" Donner asks.

"She misses him. She misses so many things from her life."

"Will you try something for me, Clara? Remind Bobbie about Dawn's baby."

"Beatrice? Why?"

"Because that's Bobbie's great-great-granddaughter. Dawn misses Bobbie, and she'd really like Beatrice to see her Nanna."

Quietly, an investigator leads Dennis, Belinda and Marnie into the doorway.

Young Barbara and Clara move over to the corner of the bedroom, watched by the group in the doorway. Clara smiles at young Barbara.

"You think this is best? But I'll miss you. Come with me. Let's be friends ... forever," young Barbara says.

"I'd love that, but I belong here with my family. And you belong with your family," Clara says.

Young Barbara smiles that smile at Clara. They move closer and begin to hug. Locked in an embrace, Barbara begins to glow, then evaporates into a bright sparkle of light.

Rollins watches the monitors in the mobile lab. As the glow fades from Clara's face on one monitor, the hospital monitor shows old Barbara Corbett's eyes flutter and open.

Rollins gives a final log entry: "Case #847117. We remained on the site for an additional two weeks after our experiment. The Prestons report no further visitations from the apparition they came to know as Bobbie. Barbara Corbett appears to have made a remarkable recovery. Although, regarding her ethereal visits to the Preston house, she has no recollection of anything that happened during the time she was in the coma."

Clara welcomes old Barbara Corbett to the house. She takes her to the back yard where the grown Barbara Corbett sits in the bench swing, lovingly holding Beatrice, her great-great-granddaughter.

Epilogue

Clara Preston's friend was indeed an ethereal apparition. But not that of a deceased human being. It was the spiritual projection of a living elderly woman whose subconscious was attempting to recapture happier past times. Perhaps the lesson Barbara Corbett learned is one we should all embrace: Appreciate the past, but live for the future. And the future is our children. **DAN AYKROYD**

To some, a miracle may be an act of God; to others it's ordinary people performing incredible feats in extraordinary situations. When the O.S.I.R. was engaged to investigate mysterious occurrences during a crisis aboard an aircraft, it was confronted with analyzing a seemingly miraculous event.

DAN AYKROYD

Angel on a PLANE

Evening at the control tower at Rich View Airfield near Plattsburgh, New York.

Tense air-traffic controllers man the radar screens as an airline emergency ensues. Head controller Bill Finlater asks for an update. "Flight 66A out of Chicago. They say they were struck by lightning head on," a controller reports.

"Where are they?" he asks.

"Coming out of the storm twenty miles northeast. Seven thousand feet and dropping. Emergency vehicles are standing by."

Finlater grabs the com mike. "Flight 66A, come in. Do you read?" he asks.

Up in the small private jet, the pilot is in the passenger cabin, passed out cold. Co-pilot Jarvis Parks is in the cockpit, trying to take over the controls. The plane is diving, rattling loudly, bucking in the wind. Parks answers, "Flight 66A, copy." He is panicked; his voice is breaking up.

"What is your current condition?" Finlater asks.

"Pilot's out cold! Controls frozen! Gages malfunctioning! We're going down!"

"Is your landing gear down 66A?"

"No way to tell! The whole panel is shorted out!" Blue-arcing electricity zaps across the switches. Parks reaches for a button and is electrocuted. He yells and slumps back in his chair.

Finlater spots the plane in his binoculars. "Jesus, they have no gear!"

"They're on final descent," says a controller. Finlater looks through the binoculars again. "Son of a gun. They must have control back. The gear just came down."

The plane is bouncing around wildly. Parks, still lying in the cockpit, opens his eyes. He's weak and semiconscious. A faint glowing yellow light illuminates from the empty pilot chair next to him.

"They're coming in pretty fast," one of the controllers says.

"Flight 66A, do you read? Flight 66A, copy?" Finlater asks.

Flight attendant Mary O'Brien rushes into the cockpit and sees Parks unconscious, the empty pilot's chair and the runway approaching rapidly out the front windshield.

Then, suddenly, the plane lands gently on the slick tarmac. The radio kicks back in.

"Flight 66A," air traffic asks. "Come in?"

"Hello."

"Who's this?"

"I'm Mary O'Brien, sir. I'm the flight attendant."

Finlater is confused. "Is everyone okay?" he asks.

"The pilot's in bad shape. Co-pilot Parks is unconscious," she answers.

"Who landed the plane?" Finlater asks.

Mary hears the ambulance's siren as it approaches the plane. She's not sure what just transpired. "I ... I don't know," Mary says.

TIME & PLACE *That same night, on the tarmac where the plane landed.*

T W O   A T T E N D A N T S   A R E loading semiconscious Parks into an ambulance. His hands are badly burned. Emergency crews are helping the passengers, Martin Cole, a computer chip magnate, and his assistant, Diane Schafer, off the plane. Cole, a well-fed businessman, speaks loudly, in short bursts. "She was there, plain as day. Right there in front of us," he is saying.

"I saw her, too," Diane says. "She had dark hair."

"We've looked everywhere," Finlater tells them.

"She saved the pilot's life. I watched her do it," Cole says.

"The plane was still pressurized when the emergency crew opened the door," Finlater says. "There is no one else on this plane."

Diane and Cole look at each other in shock.

TIME & PLACE *A few days later. O.S.I.R. case manager Connor Doyle is at Rich View Airfield.*

" F I L E   # 2 6 0 1 2 2 , "   D O Y L E reports. "We are beginning preliminary interviews with individuals off a stricken jet who claim to have experienced an aircraft landing aided by a mysterious entity."

Cole's plane sits outside the hangar. Finlater is escorting O.S.I.R. aeronautics engineer Sander Winkler and Doyle. "So you guys aren't the FBI or FAA?" Finlater asks.

"No, we're an independent agency," Doyle replies.

"I'll tell you what you're going to find," Finlater says, "this plane is a write-off."

"Maybe the damage occurred after it landed," Doyle suggests.

"The co-pilot says all the systems went dead right after the lightning struck them," Finlater says.

"Electrical system definitely looks burnt out," Winkler reports.

"I saw the landing gear come down," Finlater says. "I saw the plane land. I've been on this job for 30 years. I'm telling you, there's no way in hell this baby should have come out of the sky in one piece."

TIME & PLACE   *O.S.I.R. mobile lab, over the next few days. O.S.I.R. psychiatrist Dr. Anton Hendricks puts each of the witnesses under regressive hypnosis to recall the events of the crash.*

"WE RECEIVED THE weather report and proceeded to an altitude that should have been safely above the thunderstorm," pilot Graves says. "There was a bright flash. It seemed to come from below, yet I've never heard of lighting shooting up like that. I was blinded. I felt a sharp pain radiate up my left arm. My chest seized up like I was caught in a huge vise. Then I just blacked out."

Flight attendant Mary O'Brien is hooked up to the DE, brain-mapping equipment. Hendricks interviews her. "Jim, the pilot, just suddenly seized up like he had been jolted with electricity," she says. "I was thrown backward."

"You say you were in the cockpit when the plane landed and the co-pilot was unconscious the whole time. Who do you think landed the plane?"

Mary is torn, greatly troubled by her lack of a rational explanation. "I don't know."

Martin Cole, under regressive hypnosis, is being questioned by Hendricks. "What do you see?"

"A woman," Cole says. "She's glowing." Cole is remembering being on the plane. A woman dressed in a military uniform with a Red Cross arm badge walks toward him from the back of the plane. "She just appeared," he says. "Out of nowhere." Cole looks at Diane, who has seen the woman, too. Mary seems oblivious, as if she can't see her. The woman walks toward Graves and puts her hands over his chest. A glow comes from the woman's hands and goes into Graves' chest. The force throws Mary back, away from Graves.

He seizes up. Mary is thrown back off him.

Pilot Graves' hypnosis continues. "I'm awake. I open my eyes and see her," he says. "Blurred and dreamlike. She glows. And then everything goes black again."

TIME & PLACE   *At Rich View Airfield the next day. Doyle, Winkler and other O.S.I.R. investigators examine the plane.*

DOYLE GIVES ANOTHER case log update: "Despite our best efforts, Jarvis Parks' condition remains critical. Dr. Davison says he may not live more than 48 hours. We are proceeding to the environmental assessment phase, hoping it will clear up some of the conflicts that have arisen thus far."

Winkler is examining the control panel. Doyle checks in. "You think phantom pilots leave fingerprints?" Doyle asks.

The circuitry in these damn things is so vulnerable," Winkler says. "You'd think someone would figure out a better way to protect them."

"Don't these planes have redundant systems?" asks Doyle.

"I suppose they were lucky just the electrical system went down," Winkler explains. "A direct strike can cause structural damage and even ignite fuel vapor."

"All things considered, I say lucky is a bit of an understatement."

TIME & PLACE *Same day, O.S.I.R. mobile lab. Doyle, Hendricks and physicist/statistician Peter Axon are listening to the playback of the radio transmission and watching a replay of the radio screen from the night of the plane's emergency.*

" W H A T   I S   I T we're looking at up there?" Doyle asks, pointing to something on the main screen.

"A new class of the lightning phenomenon has recently been documented," Axon says. "Both types occur above cloud cover and are extremely rare. The first type is a red sprite as seen on the left. The second is called a blue jet. It's possible that the co-pilot was describing the latter. It appears as a blue cone of light bursting upward at tremendous speeds."

"If the plane was hit by one of these types of lightning, could it land safely?" Doyle asks.

"Not with all the electrical circuitry destroyed," Axon answers. "Landing systems, everything, shouldn't have worked."

"How about the claims of a sixth person on board—as the witnesses describe, a dark-haired woman?"

"The cabin was still pressurized when the plane landed and the ground crew did a thorough search. We don't know how she could have gotten on and off that plane."

"Unless someone is lying," Doyle says.

"Not as far as I can tell," Hendricks chimes in.

"Historical background check on the area and witnesses turned up only one interesting thing," Doyle says. "This airfield used to be a military landing site for planes during World War II. Only one plane has ever crashed here in 1945. A medical evac plane. It was apparently struck by lightning."

"Any survivors?" Hendricks asks.

"None," says Doyle.

TIME & PLACE *The hospital, the next day. The O.S.I.R. investigators have rigged Mary O'Brien up to biofeedback-monitoring equipment. Video and infra-red surveillances are at both the airplane hangar site and in Parks' room in intensive care. Parks is not expected to last the night.*

H E N D R I C K S   A N D   D O Y L E are in the mobile lab, monitoring the surveillance screens, discussing the case. "Mary is searching for some explanation," Hendricks reports. "In behavioral terms it's called 'the survivor syndrome.' She's trying to rationalize in her own mind why events turned out the way they did—to understand why she's okay and Parks is not."

"So many inconsistent stories surrounding the incident can't be very helpful," Doyle says.

"No, even for someone who doubts that there is a force capable of intervening, the desire to believe is extremely powerful," Hendricks says. "Especially in such dire circumstances."

By Parks' bedside, Mary sits, her eyes red from crying. His pulse monitor beeps slowly. Mary gets up and goes into the bathroom and washes her face. When she comes out, she sees something by the bed. She gasps, startled.

At the mobile lab, Hendricks checks Mary's biofeedback monitor. "Her pulse is increasing sharply," Hendricks says.

Doyle checks the surveillance camera. "There's a nurse leaning over Parks' bed," Doyle says.

"God, you scared me," Mary says to the nurse. "I didn't hear you come in." The nurse turns around. It's the dark-haired woman from the plane. Her nurse's uniform is from around the 1940s.

"Mary appears to be talking to someone," Hendricks says. "Yet the screen shows there's no one else in the room."

"He's doing much better," the woman tells Mary. "He's going to be just fine." She touches Mary's arm as she opens the door. Mary watches her leave, oddly moved by the woman's calm and warm quality. It's as if she glowed. Mary turns back to Parks to see him lifting his head, looking at her. Groggy, but awake.

"Jarvis?" Mary says, stunned. "Oh, my!" She runs to him and hugs him.

Later, back at the O.S.I.R. mobile lab, the investigators are discussing what they saw on the screens. "Mary is adamant that she saw a dark-haired nurse in the room," Hendricks says.

"Our security at the door saw no one enter or leave the room," Doyle says.

"Dr. Davison says Parks has made an unprecedented recovery," Hendricks says. " He's healing ... well, for lack of a better word, miraculously."

"I want a full psychological and physiological workup on Parks," Doyle orders. "Maybe he can help us understand what really happened."

TIME & PLACE *The next day, in Parks' recovery room. He's undergoing regressive hypnosis.*

"I HAVE TO do something," Parks says, reliving the plane's crisis. "We're going down!" Parks is perspiring profusely. He's alone in the small jet's cockpit cabin. The control panel is dead. Blue-arcing electricity zaps across the switches. Parks reaches for a button and is electrocuted. He screams and slumps back in his chair.

"Everything is black," Parks says. "I'm on fire. Burning. So bad. Then it felt warm. Good. Like the sun. I'm dying. I open my eyes." In his re-creation, Parks looks over at the pilot's seat. A dark-haired, golden-hued angel is at the controls. "She's flying the plane. She smiles at me," he says.

TIME & PLACE *Later that day at the O.S.I.R. lab. Hendricks, Axon and Doyle are discussing the case.*

"EXCEPT FOR MARTIN Cole, all the witnesses now believe they were touched by some sort of divine intervention," Hendricks says. "A natural reaction when a lack of a plausible explanation exists."

"Why did certain people see the woman sometimes, but not others?" Axon asks.

"Hallucinations are not uncommon in such frightening circumstances," Hendricks says. "The fact that they shared such a similar vision may be one person's power of suggestion."

"One witness hallucinates the angel, describes her, and for lack of a better explanation, the rest just believe they saw her as well," Doyle says.

"On a subconscious level, especially if the suggestion is coming from someone like Martin Cole," Hendricks says.

"Wait a minute. Martin Cole dreamed up the angel and now doesn't believe his own invention?" Axon asks.

"No, he dreamed up the image of the angel," Hendricks says. "He just doesn't believe that's what the image really represents. He's a very rational, practical person. He can't accept something he can't control."

"But how did the plane land and how did Parks recover?" Axon asks.

"The fact is we could actually be dealing with some sort of apparition or a collective PK energy," Doyle suggests.

"Diane offered another imaginative explanation. She wondered if maybe the lightning strike was some sort of cosmic mistake and that, because it was never meant to happen, it just fixed itself," Hendricks says.

"Doesn't sound like the sort of thing Mr. Cole would accept either," Doyle says.

The O.S.I.R. team decides their work on the case is done and begins packing to leave. Doyle reports in the final case log: "We are wrapping up the investigation after three months of intensive monitoring. No evidence to explain the amazing events was collected. No further sightings of the mysterious woman were reported. The only knowledge we gained was that for the passengers on the apparently crippled jet, everything worked out for the best."

TIME & PLACE *Months later, Martin Cole and Diane Schafer are on another private jet en route to a business meeting.*

COLE IS LOOKING at old black-and-white pictures of military servicemen on his laptop computer. "What are you working on?" Diane asks. "Who are those people?"

"The O.S.I.R. e-mailed me a file of pictures of people who died in the medical evac plane that crashed at Rich View," Cole says.

"In 1945?" she asks.

Cole nods. He looks at Diane and calls up a picture. Diane looks at the screen, her eyes slowly widening. She catches her breath. It's the dark-haired angel, wearing a military uniform with a red cross on it. The picture is dated 1945.

Epilogue

Do angels really exist? Several national publications have run cover stories focused on man's belief in these celestial beings. Officially this file remains unsolved, but the material contained therein certainly seems to indicate that divine forces occasionally direct messengers to positively assist us in a beautiful and comforting way.

DAN AYKROYD

Recently, researchers have studied pheromones that seem to be associated among other physiological functions with the love experience. But could such a biochemical process turn adoration into an obsessive, all-consuming and malignant force? In the following case, the O.S.I.R. discovered just how far one fan would go to pursue his object of desire.　**DAN AYKROYD**

Stalker M O O N

TIME & PLACE　*After dinner in front of Jackie Kinley's house in Vancouver, British Columbia.*

Gavin Phillips drops Jackie off at her house. "It's a TV movie, Jackie. It isn't *Citizen Kane*," Gavin says.

"Still, to go from actor to director, that's quite a jump," Jackie says, complimenting him.

"Hey, it'll be great working together again," Gavin says. "The producer is a big fan of your *Julie Bright* movie."

"Yeah, everybody loves *Julie Bright*," Jackie notes cynically.

Forgetting her purse on the floor, Jackie opens her door to get out. "Okay. See ya on the set, kid."

Jackie walks to her house, and Gavin drives off. Corben Dean watches Gavin's car get smaller. As Jackie closes the door, she dead-bolts the chain.

She goes to turn on her alarm, but it won't activate. She doesn't remember leaving a window open, but she closes it, pressing the button on her flickering answering machine on the way.

The first message is a dial tone. The second is from Gavin, from before he picked her up. The third message chills her. It is Corben Dean. "Jackie, come to the church. We must meet." As Jackie closes the window, Corben Dean materializes behind her. Jackie spins around as she hears Gavin's voice become Corben's on the machine, and she sees Corben, who motions her to be quiet. And then he is gone. But where?

Jackie scrambles for the door, but Corben is right behind her. In a panic, Jackie yanks open the door, where Gavin stands with the purse she left in his car. Jackie looks behind her. Corben Dean is gone.

The next day, Jackie sees her therapist, Dr. Ruth Godwin.

"Let's work through this," Godwin says. "If Corben Dean was there, how did he get out of the house?"

"I don't know."

"Are you sure it was him?"

"Well, he shaved off his beard but yeah, it was Corben Dean. I just can't believe it's happening again."

As she drives away, Jackie looks at her rear-view mirror. As she looks back to the road, she sees Corben Dean standing in front of her. Instinctively, she hits the brakes, but there's no way she can avoid hitting him. Strangely, her car passes right through him.

The Marriage of Julie Bright is a *Blue Velvet*-meets-*The Hunger* kind of movie, a cult favorite. Jackie, dressed in a gothic-styled dress as Julie Bright, runs toward a church.

When she arrives at the door, "Julie" checks to see if she's being followed. On the door is a church notice: "October 16, Funeral Service for Raymond Kelly."

"Julie" closes and bolts the door, approaching a casket at the front of the church, which is decorated with flowers and candles. She opens the casket. Inside is the body of Raymond, played by Gavin. She kisses the lips of the body.

"Darling, I'll be with you soon, and all this will be over. It's not going to happen anymore," she says, taking a ring off her finger and putting it on the body's hand.

TIME & PLACE *"We're ready to go," O.S.I.R. psychobiologist Lindsay Donner says, freezing the image as she sits with case manager Connor Doyle in the mobile lab.*

DOYLE RECORDS HIS first log: "Case manager Connor Doyle. File #569135. Investigation begins into a reported recurring apparition. We have been referred to the case by a former colleague of Dr. Hendricks, psychiatrist Ruth Godwin."

The investigators interview Dr. Godwin: "I testified on Jackie's behalf at Corben Dean's parole hearing. He was clean-shaven then. She wasn't there, yet she knew that he'd shaved off his beard. I saw him at the hearing. But how could Jackie have known that?"

Hendricks looks at the file, noting classic stalker pathology. "Adoration turns into obsession, obsession turns ugly, rejection turns into violence," he says.

"And violence turns into five years' aggravated assault and attempted murder," Donner adds.

"Anything further from Beaconsfield Prison?" Doyle asks.

"He was being transferred from the prison pending his final appeal. The prison authorities assure us he's somewhere in the system," Donner says.

"Earlier in the tape the psychiatrist said something about Corben Dean stealing from the subject?" Doyle asks.

"The scene you watched in the movie," Donner says. "Apparently he stole all those props. The dress, the wedding ring."

The next day, Jackie leads Doyle, Donner and another O.S.I.R. investigator, Nicholson, around the house. Jackie moves to the window, showing them where she was when she saw Dean. Doyle examines *The Marriage of Julie Bright* poster in the hall.

"I think Corben Dean saw the movie 65 times," Gavin says, shaking his head. "It's a trade-off. When you're a public figure like this, you have an identity in people's minds that's totally outside your control. All kinds of weirdoes come out of the woodwork."

"Three years ago, the night he assaulted me, he was basically waiting outside my house to kill me," Jackie says. "Essentially I think that's it. He's not going to rest until one of us is dead."

Back from Jackie's house, Doyle, Hendricks and Donner talk in the mobile lab. "It's likely she's suffering from post-traumatic stress intensified by her fear of success," Hendricks says. "There may be a link between Jackie's stalker anxiety and the fear of success: She doesn't want success because success brings stalkers."

"And her sightings began the day she learned she would be in this new movie," Doyle says.

Nicholson enters, handing Doyle a fax. "It's from Beaconsfield Prison," Doyle says. "Corben Dean won his appeal and was released two months ago. Apparently, the board failed to file notice of his release. This is the last address his parole officer had for him. Hendricks, take a security operative and stay with Jackie. Donner, you're with me. Mr. Dean is out there somewhere."

TIME & PLACE   *On the movie set the next day, Jackie stands next to her stage husband holding a glass of champagne.*

"**N O ,   T H A T ' S   N O T** how it went at all," she tells him flirtatiously. Jackie walks out of the "bedroom" and up to Gavin. The crew looks on, bored.

"How about if I'm still looking at him when I deliver that line and then I reach for the phone behind my back," Jackie suggests. "That feels more natural for me."

Telling Jackie to hold on, Gavin looks at the video assistant. Jackie looks around and notices somebody in the crew. Corben Dean is staring at her.

Jackie involuntary squeezes her champagne glass, which breaks. Seeing that Jackie's hand is bleeding, Gavin takes a step toward her. Jackie, in a trance, misinterprets his gesture and shrinks away from him. Jackie can't see Corben anywhere.

"Do you want to take a minute?" Gavin asks.

"Uh, yeah. If you wouldn't mind."

Meanwhile, an O.S.I.R. van cruises along a dingy street in Beaconsfield, British Columbia, and Doyle dictates a case log update: "In order to establish and confirm the exact circumstances of the initial stalker's whereabouts, Donner and I are en route to the last known address of Corben Dean."

The van pulls up outside a trailer home. Doyle and Donner get out and approach the trailer. Miscellaneous mail is strewn around the front door. Doyle picks up an envelope addressed to Mr. R. K. Kelly, then knocks on the door. No answer. They walk around the trailer, trying to look in the windows, but they are heavily boarded up.

"Look at this," Donner says, picking up a *Variety* trade paper, from which an article has been torn.

"That's normally the section where they list new productions with their location and when they begin shooting," Doyle says, knocking again on the trailer.

Doyle bends down, inspecting the door lock. He gives the door a sudden hoist, and it opens slightly. Doyle and Donner squeeze into the dark trailer. Doyle pulls out a penlight and flashes it around. The trailer is dirty, mostly empty of furniture except for a ratty bureau in the corner.

Disappointed that he probably won't find anything, Doyle sits down on a makeshift bed in one corner. Leaning back, he sees that the ceiling is covered in *The Marriage of Julie Bright* posters, identical to the one in Jackie Kinley's house.

TIME & PLACE *Doyle speaks into his recorder in the mobile lab.*

"**CASE LOG UPDATE.** Donner and I have just returned from Dean's trailer, where we recovered some personal effects linked to the character of Julie Bright, a role the subject made famous in a film five years ago." Doyle clicks off the recorder.

"According to the prison doctors," Hendricks tells his colleagues, "Dean's been in the advanced stages of heart disease for some time. His massive heart attack in prison persuaded the parole board to release him on compassionate grounds."

"And now Dean appears to be restalking our subject, but how did he get into a closed set?" Doyle wonders.

"And how did Jackie drive her car right through him?" Doyle asks.

"All items that Ms. Kinley was missing were recovered from the trailer, except the prop wedding ring," Donner says.

"Initiate 72-hour on-site monitoring with the subject in the controlled environment," Doyle orders. "When he comes again, we'll be ready."

TIME & PLACE *Tired after rehearsal, Jackie walks from her house to a waiting car, where Donner sits.*

"**GOD,**" **JACKIE SAYS.** "I suppose if I stopped laughing I'd go insane. Any news?"

"We're going to be setting up some additional equipment inside for the next three days," Donner explains. "And we'll need you."

"Uh, okay. Yeah, I have to confront this and deal with it myself. Otherwise it's going to own me for the rest of my life." She opens the car door to go. Nicholson, a security coordinator, and two other security operatives stand guard around the house. Doyle and Donner monitor the house from the mobile lab.

Jackie walks in and takes off her shoes. As she goes upstairs, the whispering starts: "The world wakes up for Julie Bright." Corben appears on the stairs behind her.

"Professor Doyle, there he is!" Jackie says through the comlink.

"Biostats registering a variety of responses typical of someone hearing, seeing and responding to traumatic sensory information," Donner says. "She thinks she sees him, but there's nothing."

Jackie turns toward the apparition, which vanishes. Jackie screams, "There he is!"

The O.S.I.R. investigators watch as Jackie picks up a vase and throws it down the hall. Then she flees into her bedroom.

"Electromagnetic activity on the second floor," Donner tells Doyle, who starts heading for the house. "Something's happening."

Jackie, now in a trance, stares at Corben. Nicholson and Doyle rush in. Jackie looks over at them, then collapses onto the bed. "Let's get Ms. Kinley to the lab," Doyle says.

"It was electromagnetic variance," Donner tells Doyle through the comlink. "Thirty gigahertz."

"Frequency that high..." Doyle says, taking a final look around. He walks out as the apparition of Corben Dean watches him.

The investigators discuss the incident in the mobile lab. "I don't understand. How could someone have gotten in? We had the house sealed off with someone stationed at every door," Nicholson says.

"Unless he was in there to begin with. Incorporeal," Hendricks says.

CORBEN APPEARS, WAITING FOR HER AS IF HE WERE A BRIDEGROOM, BUT HE LOOKS LIKE A CORPSE.

"It's more frustrating because Jackie is the only one to see him. It's almost as if this were a subjective haunt—when an entity in crisis broadcasts a telepathic signal to a subject who in turn casts the impulse into a tangible form but manifests no physical evidence," Donner says.

"But that doesn't really apply unless Dean is dead," Doyle says, thinking out loud. "The trailer we found the Julie Bright items in, it was rented to an R. K. Kelly?"

Doyle clicks on the remote control, and *The Marriage of Julie Bright* comes on the screen during the scene where "Julie" approaches the church. Doyle pauses it at the moment Julie opens the door of the church. The funeral notice on the door says: "October 16, Funeral Service for Raymond Kelly."

"October 16th?" Hendricks says. "That's tomorrow."

The next day, Jackie stares at the church. Her dress resembles the Julie Bright dress. She approaches the door. A notice on the door flaps in the wind, but she ignores it. She opens the door and goes inside.

Jackie walks down the aisle of the dark, empty church. There are whispers. Jackie stops and looks but sees nothing. When she looks back at the front of the church, Corben appears, waiting for her as if he were a bridegroom, but his appearance matches that of a corpse. Then he vanishes.

Jackie continues down the aisle. As she approaches the front of the church, a disturbed Corben follows her. Jackie arrives at the front of the church, where a casket lies, just as one lay in the Julie Bright movie.

Jackie puts her hand on the casket, and Corben materializes behind her. Jackie feels his "presence" but, staying focused, doesn't turn around. Instead, she opens the casket.

Inside is the two-week-old body of the real Corben Dean. In its opened hand is the Julie Bright wedding ring. Jackie looks at him a moment before grabbing the ring.

"Jackie?" Doyle calls, jolting her out of her reverie. Hendricks and Donner follow Doyle.

"It's over. Finally, it's all over," Jackie says, looking back at the casket to see the ghost of Corben Dean. The ghost begins to dissipate. "It's not going to happen anymore," Jackie says. "Thanks for letting me do that on my own. I appreciate it," she says, giving Doyle the wedding ring.

Jackie leaves. Donner bends over the corpse, taking a letter out of the casket.

Doyle, Hendricks and Donner hold a roundtable in the mobile lab. "The letter explained everything. It was about atonement, at least in his mind," Doyle says. "He was giving back everything he had taken from her while he was alive, completing what he needed to do."

"And, knowing that he was going to die, he put himself 'in' the movie. Bizarre, but consistent. That film was his whole life, and his death, too," Hendricks says, adding that the pathologist's report puts his death at October 4th, the same day Jackie received his phone call.

"I was just thinking that it was Jackie Kinley's image that obsessed Corben Dean and which in the end overwhelmed his identity," Donner says. "And in turn it was his image that terrorized and very nearly overwhelmed Jackie Kinley."

Jackie walks with Gavin on the movie set as Doyle gives a final case log: "File #569135. We have gone ahead with field-flux termination and eradication procedures at the subject's home even though no more audible or visual sightings of the apparition have been experienced by the subject. As of last week, Jackie Kinley has essentially returned to her normal life."

Months later, leaving the set one day, Jackie is accosted by a young fan. She agrees to sign her autograph. She feels uneasy. Something about the fan seems too familiar....

Epilogue

What becomes of our consciousness after death? Although Corben Dean was clinically dead, did he actually project himself in a noncorporeal state? Or did his presence exist only in Jackie Kinley's mind? Whatever the answer, working with Jackie, the O.S.I.R. was able to effectively terminate this subjective haunt.

DAN AYKROYD

Paranormal occurrences can range from the mundane, to the fascinating, to the outright dangerous. Danger was the last thing on Blaine McCallister's mind, however, when he decided to build his dream house. A place to live out his vision of family contentment for years to come. But when the partially constructed dwelling started to behave as if it had a mind of its own, dreams quickly turned to horror. **DAN AYKROYD**

Dream HOUSE

TIME & PLACE *Daytime in front of the McCallister home in Portland, Oregon.*

"There it is, the new house, in all its unfinished glory," says Blaine McCallister as he pulls his station wagon into the driveway with his fifteen-year-old daughter, Dixie. The roof is partially completed and tarped, the front yard chewed up from heavy trucks.

"Come on," Blaine says to Dixie, who is far from impressed. "Dixie, at least you can pretend to be excited."

Inside is a scene out of *This Old House*. Plywood boards, 2x4s, construction and power tools cover the floor. Blaine flicks a light switch, but there is no response.

"Dammit! If it isn't one thing, it's another," Blaine says. "Honey, I'm going to run downstairs and check the breaker box. Stay here."

Dixie, who's wandered through the front hall, hears a sound from the dining room. She calls to her dad but gets no response. Venturing toward the dining room, she sees a belt sander switch on and whip along the floor. As she turns and stares in disbelief, Dixie backs into a polyethylene sheet that wraps around her. Then wind gusts through the house. She recoils from the wind, backing up as a 2x4 slams through the wall behind her.

As Dixie runs for the door, a mini-twister forms. She hears an ominous roaring sound. From within the vortex of wind, Dixie sees a humanoid figure appear, a three-dimensional shadow. The shadow begins moving toward Dixie.

Suddenly, another, much larger three-dimensional shadow lurches out of the vortex and begins moving toward the smaller shadow, which turns and runs toward Dixie.

Stopping directly in front of Dixie, the smaller shadow throws a look over its shoulder at the larger shadow chasing her. It turns, running right through Dixie, and disappears. With the larger shadow now bearing down on her, Dixie closes her eyes and screams.

She opens her eyes, seeing Blaine standing directly in front of her. The wind gusts around them.

"Dad!" she yells, flinging her arms around her confused father, who looks up and pulls her away before a huge roll of tarpaper falls from above, narrowly missing them.

As he looks for an escape, a glass sliding door slams shut, imploding into a million pieces.

TIME & PLACE *The next day case manager Connor Doyle steps out of an unmarked O.S.I.R. vehicle. He's followed by Peter Axon, physicist/ statistician, psychiatrist Dr. Anton Hendricks, and Lindsay Donner, psychobiologist.*

D O Y L E   C L I C K S   O N the DAT recorder on his belt: "File #34112. Case manager Connor Doyle. Day one. We have arrived to investigate the anomalous activity reportedly taking place at the future residence of a Blaine McCallister and family. Preliminary interviews under way."

Doyle stops in front of the McCallister vehicle, where the nervous Blaine and Debbie McCallister are sitting. Connor leans down as Blaine rolls down the window. "You Doyle?" Blaine asks.

"We're a little shaken up by all this. Dixie's not doing too well," Debbie says.

"I thought we were just having a run of bad luck. Contractors quitting on us, on-the-job accidents," Blaine says. "Now there must be a rational explanation for all this. And I don't want to hear that our home is haunted. I don't buy that bull."

Investigators speak with Boris Bernhard, a heavyset man in his 40s. "I sold the McCallisters the land almost a year ago now. Lovely piece of property, and a real steal. They were going to build their dream house. Strange how long it's taken."

Construction foreman Barney Newcomb explains that his was the third team hired by the McCallisters: "And after what happened, you couldn't pay me and my crew enough to go back to that place. There was this one day, things just went nuts. Equipment either wouldn't run or would start running by itself. There were bizarre noises—howling, roaring sounds. And the last straw, Joey Hatz, he's walking around the outside of the house when he sinks up to his neck in this quicksand-like mud that suddenly appeared out of nowhere. We pulled him out just in time. Guy's lucky to be alive."

Dressed in environmental safety suits, Doyle, Axon, Hendricks, and investigators Whitman and Silva move through the front door the next day carrying pieces of portable monitoring equipment.

DOYLE ORDERS SILVA to run a scan for possible toxic hazards. Hendricks and Whitman stay on the main floor as the other men head upstairs. Axon and Doyle begin checking the walls and floors. Suddenly, a wind begins to blow. They slam into the wall as the wind and sounds increase.

"Electromagnetic pulses are going right off the scale," Axon yells as Doyle frantically reports rising air pressure and wind velocity.

A collective force of shrieking air screams past the two men, sending Silva crashing into the wall in the next room. Racing downstairs, Axon and Doyle hear a rattling sound.

"Look out!" Axon yells.

A box of nails explodes, spraying nails into the walls and ceiling, and hitting Whitman. "Code Black. Investigator's down!" Axon yells as the wind dies down and the sound dissipates.

Moments later, Doyle and Axon assist operatives in carrying Whitman away on a stretcher. Hendricks moves with them, checking them over. Doyle speaks into his recorder: "Case log update. Out of concern for the safety of my team, and due to the volatile and extreme nature of the phenomenon, I am requesting permission to expedite protocol and begin an immediate environmental assessment."

Once things are calmer, the investigators assess the situation. "Remarkable," Axon says. "All baseline results of the environmental readings are normal."

"And while the occurrences take place?" Donner asks.

"Gravitational fluctuations, electrostatic discharges, background radiation drops off the map. Pretty extreme," Axon says.

"Physiological assessments show nothing unusual with the McCallisters that could account for the phenomenon," Hendricks reports. "One point of interest, though. Debbie McCallister is expecting—twins."

"What about overall family dynamics?" Doyle asks.

"Stress levels are above average due to the pregnancy and, of course, the condition of their daughter," Hendricks says. "She's still hospitalized. And she shouldn't be. It's worrisome."

The next day Hendricks and Doyle visit Dixie in the hospital.

THE LIGHTS ARE dimmed. Hendricks focuses a penlight on the bridge of Dixie's nose. She's wired up to an EKG machine. Debbie is skeptical about following through with the hypnosis, but Doyle reassures her.

Hendricks holds up a hand for quiet, and Dixie closes her eyes. "Dixie, it's May 28th, about 6 p.m. Where are you?" Hendricks asks.

"My dad and I are driving up to the new house. It's a total drag. My friends are all going out together, and I'm here with my dad."

Dixie recounts moving toward the dining room. "It's getting windy and loud," she says, growing frightened. "There's someone ... in the middle of the wind."

"Be more specific, Dixie. Where is the center of this wind?" Hendricks asks.

Dixie flashes back to the shadow figure moving out of the twister vortex and rushing toward her. "No, no!" she screams. Hendricks calms her down.

The figure slows down, stopping. "It's right in front of me," Dixie says. "It's someone, but I can't tell who. Like a shadow of somebody. No face, just blackness."

The shadow figure's head slowly changes into Dixie's. She now wears glasses, has longer hair and appears a couple of years older, more mature.

Dixie tilts her head, searching, trying to figure out what she sees. Doyle walks over to Hendricks.

"It's me, but I'm different," Dixie says, stunned. Dixie sees the figure in her mind turning to look back over her shoulder, revealing the second, larger shadow figure rushing down the stairs. Older Dixie turns back and runs, as the larger shadow figure gets closer.

The larger shadow slows down but remains a shadow. In the background, by the swirling vortex, are a medium shadow figure and two small shadow figures lying on the floor of the living room.

"I'm not sure how many other figures there are. Two or three maybe," Dixie says. "But the big one isn't stopping ... coming for me. Oh my God!"

Hendricks snaps his fingers, and Dixie's eyes fly open. She looks around bewildered. Blaine and Debbie rush to her side.

"THE ENTIRE HOUSE BEGAN TO SHAKE. THEN THE FRONT DOOR EXPLODED OFF ITS HINGES. THE FLOOR BECAME SO HOT IT BURNED THE SOLES OF MY BOOTS."

TIME & PLACE *That evening, the O.S.I.R. team members compare notes in the mobile lab while Doyle speaks into the recorder.*

"FILE #34112. WE are initiating full environmental monitoring and surveillance, and proceeding with extreme caution. This complaint is a full-scale level 5. No investigator will be on-site without a partner for more than five minutes. Due to the volatile nature of the phenomenon, I am requesting additional personnel be assigned to the case."

Doyle asks how Silva and Whitman are.

"They suffered lacerations, concussions, some internal bleeding. They're recovering as anticipated, but will be hospitalized for a few more days," Hendricks says.

The team then gathers around a monitor of video footage of carpenter Rory Johnson. "The entire house began to shake," Johnson begins. "Like we was having an earthquake or something. Then the front door just exploded off its hinges just as Monty was coming in. He must have flown 15 feet. And around me, the floor became so hot it burned the soles of my boots.

"Then this black figure, I don't know, like a shadow, comes blasting through the room and throws me into a wall. I guess I was knocked out for a bit, because when I came to, Dirk had pulled me outside. We just lay there and watched the joint shake. But the worst was that high shrieking. I can't get the sound out of my head."

The investigators discuss the tape. "Any patterns developing as to when the activity occurs?" Doyle asks.

"No consistency whatsoever, except that it seems to be building," Axon says.

"The humanoid shadows figure prominently in everyone's testimony," Doyle says.

Hendricks punches some keys to reveal a photo of Dixie on the main screen beside a composite drawing of the person she described during regressive hypnosis.

"Since Dixie described the smaller shadow as being an older version of herself, I'm thinking we should play out the PK angle," Donner says.

"There's no physio or psych evidence to suggest she's responsible for all this," Axon observes.

"Except her description," says Donner. "It might be more subjective than we think."

TIME & PLACE   *At the house, three investigators stand in the front yard prepping the probe.*

"**W H A T   A R E   W E** looking for?" Doyle asks.

"Environmental anomalies, fluctuations in air pressure, irregular seismic activity, the works," Axon replies.

As Doyle and Axon return to the mobile lab, the investigators maneuver the probe into position. Axon controls the joystick of the probe as it moves through the main floor of the house. Suddenly, a bluish-black spot moves.

"What was that?" Axon demands.

"Pan right," Doyle says.

The monitor reveals that the windows are frosted up. A digital temperature gauge beside the monitor begins decreasing.

"What's the exterior temperature surrounding the home?" Doyle asks. Axon reports it's 22 degrees Celsius and holding.

The black spot reappears and starts to move about in an irregular pattern. Suddenly, investigators hear a loud thumping sound over the speaker. Axon moves to a seismograph, which registers with each thump. The thumps increase in volume as Doyle tries to determine where the seismic activity is originating.

"Temperature levels now rising rapidly," Doyle says. The monitor shows orange spots turning red. The frost starts melting on the windows.

Suddenly one of the spots becomes a humanoid shape and starts moving toward the camera. Bursts of static interrupt the image, and the camera begins shaking.

"We're losing RF transmission," Axon says. "Seismic activity on top of the probe."

The camera shakes violently, then rises into the air before apparently being flung against the wall. All monitor screens go to static.

"Damn. Probe telemetry down," Axon says. "We've lost it."

As investigators set up termination equipment at the McCallister home, another finishes putting away the

PLA. Doyle walks past them, speaking into his headset. "Case log update. At the client's request, termination procedures have been initiated. Acoustical, atmospheric and nuclear-flux technologies have all been introduced to the environment. All elimination efforts have proved unsuccessful to this point. Considering bridge procedure with O.S.I.R. AI specialist."

Doyle stops beside Blaine, who stands staring at the house. "An AI specialist?" Blaine says, confused.

"It's an operative who specializes in alternative information utilizing metaphysical techniques," Doyle explains. "A psychic."

"I'm beyond questioning anything now," Blaine says. "Just do whatever it takes to make it stop. Dixie's getting worse, and we're worried sick."

Investigators move to the mobile lab for a round table with Linda Scholtz, AI specialist. "There *is* a presence in the house, but what confuses me is that I'm receiving no information from the past. That's extremely rare," Linda says.

Axon then replays the thumping sounds recorded in the house. "And here it is after we slowed it down and filtered out all extraneous noise," Axon says, as the tape reveals the sound of a pair of boots walking across a wood floor.

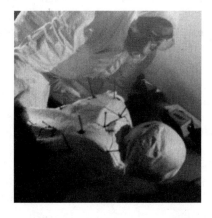

"I'M BEYOND QUESTIONING ANYTHING NOW," BLAINE SAYS. "JUST DO WHATEVER IT TAKES TO MAKE IT STOP."

"Dixie described what ... five figures?" Donner asks.

"One of them being an older version of herself," Doyle says.

"Anton, it was definitely twins Debbie McCallister's expecting?" Donner asks.

Hendricks nods, asking, "Are you suggesting this could all be related to precognition?"

"I was unable to sense anything from the past," Linda says. "That leaves the future as a possibility."

"Five shadow figures," Hendricks says. "Five members of the McCallister family, once the twins are born."

"Exactly," agrees Donner. "What if in a parallel dimension, or another time line, the McCallister family moved into this house, and lived there for several years?"

"Then something terrible happens," Hendricks warns. "A home invasion leads to multiple murders."

"Perhaps," Doyle says, "somehow the family in the parallel dimension is trying to warn our clients not to move into this particular house. And Dixie was the messenger."

TIME & PLACE *In the hospital the next day, Debbie sits by Dixie's side as she lies in bed tossing and turning. Debbie holds Dixie's hand as Hendricks enters.*

MEANWHILE, BLAINE MCCALLISTER

talks with Boris Bernhard, the previous landowner.

"Amazing. Just like that, doubling the size of your family," Boris says. "Of course I understand. The house isn't big enough anymore."

As the men talk, Donner and two investigators monitor the conversation in the mobile lab. Another monitor shows AKA activity with shrieking and stomping and windows smashing.

"So what are you proposing?" Boris continues. "You want me to take the property off your hands?"

"You'd be doing me a hell of a favor," Blaine says.

Doyle continues to monitor the AKA activity at the house. The noises and destructive activity increase in intensity.

At the hospital, Dixie murmurs in her sleep. The EKG machine beeps faster and faster. Debbie looks at Hendricks, and Hendricks gets up to look at the EKG reading.

"This is a big one," Doyle says at the mobile lab. "Dammit. Bernhard is going to blow this."

"So make me an offer," Blaine says.

"I don't think I can do any better than 10 percent under market value," Boris says. Blaine agrees right away, and they shake on it.

Doyle and Axon turn to monitor two. As Blaine and Boris release hands, the stomping and shrieking cease.

In her bed, Dixie tosses and turns. Then she lies still, and her eyes snap open.

TIME & PLACE *A few weeks later, a new couple pulls up in front of the house, which displays a "For Sale" sign.*

THEY STAND ADMIRING their new home.

Doyle presents his final log update: "After the land transaction was finalized, and after several more experiments, we have determined that the McCallisters' selling the property resulted in the disappearance of the phenomenon. Counseling with Dixie continues as she tries to put her experience behind her. Helping her parents take care of her new brother and sister has had a positive effect on her state of mind. Case manager Connor Doyle, out."

Epilogue

Was this simply an extremely active poltergeist/haunt case in which the McCallisters were being warned about dire events to come by future visions of themselves should they move into their dream house at 5214 Corvallis Crescent? Well, this is one speculation investigators could formulate. When the O.S.I.R. made it clear that his family's safety might depend on it, Blaine McCallister willingly sold the house. Blaine learned the sometimes elusive but ultimately obvious truth that a dream home is not built with wood, brick or stone, but rather on the foundation of love and the happiness of one's family.

DAN AYKROYD

THREE   SUPERNATURAL MAN

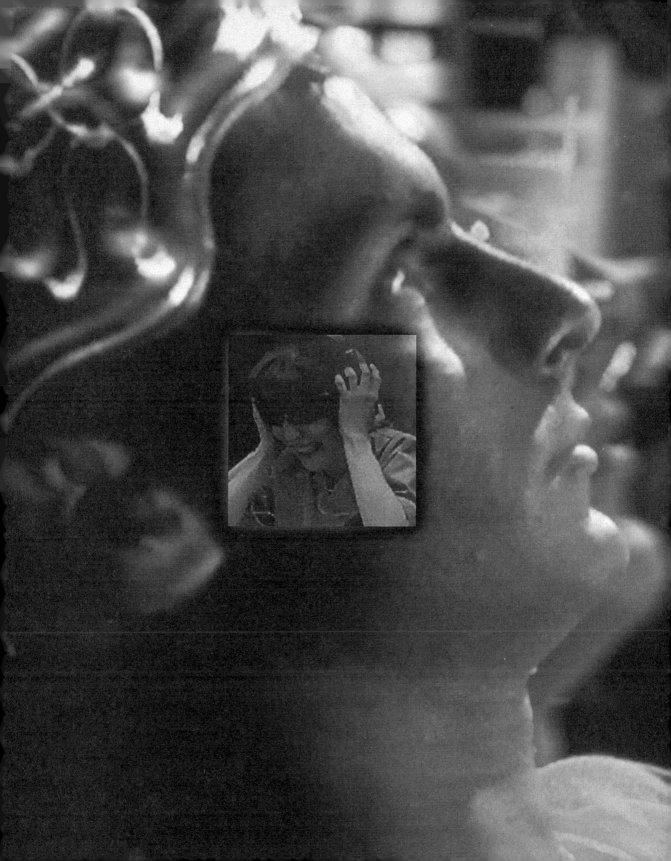

Time travel—it's a concept that captivates our imaginations. For science fiction writers, time travelers are usually depicted as courageous adventurers willing to conquer an unknown future or alter a troubled past. But what of the ordinary man, snatched from his own time and thrown into an unfamiliar future, there to be tortured by the loss of his family and tormented by a strange and threatening world? Within thirty-six hours after the discovery of a disoriented man in the English countryside, the O.S.I.R. was on the site, attempting to determine whether his ravings were the delusions of a madman or the desperate pleas of a reluctant traveler, a man out of time. **DAN AYKROYD**

Man Out of TIME

TIME & PLACE *Late evening, on a small narrow road in Bedfordshire, England.*

On an English countryside, a narrow two-lane blacktop winds through the rolling farmland. The air is still, ominous; something's brewing. A car appears in the distance. Chester and Madeline Boswell, an upper-class couple dressed in formal attire, are returning from a dinner party at a country estate. Classical music emanates softly from the car's speaker system. They are both a bit tipsy.

"What a bloody waste of time that party was," Chester says.

"Now, dear. As you always tell me, it's the price of doing business," Madeline replies.

"Price of doing business!" Chester snorts. "Next time I see that Ralphie Fenwick and his stuck-up business partners, I'd like to give him a piece of my loafer."

"Please," Madeline begs, "keep at least one eye on the road!"

Suddenly in front of them, a bright light flashes. Chester blinks and shakes his head.

"Did you see that? Up ahead, on the road?" Chester asks. Madeline shakes her head no.

Suddenly before them, a figure appears, standing on the center line. Chester slams on his brakes. The car screeches to a halt, stopping inches from a bewildered-looking man. He is in his mid-thirties with long, straggly hair, wearing strange farmerlike clothing and holding an odd-looking farm tool. Chester beeps at the man and he jumps back. Chester gets out of the car.

"What's your problem?" Chester asks the man.

The man, in an unrecognizable dialect, says, "Oh, Lord! Where be I now?"

Chester, not understanding, asks, "You deaf or something?"

The man, in great distress, answers, "In the name of God, help me!"

TIME & PLACE *McMartin Institute, a psychiatric facility in Bedfordshire, England, daytime. The O.S.I.R. team—psychiatrist Dr. Anton Hendricks; Peter Axon, physicist/statistician; Dr. Lindsay Donner, a psycho-biologist; and case manager Connor Doyle, also a professor—are discussing a report submitted by Dr. Robert Steen from the McMartin Institute.*

DOYLE REPORTS THE case: "Subject found wandering
on a road in Spotswood, Bedfordshire, England. A preliminary evaluation by Dr. Robert Steen led him to transfer the patient to the McMartin Institute. Upon reviewing the police report and the subject's statement, Dr. Steen contacted the O.S.I.R. According to Dr. Steen's report, the subject is stable but confused. He can apparently communicate in English but the dialect is obscure. Ms. Donner, we will need to identify its origin."

Donner nods.

Hendricks says, "I read Steen's report. This ... who does he say he is ... Mr. Hanrahan? His story isn't that clear."

"It's quite simple," Doyle says. "A Mr. John Hanrahan purports to have been on his farm one minute and facing a metal beast the next."

"Metal beast?" asks Donner.

"An automobile," Doyle says. "A couple driving home."

"The Boswells," Donner says. "Their statement wasn't very extensive. We'll talk to them as well."

"Let's determine the validity of the story," Doyle says. "Hopefully we haven't come a long way for nothing."

TIME & PLACE *The O.S.I.R. mobile lab, several days later. Doyle is watching video footage of the subjects who have been interviewed regarding this case.*

INSPECTOR WILLIAM HANEY reports:
"We responded to a call from the Boswells at around 2:30 a.m. We arrived to find this Mr. Hanrahan raving like a lunatic, wandering around the fields near the road. He said he'd been wandering for hours. Claims to be in hell, a lost soul as it were. He had no identification of any kind. We did a background check on him. Found no record of the man at all. No fingerprint matches. Even checked for his dental records. Strangest thing ... he has none. We turned him over to the McMartin Institute

for observation. We felt he could present a danger to himself or to others. He was in quite a state, I tell you. Terrified. Everything seemed to petrify him."

Doyle then watches footage of Hendricks' interview with Dr. Steen. "When the police brought him in, he was raving, paranoid and terrified at almost everything he saw," Dr. Steen says. "He began mumbling about death and purgatory. Asking if he was indeed in hell. I assumed it was a form of schizophrenia and admitted him to our constant care ward."

"What made you contact our office?" Hendricks asks.

"His statement," Dr. Steen says. "His accent is difficult to understand if he's excited or nervous. Once he's calm, though, he does make sense. He was quite consistent over several interviews. It isn't every day that a man appears claiming to be from the 17th century!"

TIME & PLACE   *The McMartin Institute observation room, later that day. The O.S.I.R. team is watching a video of Dr. Hendricks interviewing Hanrahan. Hanrahan is hooked up to a digitally enhanced polygraph DEP machine.*

"WHAT IS YOUR name?" Hendricks asks.

"I be John Hanrahan of Bedfordshire, sir," Hanrahan responds.

"And what is your current age?"

"I am five and thirty year."

"Where do you live?"

"Me farm be near the town of Spotswood."

"Date of birth?"

"I was born on five of April, in the year of our Lord sixteen and twelve."

"How did you get here?"

"I do not know that, sir," Hanrahan responds, very distressed. "God help me ... "

Doyle turns away from the video and addresses the O.S.I.R. team.

"The physiological tests on the subject reveal no traces of modern bacteria or synthetic antibodies in his system."

"That's remarkable," Donner says.

"But not impossible," Doyle answers. "If he's from a remote region of the earth, his system could be this clean. Peter?" Doyle turns to Axon.

"No environmental anomalies in this area," Axon reports. "No hazardous materials or toxic gases. No abnormal concentrations of energy fields. All baseline results are fairly typical."

"The subject's accent and speech patterns are strange," Donner says. "It's not Irish as it turns out. Our linguistics experts reviewed the tapes and concluded the speaker was either from a remote area in the Cotswold uplands ... or he has language patterns inherent to a Bedfordshire farmer from the 1600s.

"There's more," Donner continues. "According to local archives, a farmer named John Hanrahan did exist in Spotswood around 1612."

"The subject could have had access to this information?" Doyle asks.

"It would have taken some work but ..." Donner answers.

"So the possibility of a hoax remains high," Doyle interrupts.

Donner nods. "As we discussed," she says, "I'm starting a covert investigation into the local homesteads in the area. Trying to cross-reference the archival findings."

"Good," Doyle says. "Hendricks?"

"Hanrahan is still quite distressed," Hendricks says. "Repeated DEP testing was required to interpret his psychodynamics. But the data collected so far back up the subject's story."

"What about regressive hypnosis results?" Doyle asks.

"No luck yet," Hendricks says. "I haven't been able to relax him into a preconscious state."

"Do whatever it takes to put him under," Doyle says. "If he feels more relaxed having a tea party, then do it."

TIME & PLACE *McMartin Institute observation room, the next morning.*

HENDRICKS IS ATTEMPTING to put

Hanrahan under hypnosis. He's successful.

"Tell me what you see," Hendricks says to Hanrahan.

"Me farm. I must go clear the path."

"Why?"

"A tree has fallen from the storm."

"When was there a storm?"

"It be the night last," Hanrahan says. Then, after

"HE'S VERY UNSTABLE. HE CAN'T EVEN COMPREHEND WHAT MAY HAVE HAPPENED TO HIM."

a pause, Hanrahan shouts, "Good Lord!"

"What is it?" Hendricks asks. "What is happening? What do you see?"

"A light. Like a pebble in the water but there be no water. It surrounds me. Help me!"

"Please continue. What do you see now?"

"It has vanished! Me house ... me family ... is gone."

"Now what do you see?"

"I'm in my field. But all looks different. A bright light. A roaring beast on the road. Where am I ...?"

TIME & PLACE *The Lester estate, later in the day. Donner and two other O.S.I.R. investigators are ushered into the estate's main house by its owner, Lucille Lester.*

"WE REALLY APPRECIATE you taking the

time, Mrs. Lester," Donner says. "This is a very important project for the university's historical society."

"Always glad to help maintain our heritage," Mrs. Lester answers as she guides them on a tour through the house. "The main house was built in 1809."

And prior to that, what was here?" Donner asks.

"Just farmland."

Donner looks at one of the hanging portraits and sees a man who is the spitting image of John Hanrahan. She excuses herself to call Doyle on her cell phone.

"It's remarkable," she tells Doyle. "It's him."

"You mean you think it's him," Doyle says.

"Point taken," Donner says. "Shall we maintain our cover?"

"Don't tip them off just yet," Doyle orders. "Find out what you can about the family's history." Just then an investigator hands some documents to Doyle. "Hold on. The genealogical trace report indicates the Lesters are the descendants of one John Hanrahan."

Donner hangs up with Doyle and walks back to the main parlor. Lucille Lester is now joined by her daughter, Meagan.

"If I may inquire, who is the striking figure in the portrait?" Donner asks, pointing to the Hanrahan-like figure.

"That would be Sir Stewart Lester," Meagan answers. "It was painted by a local artist in 1731. Sir Stewart established the first barley mill in this region in 1702 and was knighted by Queen Anne."

"And who were Sir Stewart's parents?" Donner asks.

"Sir Stewart's mother, Regina, was orphaned at age seven after her father disappeared and her mother died of consumption," Mrs. Lester answers. "She was raised by an aunt."

"You wouldn't happen to know the name of her father?" Donner asks. "The one who went missing?"

"No, he didn't go missing," Meagan says. "He ran off. Apparently to America."

"Now, now, Meagan," Mrs. Lester chides. "That's just folklore. The truth is that no one knows why John Hanrahan left his family."

TIME & PLACE   *McMartin Institute, evening.*

THE O.S.I.R. TEAM is gathered for a round-table discussion.

"He's very unstable," Hendricks says. "He's exhibiting all the symptoms of post-traumatic stress disorder. He can't even comprehend what may have happened to him."

"I've got a lab report on the subject's clothes and personal effects," Axon says. "They appear to be authentic. But not vintage pieces. The fibers match exactly with fibers of the period yet they haven't aged more than five or ten years."

"That would be difficult to do," Hendricks says.

"It might be possible," Doyle says. "I'm going to talk to Mrs. Lester myself and explain our situation. We need the family's cooperation."

TIME & PLACE   *The Lester estate, the next day.*

DOYLE EXPLAINS THE situation to Mrs. Lucille Lester and her daughter, Meagan.

"This is absurd!" Mrs. Lester says. "Are you implying this man is actually *the* John Hanrahan? That's rubbish!"

"There is some evidence supporting his claim," Doyle says calmly. "What might help is a comparative DNA test."

"I've heard quite enough!" Mrs. Lester says. "I think it's time for you to go!"

"Please," Doyle says, "think about it." Understanding that Mrs. Lester is upset by the information, he leaves the house. As he stands by his car, ready to get in, Meagan approaches.

"I must apologize for Mother," she says. "She can be very closed-minded."

"You understand we are trying to help, Meagan?"

"Professor Doyle, this man ... could he really have traveled through time?" Meagan asks.

"That's what we're trying to find out."

"And that DNA test you mentioned ... that would help your investigation?"

"Yes, it would."

"Then I'll do it," Meagan responds.

TIME & PLACE *Back at the McMartin Institute, later that day.*

DOYLE ENTERS INTO his case log that Meagan's DNA is a consistent match to Hanrahan's. Hendricks is sitting in the observation room with Hanrahan.

"Mr. Hanrahan," Hendricks says.

"Sir, call me John, if you like. It be the name me friends call me by."

"Do you know where you are?"

"I know now that I be in purgatory. Limbo to either the gates of heaven or to hell's damnation."

"You believe you are dead?"

"Of that I have no doubt. And you, sir, be my judge. To see fit where I spend my eternity."

"John ... I assure you ...."

"Spare me the ruse, sir. I will do well by you, I swear to that. I know you are of good spirit. You will help me find the way to the angels' chorus."

"But I'm not an angel. Or a saint. I'm a man. A doctor."

"I see by the very glow in your eyes, sir, that you have knowledge of the vast unknown that is man's final journey. I know you will show me the way."

TIME & PLACE *The O.S.I.R. mobile lab, late in the evening.*

THE O.S.I.R. TEAM is meeting. Donner is exhibiting a current map of Bedfordshire on a screen. She flicks to the next image. "This transparency is a map from 1638." She points to an area on the map. "This is Spotswood, where Hanrahan's property would likely have been. And this," she says, pointing again, "is where the Boswells found him."

"Professor Axon, was the property area covered by our initial assessments?" Doyle asks.

"We've run all possible on-site tests," Axon answers. "All came up negative. It would help if Mr. Hanrahan could show us the exact spot where he appeared."

HANRAHAN IS WEARING a biofeed that monitors

all aspects of his biophysical state. "John, we need you to take us to the place where you found yourself after seeing the bright light," Hendricks tells Hanrahan.

"I do not know if I can. But I shall try me best," Hanrahan says. "You'll be testing me again, sir. I shall win your favor over if it takes a thousand years."

"John, " Hendricks says, "we're just trying to help you."

Something catches Hanrahan's eye. He gasps and runs forward. Hendricks follows. Hanrahan is approaching the ruins on the land. He touches the stone wall of the dovecote.

"But this is my land!" Hanrahan cries out, anguished. "I built this dovecote here with me own hands. I know it well!"

Doyle shakes his head. Hendricks puts his hand on Hanrahan's shoulder to comfort him. Hanrahan looks at them with tears in his eyes.

"There's nothing more we can do here," Doyle says.

"I've failed then, sir," Hanrahan says. "All is lost."

THE TEAM IS in a conference. "Any theories?" Doyle asks.

"Hard to say," Axon offers. "Subconsciously, he could have transported his corporeal state subatomically from one point to another: the psychokinetic vortex theory."

"What about corporeal duplication? A form of reincarnation?" Donner asks. "Through subconscious compulsion, he gains ethereal awareness of a past life and synthesizes it into his current one."

"We just don't have enough evidence to support a scientific theory," Doyle says. "And since we don't know how to return him to his home, if he is from the past, then we have an obligation to help him adjust."

"Hanrahan is still suffering from some kind of highly traumatic experience," Hendricks says. "Our focus should be on counseling him. I'd like to see him moved to friendlier surroundings."

DOYLE AND HENDRICKS are en route to

Hanrahan's room. "This news should lift his spirits," Doyle says.

"I think he'll only be too happy to leave this place behind," Hendricks says.

The guard unlocks the door to Hanrahan's room. Hendricks steps inside to find Hanrahan dead. He's hanged himself.

" F I L E # 1 0 1 0 3 .   F I N A L   case log," Doyle reports. "An autopsy was performed on the body supporting the theory that John Hanrahan lived nearly 400 years ago. Cell structure, stomach enzyme analyses and blood count are consistent with that of a 17th-century adult male. As for how he came to appear in our present, we can only speculate that he encountered a phenomenon that instantaneously brought him forward in time. This phenomenon, whatever it may be, remains unidentified. Doyle, out."

Epilogue

The O.S.I.R. discovered no conclusive evidence of how John Hanrahan's unhappy journey occurred. But if, as the work of Einstein, Rosen and Hawking suggests, the fabric of space and time is one which can be bent, then perhaps he was unlucky enough to stumble through a compressed fold in that fabric. Whatever the reason, Hanrahan's tragic experience is a disturbing antidote to science fiction's premise that time travel is an exciting and glorious adventure.

D A N   A Y K R O Y D

Newton's first law of motion: An object remains at rest, unless acted upon by an external force. But what if an object moves without any visible evidence of force acting upon it? This was the disturbing complication that further upset the life of Matt Peck after he suffered the tremendous physical loss of his right arm. A complication that drove him and his family to reconsider the laws of motion— as we generally understand them—with the help of the O.S.I.R.

DAN AYKROYD

P h a n t o m L I M B

TIME & PLACE *Midday on a farm in Jardine County, Pennsylvania.*

Matt Peck, forty-nine, oversees his son, Brad, twenty-eight, a tall broad-shouldered young man, working at a grain silo. "Take the tractor out to the northwest quarter, Brad. I'll meet you out there," Matt says.

As Brad drives off, Matt notices something caught between the drive shaft of the seeder. "Hold on! Something's jammed in there," Matt says.

Brad stops the tractor. Matt jumps on the seeder, opens up the drive shaft and reaches inside. Brad stands on the tractor and watches his father pull at the machinery. Then without warning, the seeder starts running. Before Matt can pull away, his shirt sleeve gets stuck in the revolving pieces of machinery, pulling his right arm into the seeder's blades.

"Brad!" Matt yells.

Jumping down from the tractor, Brad starts screaming. Suddenly the seeder stops. Matt's right arm is locked into the blades of the seeder up to his shoulder. Brad gasps in horror as he sees the sleeve of Matt's jacket absorbing blood. Matt slowly loses consciousness.

"NICE CATCH, GRANDPA," Joshua says.

Matt grunts and throws the ball back to Joshua with his left hand. Matt's wife, Sarah Peck, 45, brings out some lemonade. Matt faces her, revealing that his right arm has been amputated at the shoulder. Matt takes some lemonade, and Joshua throws the ball back.

Matt grits his teeth and gives his best effort with his wrong arm. The ball lands in front of Joshua and bounces by him. "Sorry, Joshua," he says.

As Matt sips his lemonade, Joshua yells at him to watch out. Matt turns in time to see the softball speeding for him. Before it hits, the ball stops in midair, inches from his face. Impossibly, the ball hovers in front of Matt and Sarah. It gently drops onto the grass. Matt and Sarah look at each other, amazed and frightened.

IT IS EARLY evening and Matt is watching television when his son Brad walks in. "Dad, I was talking to Earl Johnson at the hospital today. He tells me those new prosthetic arms are just like the real thing."

"They got fingernails on the fingers and hair on the arms and blood in the veins?" Matt asks. "They're not just like the real thing, are they?" His anger building, Matt reaches for the TV remote control. Clumsily using his left hand, he knocks it to the ground. He stands up, swears, and ... a hole punches itself into the living room wall.

The next day, technicians scurry around the O.S.I.R. mobile unit, which is parked on the farm property, and case manager Curtis Rollins speaks into a recorder: "Case manager's log. File #52113, 0900 hours. Initial contact made by Dr. Paul Slater, professor of biophysics, Penn State University. Dr. Slater was apprised of this claimed anomalous activity by one of the subjects and a former student, Brad Peck."

Dr. Anton Hendricks greets Rollins near the front door. "I'll start on physiological and psychological assessments as soon as the preliminary interviews are done," Hendricks says.

The first person interviewed is Professor Paul Slater, Ph.D. "Brad Peck asked me to come over and take a look," Slater says. "I found structural damage to the house and property. Objects freezing in midair. It was ... I don't know what it was, but it violates every principle of physics."

The Pecks also give interviews. "Dad was the classic football hero in college. Then he played top-tier baseball in the service. He was good with his hands, you know? A natural," Brad says. "So it was really tough on him, you know, the accident. I thought he might be coming around a bit. Dealing with the loss. But then all this stuff flying around, coming from nowhere."

"Maybe it's ghosts," Matt says sarcastically. "Maybe it's little green men from outer space. You people say you can figure it out. Good. Go to it. Figure it out and get rid of it. I've got enough to worry about running this farm."

Sarah also speaks with investigators. "This is going to sound odd," she says, "but I was walking with Matt when I stumbled. Then I felt a hand grab my elbow and steady me, but there was nothing there. It couldn't have been Matt because I was on his right side."

After the interviews, an O.S.I.R. physician performs a physical examination on Matt while Hendricks talks to him. "How did you feel when you first woke up in the hospital?" Hendricks asks.

"What do you think? I didn't want to be there," Matt says.

"When exactly did this injury occur?"

"'Bout six weeks ago. Guess it healed up pretty well."

"Remarkably, I'd say."

Out on the farm, O.S.I.R. physicist/statistician Peter Axon rides shotgun as Brad drives. Another investigator, Gerrard, rides in the back, holding various scanners. "What's all this stuff for?" Brad asks.

"Well, everything has a different purpose," Axon explains. "This is a magnetometer, which measures fluctuations in different parts of the magnetic spectrum. Science geeks like us use these a lot."

The pickup truck approaches the seeder and stops on an incline. Axon, Brad, and Gerrard get out and move near the granary. Axon waves the probe around the area while Gerrard examines a scanner.

"This is where it happened. I shut everything down. I know I did. It just started up on its own," Brad says.

"I'm picking up some inconsistent readings," Axon says.

Axon stares down at the magnetometer, noticing that the numbers are surging. He turns back to the granary, moving the probe along its surface. On the incline, the pickup truck rolls slowly backward toward them. With their backs turned, they don't see it; with its motor off, they don't hear it. The truck is almost on top of them, when, at the last moment, Gerrard sees it. "Look out!" he screams.

Axon pushes Brad out of the way, and the pickup truck crashes into a combine.

TIME & PLACE   *At the mobile lab unit, Rollins gives a case file update.*

"BACKGROUND, HISTORICAL, AND archival assessments now under way. Nothing we have found so far suggests we are dealing with a hoax. Soil and water samples, glass and plaster fragments will be enclosed in data pouches labeled DD52113 en route for analysis."

Rollins returns to the farm near the rest of the team.

"An unusually large area of tissue was destroyed near the amputation site. Rather than simply stitching the stump over, a skin graft was applied which, incidentally, has been healing at an incredibly fast rate—three weeks ahead of schedule," Hendricks says.

"No evidence of any toxic or hazardous substances capable of inducing hallucinations or perceptual abnormalities," Axon says. "Environmental scans have found no geophysical anomalies, with one exception. The scan picked up a localized deposit of magnetite. It produced a field strong enough to momentarily throw the magnetometer out of whack. I ran more tests and found the deposit was concentrated enough, along with a faulty emergency brake, to pull the truck. I think it could have caused the seeder to start spinning again, even though the motor was off."

"So the magnetite may have caused Matt's accident," Rollins says. "Could this deposit have caused the other occurrences as well?"

"The field it generates is too localized. It only affects objects in close proximity," Axon says.

That evening, Matt nurses a beer in the kitchen while Sarah sips lemonade. Both wear biophysical-monitoring equipment.

"Yeah, well, how long is this going to take?" Matt asks.

"They're trying to help," Sarah says. "Please, give them a chance."

"This ain't a research center for the lame and crippled. I just want to be done with things moving around by themselves."

Matt bangs the table for emphasis with his left arm. He knocks over his glass of beer. Suddenly the glass flies across the room, smashing against the far wall.

TIME & PLACE *The next day, Rollins and the investigators gather around a bank of television screens in the mobile unit.*

"AT 2200 HOURS on day six of this investigation, something extraordinary occurred," Axon says. "It was witnessed by both Matt and Sarah Peck as well as Curtis here. The event registered on a variety of monitoring equipment. We best captured what happened on thermal imaging."

Axon dims the lights and starts to play a videotape that has captured the last moments of the scene in the Peck kitchen. It shows Matt spilling the drink. Then, thousands of sparkling points of light appear at Matt's right. They coalesce into a greenish-purple energy form, and the shape of an arm emanates from Matt's right shoulder stump. Matt, who appears unaware of the limb's movements, uses this "phantom limb" to fling the glass against the wall.

"Remarkable. Here, take a look at his biostat readout during the incident," Axon says. The biostat readouts surge as the phantom limb takes shape.

"Well, we've covered all other plausible explanations for this phenomenon. Any other theories?" Rollins asks.

"The appendage may be a subatomic energy matrix generated by Matt Peck," Axon says.

"This suggests Matt could be solely responsible for the phenomenon," Hendricks says.

"That could be what the data are telling us," Axon says.

"But someone else in the house could be using latent PK ability to produce the appendage," Rollins says.

"Matt Peck's psych profile suggests that if he were doing this consciously, he'd tell us up front. Honesty is a high priority with him," Hendricks says.

"So last night, Matt saw the glass falling and without thinking just threw it," Rollins says.

"So it's conceivable this traumatic loss has caused Matt to access innate but unconscious psychokinetic powers in situations where he reacts involuntarily," Axon says.

Later, the investigators replay the looping thermo image for the Pecks. "Turn that damn thing off!" Matt yells.

"Dad, didn't you see? It's you. You did it."

"If I was making things move, I'd know it," Matt says, "and I know I had nothing to do with that."

"We need to run more tests to help you, and us, better understand this phenomenon. And, hopefully, assist you in using it with more control," Rollins says.

"That freak show is not me," Matt says, storming out.

That evening, Rollins is alone in the mobile lab unit. The tape of the kitchen incident loops through one of the monitors while Rollins talks into his comlink headset: "Case log update. We have been given an extraordinary opportunity to observe and research an unusual form of PK activity. But the meeting this evening with Matt Peck was disappointing. I'm concerned we may lose this opportunity to study this phenomenon."

Rollins clicks off the recorder, moving to another part of the lab, where Axon and Hendricks are examining a 3-D computer image of a one-armed male figure.

"If Matt Peck will cooperate, I recommend further testing," Axon says. "I'd like to determine exactly how much of his ability is a result of reflexive, involuntary action and how much can be controlled."

"Remember that it takes some time for someone to dissociate themselves emotionally from the trauma of the actual event. My emphasis would be on counseling him. If he were willing, I'd start a program of hypnotherapy," Hendricks says.

"YOU ARE NOT A FREAK. SOMEHOW, GOD GAVE YOU THIS GIFT. LET THESE PEOPLE SHOW YOU HOW TO USE IT."

"He could be eased into his own method of controlling his phantom limb," Rollins agrees.

Responding to a cue from his headset, Rollins exits the lab and goes outside, where a security operative is standing with Sarah. "If Matt knew I was talking to you about him, he'd throw one hell of a fit. Are you sure he's responsible for all of the strange occurrences?" Sarah asks.

"Pretty sure, but we need to run some more tests," Rollins says.

"And you can teach him how to use this power?"

"I can't guarantee that, but we'll try. But first Matt has to stop denying his life is different now. If we could get him to accept his new-found ability, it could become as good as a real arm," he explains.

That night, Matt sits in the kitchen staring at a photo album in his lap.

"You have to let them help you, teach you about this power you have," Sarah says.

"I don't have any powers, Sarah."

"You would rather live the rest of your life bitter and frustrated. They have proof, Matt. You are not a freak. You are my husband. Somehow, God gave you this gift. Let these people show you how to use it."

"I don't want a gift, Sarah. I want things to be the way they used to be," Matt says. "I didn't do all those things. And no matter what you say or they say, I won't change my mind. These scientists have solved nothing, and they've fed this family a bunch of lies and false hope. I want them to leave."

"YOU AND YOUR team have been here a week turning this place into a fun house," Matt says.

"If you want us to leave, we'll be gone by noon," Rollins says.

Finally satisfied, Matt walks toward the barn. As he enters, he looks up to see Joshua high on a wooden beam. "Joshua! You come down from there right now!" Matt says.

Just as Joshua moves back to the ladder, he slips and falls off the beam, hanging on only by his fingertips. He cries out to Matt, who runs to a ladder. Joshua cries out again, louder. As Matt pulls himself up onto the beam, Joshua is barely hanging on.

"Joshua, don't move. Grandpa is going to come get you," Matt says. Matt moves toward Joshua, and the boy's grip loosens. He begins to fall. Without thinking, Matt grabs a nearby post and leans out as much as he can. Joshua stops in mid-fall, frozen in the air above the barn floor.

Rollins and two operatives, along with Sarah and Brad, who heard Joshua's cries, enter the barn. The group watches as Joshua is pulled back onto the beam by some invisible force. Matt clutches his grandson.

"Grandpa!" Joshua cries.

"I gotcha. It's all right. Well, I'll be damned," Matt says, incredulous.

After the incident, the investigators replay the thermal-imaging videotape in the mobile lab. Matt's phantom limb, his right arm, takes shape as it did before in the earlier thermal-imaging. It grabs Joshua at the last second, pulling him up safely.

"Final case log entry," Rollins says into his recorder. "Since the final barn incident, Matt Peck has become an enthusiastic participant in the O.S.I.R.'s program to study his psychokinetic powers. Closing case file #52113. Curtis Rollins, out."

Epilogue

After nineteen months of training with the O.S.I.R., Matt Peck refined the involuntary energy of his phantom limb and learned to control it. Has what we've just read violated Newton's first law, that an object remains at rest unless acted upon? Well, not really. Matt Peck was able to concentrate this new-found psi-kinetic force to take the place of his missing limb and act upon objects in the world around him.

DAN AYKROYD

Dimensional portholes enabling matter to move instantly from one place to another, great distances away, have been frequently exploited by science fiction writers. Unproved by existing technological means, the concept remains possible if one considers the super-string theory. But for a stressed-out single mother, Angela Corbeil, and her seven-year-old daughter, Sabine, encountering a dimensional rift became more than a mere theoretical possibility. It became a disturbing reality that would ultimately change their lives forever.

DAN AYKROYD

Human APPORTATION

TIME & PLACE *Late afternoon at the University of Toronto, Ontario, in the heart of the city.*

Walking along the sidewalk, a campus police officer comes across two drunk students drinking beer and picking up some CDs, which have fallen to the ground from a speaker on the dorm's second floor.

"I think it's all right. The case is broken; that's all," the first student says.

"Good evening, fellas," the officer says.

"Hey, Kenny, how you doing?" the second student says.

"Okay, guys, I'm going to have to ask you to turn down the music because there are some people who haven't finished their exams." The students gather their CDs and go inside.

TIME & PLACE *It's 10:15 P.M. Jake and Howie are cramming for finals in a nearby dorm room.*

PAPERS, BOOKS, AND remnants of junk food litter the floor. As the music goes down, Howie comes away from the window. "Finally. What'd you get for the last question?" Howie asks.

"If I tell you," Jake says, "will you remember it this time? You asked the same question four hours ago."

Howie sighs and moves to a small fridge in the corner, where he gets a soda. A strange light breeze ruffles the phone bills on the fridge, and for an instant, an odd blue light appears. Howie closes the fridge. In the mirror above the fridge are two figures on the dorm room floor.

An African-American woman clutches a small girl in her arms. Angela Corbeil, dazed and confused, trembles as she holds her daughter, Sabine. Howie slowly turns around, calling to Jake.

Jake notices Angela and stands in shock. Angela looks around in total confusion and fear. "Where am I?" she asks.

"Lady," Howie says, "how did you get in here?"

TIME & PLACE *The next day, case manager Connor Doyle, psychiatrist Dr. Anton Hendricks, physicist/statistician Peter Axon and psychobiologist Lindsay Donner of the O.S.I.R. walk along the sidewalk as Doyle speaks into a recorder.*

"FILE #87015. CASE manager Connor Doyle.

We are launching an investigation into the mysterious appearance of one Angela Corbeil. She claims she was in her home in Eureka, California, one second and in Toronto, Ontario, the next."

They arrive in front of Dean Allan Cudmore, who welcomes them.

"Where is she now?" Doyle asks.

"The police have been keeping her here, pending charges of trespassing, and for the safety of her daughter," Cudmore says. "Two students discovered them."

"We'll do all we can to help," Doyle says, ordering the preliminary interviews.

Hendricks sits down with a nervous and silent Angela, smiles warmly and introduces himself. "I already told the cops everything," she says. "All I want to do is get my daughter and go home."

Hendricks convinces her to tell him what happened. "Look, I was at home with Sabine one minute and the next I'm here, in another city, under arrest."

Investigators also speak with a Toronto police officer. "We had to charge her with trespassing. We asked her to move on peacefully, but she was extremely resistant. We couldn't calm her down. Said her name was Angela Corbeil. From Eureka, California. But she had no identification, couldn't tell us how she got to Toronto, let alone how she got into the residence. We asked the university hospital psychiatrist to have a look at her. Later I checked with the California Department of Motor Vehicles. A woman named Angela Corbeil does live in Eureka, California."

The university psychiatrist, Dr. Brillstein, provides her take on the situation: "She presented signs of shock from psychological trauma. Paranoia bordering on hysteria at first. But once she calmed down, her story, although implausible, remained lucid and consistent. From my brief session with her, my opinion is she's not unstable. Whatever happened to her was very disturbing for her."

Investigators speak with Sabine Corbeil, seven, who says she was simply watching TV at home. "Then the door opened," she says.

"Which door?" Hendricks asks.

"The one to the sunlight. And then we were here."

Jake and Howie show Donner and two O.S.I.R. operatives their dorm room. One operative videotapes the proceedings while Jake and Howie act out what happened.

"So I was right here, like getting a pop, and I turn around and poof! Right where you are. I thought they came in through the door."

"But that couldn't have happened, Howie, because I would've seen them," Jake says.

TIME & PLACE *Later, Donner, Axon and Doyle are in the mobile lab.*

"ACCORDING TO THE desk monitor on duty, Howard and James were in their room studying from 5 P.M. on. At around 10:15, they ... showed up. And no person matching their description had entered the building," Donner says. "I've run West Mat, Central Scan, Interpol and CIS. All airline bookings, bus, train, even car rental companies. Nobody has an Angela Corbeil traveling on that day."

"She could have traveled under an alias," Doyle says.

"Possibly. Although customs has no record of anyone matching their description."

The next day, Angela is hooked up to a DEP machine, as well as other machines that record her heart rate and vital signs. Hendricks sits across from Angela, asking questions.

"Try to answer everything as directly as possible," Hendricks says. "Your name is Angela Corbeil and you live at 342 Lightbourne Crescent in Eureka, California?"

"Yes."

"Do you have any living relatives?"

"Just Sabine and my sister, Mary."

"What do you do for a living?"

"I'm a secretary at an accounting firm in Eureka."

"Are you married?"

"Divorced. Dr. Hendricks, I want to get my daughter back to her home. All the questioning in the world isn't going to make that happen."

"You are free to go at any time, if that's what you want," Hendricks says.

"Okay. But can you find out what happened to us?"

"We'll try our best. Right now, we're simply assessing your psychological profile."

"My psychological profile? I'm sick of people treating me as if I were a liar."

Hendricks reassures her, explaining that she may have undergone an event that defies conventional understanding.

After the interview, Doyle, Hendricks and Axon discuss the situation in the mobile lab.

"Do you agree with the university psychiatrist's assessment?" Doyle asks. Hendricks nods. "I dispatched Lindsay Donner and a Bravo team to Eureka, California, to investigate further," Doyle continues.

That day, Donner reports back via satellite. "Preliminary on-site inspection of the Corbeil house is under way. I've also talked to neighbors and relatives, including the subject's sister, Mary."

Doyle punches a keyboard for Mary's interview. "I phoned Angela at about 7 P.M. We spoke for around ten minutes. I was supposed to baby-sit while Angela went to her class, and I was going to be a bit late, so I called back half an hour later and there was no answer. I went right over. Dinner burning on the stove, TV still on, but no Angela and no Sabine. I called the school, friends, workplace, then the police. Nothing. Finally at around 10 I get the call from Toronto."

*In a low-lit room
at the university dorm, Hendricks shines a penlight
into Angela's eye. She appears peaceful as she recounts
the May 5th incident.*

"I'M IN THE kitchen making Imperial Chinese Chicken, Sabine's favorite," Angela says. "My sister just phoned me to say hello. I have to hurry to get to my class."

"Where is Sabine?"

"Watching TV in the living room. As I call her in to dinner, there's a small breeze coming from the living room. Then a blue light so bright ..." Angela cries out.

"What's happening?" Hendricks asks.

"We're somewhere else," Angela answers, trembling. "Strangers yelling at us. I'm so frightened ... What happened?"

Later, two operatives drop off some data for Doyle, Axon and Hendricks, who sit in a round-table meeting in the mobile lab. On the wall screen is a map of North America with Toronto and Eureka distinctly marked.

"Headquarters had the trespassing charges dropped to assist our investigation," Doyle says. "I think the university wants this one off their books. What are the results of your environmental scans of the dormitory?"

"Nothing," Axon says.

"And conclusions from the hypnosis?"

"I believe Angela Corbeil experienced something quite traumatic," Hendricks explains. "Counseling is in order regardless of the outcome of the investigation."

The next day in Eureka, California.

DOYLE SPEAKS INTO his recorder: "Day six. So far our initial environmental scans of the Corbeil house have turned up normal baseline readings. We are preparing Angela and her daughter for real-time bio-monitoring scans in conjunction with uninterrupted surveillance of the house."

Axon and Doyle search the house while operatives set up surveillance cameras in several rooms. "There is no indication of toxic gases, hazardous materials or abnormal concentrations of energy fields," Doyle says.

"It doesn't make sense," Axon says. "You'd think there might be some residual electromagnetic radiation."

In the living room, technicians hook up biofeedback wires to Sabine and Angela, who asks Doyle what he's looking for.

"Anything out of the ordinary—in the environment and in your own bodies," Doyle replies.

"You mean we could have caused it to happen?" Angela asks.

"We can't rule that out. If it does happen again, your vital signs will be recorded during the phenomenon. They can offer us a clue as to what kinds of things may be at work."

That night, technicians man various video monitors in rooms in the Corbeil house. Angela and Sabine sleep as bio-monitors track their vital signs.

The next morning, Mary visits. "Don't know why I had to wait a week to visit my own sister," Mary says.

"It's called maintaining a controlled environment. These O.S.I.R. people insisted upon it."

"Have they found anything?" Mary asks.

"Nothing," Angela says as they walk into the living room. "This is where it happened. I don't like being in this room. I wanted to move the TV, but they wouldn't let me alter the environment."

Doyle, Hendricks, Axon and Donner sit at a conference table in the mobile unit. "All right, people. It's been two weeks. If any of you has theories, now's the time to put them on the table," Doyle says.

"Peter has a theory," Donner offers with a smile.

"Uh, thanks." Axon clears his throat, a bit nervously. "Well, it's a little out there," Axon says, "but we may be dealing with some form of apportation. Instantaneous movement through physical space. One moment you're in California, the next you're in Canada. How? My first hypothesis was psychokinetic apportation. Either Angela or Sabine subconsciously accessed psychokinetic energy to transport themselves."

"But neither of them has exhibited any PK abilities," Hendricks says.

"WE MAY BE DEALING WITH SOME FORM OF APPORTATION. INSTANTANEOUS MOVEMENT THROUGH PHYSICAL SPACE."

"Right," agrees Axon. "So, second hypothesis. Whatever energy involved wasn't internal but external—some concentrated flux in the space-time continuum."

"You're talking about the fabric of space being bent," Hendricks says.

"Yes, and a conduit forming between two distant points: a worm hole. Now, can I prove it? With more time ..."

"Peter, as of today you don't have anything," Doyle says. "I recommend we scale back the investigation. Pull out. Maintain periodic contact with the subjects."

Axon asks why. "You said it yourself," Doyle says. "No hard evidence. Let's close up shop first thing in the morning."

The next morning, Doyle and Hendricks sit with Angela as technicians dismantle surveillance equipment. "So that's it. You still think I'm lying, don't you?" Angela says. "What if it happens again?"

"We don't think you're lying," Doyle says. "This could have been a one-time occurrence."

"What more would you have us do, Angela? We've given you counseling; your psychological state has been stabilized," Hendricks says. Angela agrees but the fear does not subside.

"You can contact our office in an emergency," Doyle says. "And we will maintain regular contact with you for the next six months."

Angela watches Doyle cross the front yard to the van. Doyle looks back at Angela briefly, then climbs into the van. The O.S.I.R. vehicles fire to life and pull away. Sabine joins her mother in the doorway.

Later, Mary and Sabine are sitting in the living room watching TV when Angela gets home from her night course.

"We saved you some dessert," Sabine says. They sit down at the dinner table just as a light breeze blows through the room. A blue light covers Sabine's face.

███TIME & PLACE███ *Two months later in a black sedan, Doyle summarizes a case update.*

"FILE #87105. CASE manager Connor Doyle's log supplement. Have maintained periodic contact with Angela over the past two months. We became concerned when she didn't check in over a two-week period and repeated attempts to contact her failed. Two investigators were dispatched to re-establish contact."

The car moves along the street until it reaches the spot where Angela Corbeil's house once stood. Dirt foundations are all that remains. Donner and another operative get out of the car and stare at the empty lot. Donner pulls a cell phone from her jacket and makes a call.

Two O.S.I.R. vans and a mobile lab are parked on the road while investigators swarm the vacant site. Donner talks to a neighbor, who appears nervous, trying to end the interview as quickly as possible. Hendricks makes notes before surveying the empty lot.

"Neighbors all say the same thing," Donner tells Hendricks. "Two weeks ago they all woke up to find the house gone. No one saw or heard a thing from Angela or her daughter."

"What about the sister?" Hendricks asks.

"I sent a team to her apartment, but there's no sign of her at all," Doyle says.

Axon approaches them, note pad in hand. "Initial environmental scans do indicate evidence of heavy machinery in and around the site. But neither the department of works nor the state development commission issued a permit for demolition on this site," Axon reports.

"What exactly did you find?" Doyle asks.

"Industrial-grade tire tracks. Probably a caterpillar and a couple of flatbeds. Two weeks old," Axon says.

Just then, Gerrard hands a cell phone to Doyle. Doyle has a terse conversation with Frank Elsinger, the imposing Director of Operations for the O.S.I.R. "I see," Doyle says into the phone before hanging up. "Headquarters wants us to pull out," Doyle tells Axon and Hendricks. "No explanation given."

Doyle climbs into his car, turns and stares at the empty lot. That night, he dictates a final case log entry: "We have been unable to determine what happened to Angela, Mary and Sabine Corbeil. The traces left at the site of her home have been left unexamined due to direct orders from O.S.I.R. headquarters. This investigation has been terminated."

Epilogue

The O.S.I.R. never saw these subjects again. The cause of what occurred to Angela Corbeil and her daughter could not be determined conclusively. Their journey from California to Toronto without any known material conveyance and the subsequent tragic permanent disappearance of Angela, her sister and Sabine is only one small example of the mysteries in this infinite universe we share.

DAN AYKROYD

Every culture has its shamans, medicine men, and healers. In modern society, it is the medical practitioner. But increasingly, today's medical community acknowledges the value of creative visualization and positive affirmation—the spiritual aspect of successfully treating illness. Here in North America, the laying on of hands is a ritual utilized by some believers, and when results are achieved, it often warrants investigation and verification.

DAN AYKROYD

T h e
HEALER

TIME & PLACE *Daytime at the intensive care unit in a hospital in Tullahoma, Tennessee.*

Duwayne focuses on the burn victim, regarding him with great sympathy. "You're gonna be okay," he says.

Keeping his eyes fixed on Duwayne, the burn victim takes a deep breath. Duwayne's mother, Marsha, and a stern Dr. Ferber look over Duwayne's shoulder.

"Close your eyes," Duwayne says. As he speaks, Duwayne peels back the bandage covering the severe burns across the patient's stomach and chest. Duwayne shuts his eyes and lowers his head. Then he moves his hands about six inches over the burn victim's body. He breathes deeply, occasionally catching his breath as if startled, but always returning to an even rhythm. Duwayne's hands move closer to the patient's body as Duwayne sways to a rhythm only he can feel.

Duwayne lays his hands on the patient's burned stomach. Continuing to sway, he suddenly raises his head and looks straight ahead as if in a trance. Beneath Duwayne's fingers, the burn starts to disappear. It fades until there is no scar. The burn is completely healed.

Dr. Ferber gapes in astonishment as Marsha smiles proudly. Beads of sweat roll off Duwayne's forehead. His slight frame practically vibrates with energy. The burn victim opens his eyes and smiles.

"CASE #969121, CASE manager Connor Doyle. We have arrived to investigate the case of Duwayne Morris, a 16-year-old male who has healed a severely burned patient through alleged nonmedical powers. Our contact is Dr. Brad Ferber of Tullahoma County Hospital. O.S.I.R. M.D. Linda Davison is reviewing his report."

Dr. Ferber tells the investigators of his amazement. "Mr. Wilson had third-degree burns over 36 percent of his body," he says. "Now there isn't a trace of scarring. I watched it disappear, and I still can't believe it."

Russell Wilson, the completely healed burn victim, believes he's been blessed. "It was like I actually came out of my body for a moment and when I came back, everything felt fresh and new again," Wilson says. "I've never been a real religious kind of guy, but this was a miracle."

HE PRESSES HIS HAND TO DAVISON'S WOUND. SHE LOOKS DOWN AT HER HAND. THE WOUND IS GONE.

The next day, Duwayne reclines in a chair with brain-mapping equipment attached to his head, face, and arms. The cables extend out of the room.

"Why do you think you are able to heal people, Duwayne?" Hendricks asks.

"Momma says it's on account of being chosen by God," Duwayne says.

"How do you feel when you heal someone?" Hendricks asks.

"Sometimes I can feel their pain. I haven't done it that many times. Mr. Wilson, the man who got burned, he was the first person I didn't know."

"Your mother told me your father died last year," Hendricks says, moving closer to Duwayne.

"He had a heart attack. He worked very hard."

"Did you try and save him?"

"I tried, but he was too sick."

"Did it hurt when you tried to heal him?"

"Can you really read my brain with all this stuff?" Duwayne asks, looking around.

"We can only see if you're telling the truth," Hendricks says.

"Why would I lie?"

A few hours later, Duwayne, wearing a hospital gown, lies on an examination table while Dr. Davison completes a checklist of questions. She then puts down her clipboard and begins to examine Duwayne.

"Do you have a girlfriend?" she asks.

"No," Duwayne says, embarrassed. "I could. Momma says I have to be careful who I trust now that people know what I can do."

Davison opens the cupboard, and a glass container inside falls out, shattering on the counter. Davison winces in pain, her hand cut and bleeding. Duwayne quickly grabs the gauze from the tray beside the exam table and takes it to her.

"Thanks," she says.

Trying to be helpful, he presses his hand to Davison's wound. Before she realizes what he's doing, he closes his eyes. Aware that the pain has disappeared, Davison yanks her hand away.

Duwayne looks startled but not as startled as Davison. The wound is gone.

"Duwayne!" Davison yells. She looks down at her hand again in amazement, unable to form any rational explanation.

TIME & PLACE *Later that day at the Morris trailer on a deserted farm, Doyle knocks on the door. Marsha answers.*

"WE NEED TO talk, Mrs. Morris," Doyle says. "Can I come in?"

"Duwayne's resting. We've got a big day tomorrow," Marsha says, coming outside.

"Would it have anything to do with the amazing powers of Duwayne Morris and a healing fair?" Doyle asks, removing a flyer from his pocket.

"So what if it does?"

"Mrs. Morris, this could interfere with our investigation," Doyle explains. "With our attempts to understand your son's abilities."

"Duwayne's got an obligation to do what the Lord means him to do," Marsha says. "That purpose is far greater than anything you people think you're here to do."

They both turn as a beat-up car pulls up. Alice, who had been driving, gets out, leaving the man, Buddy, behind. She walks to the trailer.

"Pardon me, my name is Alice Brooks, and that's my husband, Buddy, over there in the car. Excuse him, but he isn't feeling too well. Also, he isn't much of a believer if you know what I mean. But then, anyone might have some doubts if the Lord did to them what he's gone and done to Buddy."

"You came to see Duwayne," Marsha says.

"I have heard about your son, yes. The doctors have tried everything they know."

Marsha takes the flyer from Doyle's hand and gives it to Alice, telling her to return the next day.

That evening, Doyle examines Davison's hand in the mobile lab. Davison would not have believed her own hand healed that quickly if she had not experienced the event herself. "If we can unlock Duwayne's secret to human cell regeneration, the potential medical benefits are incredible," Davison explains.

"I've discussed the situation with headquarters, and we've decided to allow them to proceed with the healing fair," Doyle says. "As highly unusual as it is, there's too much at stake to let the opportunity to observe Duwayne in action slip away. We can set up a covert operation so Duwayne won't feel like he's being watched and the community won't know we're there."

TIME & PLACE *In the morning, a line of people waits outside the decorated barn.*

92

who is dressed as a local. Davison approaches people apparently on behalf of the Morrises. "Hi, my name's Linda. I'm a friend of the Morris family," Davison says. "Before Duwayne sees you, we need to find out a little bit more about what's wrong with you so that he can prepare," she adds.

In the mobile lab, Doyle, Donner, and Hendricks watch the monitors as hidden cameras show the inside of the barn where Duwayne works his magic on a patient.

Suddenly, everyone is distracted by the sound of a roaring engine. An old pickup races up to the barn, and a panic-stricken farmer leaps out. "Help! You gotta help me!"

He runs to the other side of the truck and yanks open the door, reaching in to pick up a seventeen-year-old girl lying unconscious in the seat. Her forehead has a large bleeding contusion.

"It's my daughter. Her horse threw her," the farmer says.

Leaping in instinctively, Davison rushes over. The crowd gathers around.

"I'm a doctor," Davison says. "Please, lay her down."

Davison checks the unconscious girl's pupils and pulse. Thinking the girl may have intracranial hemorrhaging, Davison tells the farmer to take her to a hospital immediately. Hendricks and another investigator hurry out of the mobile lab, but Duwayne reaches the scene first. Duwayne looks at Davison with intense conviction.

Davison backs away, and Duwayne places his hands on the girl's forehead and concentrates. The crowd looks on. Duwayne shakes with effort while Davison monitors the girl's pulse.

A spike suddenly streaks across the biofeedback monitor in the mobile lab. The girl's eyes open, and Duwayne slumps back, drained of energy. The contusion is completely healed.

The farmer grabs the stunned girl, hugging her tightly. Davison and Donner stare at Duwayne, who continues to waver, slumped in exhaustion.

TIME & PLACE   *The next day in the mobile lab, Doyle, Donner, Hendricks, and Davison examine an X ray of the girl.*

" W E   S A W   T H E   biofeedback event that occurred while he was healing the girl because it was so significantly larger than the others," Donner says.

"He seemed to be quite drained after the experience," Davison says.

"Donner, what is the status of our covert surveillance?" Doyle asks.

"Our cover was maintained, and surveillance of the Morris residence is in place and active."

Back at the Morris trailer Marsha talks to Duwayne in the kitchen. "You did a good job today," she says. "You just got to work a little faster. We gotta support ourselves now that your father's not around."

A four-person surveillance team in the mobile lab records the dialogue and activity in the home.

As Duwayne starts to change for bed, he winces in pain. Blood oozes from his closed fist. It's the same hand that Davison cut and Duwayne healed. Duwayne opens his fist, seeing a fresh cut. He closes his fist again and shakes, trying to fight an even greater pain building inside him.

The next day, Davison approaches Marsha at the fair and tells her Doyle wants to see her. As Marsha walks toward the trailer, Alice Brooks intercepts her. Buddy doesn't look good and seems embarrassed to be there.

"I am so sorry to bother you," Alice says, "but we were here yesterday, and we were almost at the front of the line. I'm not saying that Buddy is in any greater need than any of the others here today ..."

"I understand completely," Marsha says. "When I get back, I'll have Duwayne see you right away."

Doyle explains the situation to Marsha. "Duwayne seems to be near exhaustion," Doyle says. "We feel that he shouldn't be pushed too hard."

"Duwayne is doing the Lord's work. He will be protected," Marsha says.

A commotion from the crowd interrupts their conversation. Marsha and Doyle race toward the barn. Marsha stops in her tracks when she sees the crowd gathered around Duwayne, who is collapsed on the ground. Davison and Donner are attending to him. Frantically, Marsha pushes through to Duwayne.

"Duwayne! What's happening to him?" Marsha screams, noticing that Duwayne's forehead is bleeding. A dark contusion has also formed.

TIME & PLACE   *Later in a hospital waiting room, Davison walks in.*

" D U W A Y N E ' S   V E R Y   S I C K , " Davison says. "We managed to relieve the subdural hematoma. We're treating the appendicitis with antibiotics and the burn as best we can, but there's so much to deal with. He's displaying what appear to be the symptoms of all the afflictions he's healed."

"Is he going to be okay?" Marsha asks, looking back and forth between Doyle and Davison, her concern growing at their lack of positive response.

The weakened Duwayne is hooked up to all kinds of machines and monitors. "I'm amazed he's hung in this long," Davison says. "We're actually starting to see some signs of improvement."

"It seems as if he somehow manifested a physiological transference of the ailments he was appearing to heal," Donner says.

That night, Marsha holds Duwayne's hand. Hendricks sits with them. "I'm sorry we don't know enough about how you do what you do yet, but be patient, we're working very hard on it," Hendricks says.

The next day, Davison and Hendricks talk outside Duwayne's room. Still very weak, Duwayne opens the door. "Duwayne, you shouldn't be out of bed," Davison says.

I feel much better. Can I go for a walk?"

"If you really feel up to it. We'll join you."

"When do you think I can start healing people again?" Duwayne asks as they walk down the hall.

"Duwayne, people get sick, and everyone eventually dies," Hendricks says. "You're going to have to learn that you can't help everyone."

Donner comes down the hall behind them with some data results. Duwayne continues down the hall.

"The size of the spike on the biofeedback readouts is directly related to the severity of the illness Duwayne was curing at the time," Donner says. "If the spike represents the energy Duwayne expends, the more ill people are, the more energy it takes for Duwayne to heal them."

Down the hall, Duwayne stops and stares at Buddy Brooks, who is lying in a hospital bed, deathly ill. Alice, who sits by his side, catches Duwayne's eye.

Hendricks looks down the hall but can't see Duwayne. Then a scream echoes down the hall. Hendricks, Davison, and Donner run down the hall.

Duwayne is lying on the floor, and Alice Brooks is standing on one side of the room, her hand at her mouth in horror, tears streaming down her face. Buddy Brooks is sitting up in his bed. He looks healthy, but shocked.

Davison yells for a crash cart as she bends down, feeling Duwayne for a pulse. "He's dead," she says.

That evening, Alice and Buddy leave the hospital. They walk arm in arm, happy that Buddy's going to live. Yet they know the cost, and they will carry it with them.

"Final log entry," Doyle says into his recorder. "The mystery surrounding Duwayne Morris' extraordinary power remains unsolved. Cause of death was officially recorded as heart failure. An autopsy revealed no further explanation of his abilities."

Epilogue

Duwayne Morris died a quiet hero. He sacrificed his own life in the process of absorbing the illnesses of those he helped. Marsha Morris never realized fame and fortune through her son's beautiful power. But perhaps she gained something more valuable. Something that can't be measured in dollars: an understanding of human kindness and compassion like that which Duwayne intrinsically and unselfishly imparted to others. **DAN AYKROYD**

Skydiving—it's described by enthusiasts as an exhilarating release from all worries and concerns. Skydivers know that the law of gravity governs all objects and bodies in our world and that's why they wear parachutes. But this law didn't hold true in the case of Peter McGrattan. For in the midst of seeking to overcome his own personal insecurities, he discovered that he was an incredible exception to one of life's universal rules. **DAN AYKROYD**

Free
FALL

A clear day in Emerson, Manitoba.

Three skydivers, Peter McGrattan, Andy Askwith and Nick Barrie, all in their mid-30s, prepare to skydive. A green light flashes, signaling that they have reached 10,000 feet, their jump altitude. Barrie and Askwith move to the double doors of the airplane, and Askwith turns to the nervous McGrattan.

"Come on, Pete. This is it," Askwith says.

"Andy, I don't know," McGrattan says. "I'm feeling kinda ... What's the checklist again?"

"Arch thousand, two thousand, three thousand, pull thousand. You've learned all that," Barrie says. "You promised. You would either jump today or ask Wendy out on a date. Now I haven't heard any details about Wendy, so ..."

Askwith opens the doors, and a massive gust of air rushes in. The three men brace themselves, and McGrattan looks out. "I'm not jumping," he says.

"Well, I am," Askwith says, yelling over the wind. He looks out and jumps. McGrattan backs away, cowering against the wall of the plane. Barrie moves to McGrattan.

"Pete, you came all the way up here. Live a little. You want to sit in front of a computer the rest of your life?"

McGrattan looks down at his feet, then out the open door. He gets up, moving toward the door. Mustering everything he's got, McGrattan takes a breath and jumps.

After a moment, his panic gives way to exhilaration. At about 2,000 feet, he pulls on his ripcord to release his parachute, but nothing happens. He tugs furiously. Nothing. He looks around for his buddies.

"Hey!" he yells to Andy, below him, but his voice is lost in the wind. He locates his backup cord on his chest and frantically pulls it. Nothing. He starts panicking, his face contorted in fear.

Barrie spots McGrattan, and he calls to him, but his words are swallowed up by the free fall. He shifts his weight to maneuver toward McGrattan, who's still tugging at his ripcords.

Barry can't get close enough to McGrattan to help. Finally he has no choice but to pull his own ripcord.

McGrattan, looking at the fast approaching ground below, prepares for the worst. Suddenly, about 100 feet from the ground, he feels himself slowing down. He looks around astonished, then lands smoothly and safely one foot at a time.

Askwith floats to the ground, staring in disbelief at McGrattan, who registers relief before collapsing in a dead faint.

TIME & PLACE *The next morning, a van pulls up to St. John Hospital, and a group of O.S.I.R. investigators emerges.*

R O L L I N S   D O E S   H I S   log: "File #47129. Case manager Curtis Rollins. After being contacted by Dr. Leslie Stafford of St. John Hospital, the O.S.I.R. has begun an investigation into the reported phenomenon experienced by Peter McGrattan: Mr. McGrattan has allegedly completed a successful skydive from 10,000 feet without the use of a parachute."

The team enters the hospital, proceeding to Dr. Stafford's small office. "I was on call when he was brought in," Stafford says. "He had already regained consciousness and seemed quite lucid."

"And you found nothing unusual?" psychobiologist Lindsay Donner asks.

"Aside from slightly elevated blood pressure, Mr. McGrattan was in perfect health. I didn't believe his story until I saw it the second time myself."

"You witnessed a second jump?" Rollins asks.

"Yes. One of the nurses told me he was going to jump again, and I was concerned Peter might be suffering from a head injury, subdural hematoma or diffuse axonal injury. He had been in a strange state of exhilaration." The doctor continues, explaining that she tried to stop him but arrived too late.

Andy Askwith elaborates: "Pete's always been the sorta guy who's happy to play second-string goalie on the hockey team. A buddy and I bet him that if he didn't ask our receptionist out, he'd have to skydive with us. When I saw him plummet right by me, I thought, man, we're going to be scraping this guy off the tarmac. But then he lived, and he goes out the next week to do it again!"

Nick Barrie is less enthused. "I think he really changed after that first jump," he says. "It's like two different people, the before and the after Pete. He's just more focused, assertive."

Walking past the receptionist in the afternoon, McGrattan and Askwith take some mints. McGrattan moves with a confidence he did not show before.

"NICE TIE," SAYS Wendy, the receptionist.

McGrattan tells Wendy to keep Saturday open to watch him skydive, and she writes it down in her book. Just then, Rollins and Donner walk in, requesting to speak with McGrattan.

McGrattan introduces himself and leads Rollins and Donner to a conference room. "I've jumped too, but I've always landed with the aid of a parachute," Rollins says. "Mr. McGrattan, we're proposing a series of tests to help verify and explain the phenomenon that allegedly occurred."

"Has anyone else that you're not acquainted with witnessed your feat?" Donner asks.

"Just the guy who shot the videotape I gave you. Look, why don't I just jump again and we can do all the tests you want?"

That night in the mobile unit, Donner pops in the videotape while Rollins gives a case update: "Case #47129. Day four. Peter McGrattan has completed a series of physiological tests covering all perceptual and neurological factors. He is in perfect health. No extreme or unexpected conditions were found. "

The investigators watch the videotape. "Well, McGrattan wasn't lying about the poor quality of the video," Donner says.

"Too many stops and starts, tape glitches. Even with digital enhancement, the distance from the subject is too great to make out that it's McGrattan, not to mention that the landing is obscured by trees," Constantine says.

"Lindsay, send the tape back to headquarters to see if it's been doctored," Rollins says. "I can't sanction a test jump until we've gathered enough data to substantiate his claim."

The next day, McGrattan reclines in a chair after a physical examination, which two video cameras have recorded.

"What were you thinking when the parachutes failed?" Donner asks.

"I was rushing toward the ground, thinking these were my last moments alive, when this total-relaxing euphoria overcame me. Then it goes, and you try to remember it, but you can't."

"Why'd you jump again?" Donner asks, really intrigued.

"I don't know. I think I had to, to make it mine, you know?"

Wearing headsets, Sandor Winkler, O.S.I.R. aeronautics engineer, and a team of six investigators comb the landing area of McGrattan's second jump, looking for environmental abnormalities. A high-tech environmental-scanning balloon is being prepared. An O.S.I.R. investigator tells Sandor that data analysis has begun.

"Thank you," Sandor says. "Do we have a sounding from the first balloon?"

"There's a ridge of high pressure at 160 feet and some thermal updrafts, but no uncharacteristic elements," the O.S.I.R. investigator says.

At the training facility after his interview, McGrattan is hovering over a crash mat. He's wearing a safety harness manned by two investigators.

ROLLINS, WEARING A ~~FREE~~ FALL

headset to communicate with investigators in the mobile unit parked outside, watches while a third investigator holds a radar gun to gauge McGrattan's speed. Suddenly, Rollins stops the fall.

"You weren't decelerating," Rollins says, signaling the assistants to ease him down.

"Look," McGrattan says, "this harness thing isn't working. Can't we just arrange a jump?"

In the mobile lab, investigators monitor McGrattan's biophysical state, while anthropologist Natasha Constantine and Donner talk in an adjoining unit.

"Have you wondered if this isn't the result of some kind of Superman complex, that he thinks he's invincible?" Constantine asks.

"Could be," Donner says. "It's also possible that the psychological complex developed as a result of the event."

Constantine notices McGrattan's heart rate accelerate, and she and Donner go to the training facility, where McGrattan is climbing to the top of a 35-foot tower. He's still wired but not wearing a safety harness.

McGrattan takes a deep breath and jumps. As he starts to fall, he looks confident, but he proceeds to crash into the mats at full speed.

"SKYDIVING IS LIKE A ZENITH OF EXHILARATION, LIKE A FEW MOMENTS THAT REMINDED ME WHY I WANTED TO BE ALIVE."

Later in the mobile lab, investigators replay the test jump, noting no sign of deceleration. In the training facility, McGrattan vents frustration to Rollins.

"These tests, they're rinky-dink," he says. "We're not going to get anything useful under these conditions."

"Go home, relax and get a good night's sleep," Rollins says. "We'll get back at it tomorrow morning."

Dejected, McGrattan stops by the office on the way home. Wendy holds up a note from Andy Askwith. "Oh, I'm sorry, but I can't make it Saturday," she says.

"Oh," McGrattan says, about to say something else until he notices the that the door is locked.

"Hang on. I gotta buzz you out," Wendy says. "So what was it like, anyway, skydiving?"

"Only a kind of zenith of exhilaration, like a few moments that reminded me of why I wanted to be alive."

Wendy tells him she'd like to try it sometime, then buzzes McGrattan out.

The next morning, Rollins and his team look at diagrams from the weather balloon soundings. The data show a stable atmosphere over both jump locations.

"He's moving from terminal velocity, 55 meters per second, to zero velocity in one and a half seconds. Where would that kind of energy come from?" Sandor wonders.

"Lindsay," Rollins asks, "you feel the phenomenon could be related to some sort of PK gravitational distortion induced by the subject?" She says it's a possibility that McGrattan's emotional state could trigger the phenomenon.

"The hypothesis being that Mr. McGrattan's high level of endorphins during free fall triggers the PK shift?" Rollins asks.

"Exactly," says Donner.

"Tell McGrattan we're going to let him jump," Rollins says.

TIME & PLACE *That afternoon, McGrattan stares at the plane sitting at the airfield. He takes a mint out of his pocket and, surveying the sky above him, puts it in his mouth.*

ROLLINS, WEARING A parachute jumpsuit and carrying his helmet, walks over to McGrattan. "You'll be rigged with total remote biostat monitoring, and you will wear a parachute. I'll be jumping with you," Rollins says.

As the small plane taxis down the runway, Wilkinson hooks McGrattan up to the biostat unit on his jumpsuit. "How long since your last jump, doc?" McGrattan asks Rollins.

"Long enough," he answers, telling McGrattan to focus on the procedure.

"But can you think of a better way to go?"

"Do you want to die, Mr. McGrattan?"

McGrattan and Rollins check their chutes as the plane lifts off. Ensuring contact with the mobile unit, Rollins speaks into a radio headset mounted on his jump helmet. As they approach the drop zone, Rollins stands up, ready to jump. McGrattan is nearby, his excitement barely containable.

"At 2,800 feet, pull your ripcord," Rollins instructs McGrattan. "By then we'll have all the data we need."

The green light comes on, and an operative opens the plane's side door. Rushing air roars through the cabin, and McGrattan jumps. After looking down for a moment, Rollins leaps out as well.

At the landing site, Donner follows them through her binoculars. McGrattan freefalls, bold and confident. Rollins swoops down through the air, trailing him.

"Oh my God," Donner says. "McGrattan's taking off his chute."

McGrattan manages to wrangle the chute off his body. Rollins, worried but intent, watches the chute fly away. He then angles himself to go after McGrattan.

The O.S.I.R. team watches McGrattan's free fall. "Terminal velocity reached," Donner says. "Curtis, you're below 1,000 feet. Pull your chute!"

Rollins checks his altimeter and, after a last look at McGrattan, pulls his ripcord.

Sandor shakes his head sadly while Donner watches McGrattan with increasing horror. Suddenly, McGrattan bumps down to a much slower speed.

"He's slowing down," Donner says into the headset as Sandor verifies that there are no atmospheric abnormalities or energy fields present.

McGrattan continues to descend slowly and in control. After a few moments, he touches down safely, shaking off the effects of the sudden deceleration. He then raises his fist in the air. The O.S.I.R. team races over, surrounding McGrattan.

"Now you believe me! I told you I could do it!" McGrattan yells triumphantly.

"That was totally irresponsible of you," Donner says. "You could have gotten Dr. Rollins killed."

"He's alive, I'm alive and you got your data. We all got what we ▪■:R■■■■ F A L L wanted."

▰▰▰▰ & PLACE▰▰▰ *Gathering to discuss the case that evening, the investigators admit they still have no explanation.*

"MAYBE MCGRATTAN EXPERIENCED

some type of anomalous geophysical gravity surge. It's just that we have no geophysical or environmental evidence to support that," Sandor says.

"But what if, as McGrattan passes through the vortex of this surge, he's affected on a cellular level, briefly altering his body weight composition?" Donner suggests.

"But the hard data just aren't there," Rollins says. "At the end of the day, all we have is an unexplainable anomaly."

The next day, Rollins meets with McGrattan at the airfield, and Rollins makes a final log entry: "Case #47129. All test results on the subject are inconclusive. Due to his violation of the O.S.I.R.'s mandated investigation procedure and his irresponsible actions, all on-site investigations regarding this case will be discontinued. However, the O.S.I.R. will continue to monitor the subject from time to time."

"So are you going to keep jumping without a parachute?" Rollins asks McGrattan.

"Not today," he says, as Wendy walks over in a flight suit with a parachute on her back. She hands another chute to McGrattan.

"Word of advice, Mr. McGrattan. Your ability could disappear without warning. Be careful."

"Or it could last forever, but I'll be careful."

They shake hands. Rollins and Donner watch McGrattan and Wendy jog to the plane and climb aboard.

Epilogue

Were unknown external forces the cause of this amazing phenomenon, or was it generated from within Peter McGrattan? Well, the limits of human potential have yet to be fully explored. In fact, we're just beginning to realize the innate powers that lie within ourselves and all our capacities. Only the O.S.I.R. knows whether Peter continues to tempt fate or whether he became a small headline in a local paper: "Chute Failure Ends in Tragedy."

DAN AYKROYD

Past life regression under hypnosis has been explored by therapists with varying degrees of success. In this research some people claim to have traced back and discovered who they might have been in a previous incarnation. But what if hypnosis revealed a parallel existence? Explaining this perplexing phenomenon was the challenge in the following case of two men who seemed to be experiencing intersecting lives. **DAN AYKROYD**

R e i n c a r n a t i o n

TIME & PLACE *Lisa Dressler, a hypnotherapist in her 30s, chats with 27-year-old Garth Lindenaur, a parking attendant, in her office in Edmonton, Alberta, on October 20, 1995.*

"**I** hope you're doing this because you think it will help you, not because it will give you excuses," Dressler says.

"I'm doing it for Annie. It's almost like she's obsessed now that she's done it, and she's everything to me."

"Go ahead and get comfortable," Dressler says. "Close your eyes, and try to wipe everything from your mind. As you listen to my voice, you're going to become more and more relaxed."

It's 2:30 p.m. and Lindenaur is deeply under. "It's my fifth birthday," he says, seeing a birthday cake with five candles. "My parents are there. I'm blowing out the candles, but they're not watching. They're fighting."

"I want you to go even farther back now to the time before you were born."

"I'm in a hospital room," he says, "and my name is Ian Vethamany."

"How old are you?"

"Eighty."

"What year is it?"

When he says 2040, Dressler does a double take. "Okay, let's go back farther, to 1995. October 20th. Where are you?" Dressler asks.

"I'm walking down Michigan Avenue in downtown Chicago," he says, seeing himself, thirty-five, as Ian Vethamany.

TIME & PLACE *Six days later, O.S.I.R. case manager Connor Doyle and psychiatrist Dr. Anton Hendricks meet with Dressler outside her office building in Edmonton.*

"YOU SAID YOU haven't told Mr. Lindenaur about the unusual nature of his past life?" Doyle asks.

"I felt it might be damaging to him."

"I agree, and I'd like to keep this investigation covert," Doyle says.

"I'll just tell Garth that Anton's an old colleague who's interested in the regression procedure," Dressler says.

That afternoon, Lindenaur is deep in hypnosis. Dressler looks on as Hendricks talks Lindenaur through a session. "What year is it?" Hendricks asks.

"2001."

"Who are you?"

"Ian Vethamany," Garth Lindenaur says.

"Where are you?"

"I'm in jail. Five years ago I was an investment broker. I made a few short-term investments that went sour," Lindenaur says.

"But that's not illegal," Hendricks says.

"It is when you borrow your client's money and make the investments on your own behalf."

"Okay, I want you to go back to 1995. It's the morning of October 26th. What's happening?"

"I'm listening to the radio on my way to the office," Lindenaur says. "There was a big quake in Chile this morning. The Panthers beat the Leafs last night 6-1. Oh man, I'm in big trouble."

"Why?"

"Gold futures took another dive. That wasn't supposed to happen. Marty told me it was a sure thing."

"Okay," Hendricks says, "you're going to wake up slowly now and when you do, you won't remember anything we've just talked about."

After the hypnosis, Hendricks meets Axon, Doyle, and Donner in the mobile lab.

"Ian Vethamany is alive and living at 355 Armoury Lane, Chicago, Illinois," Doyle says. "He's 35, married, no children. He's an adviser at Tilwood and Brock, a mid-sized investment firm."

"Just came over the wire service," Hendricks says, checking a computer. "A quake measuring 6.8 on the Richter scale hit Santiago, Chile about an hour ago."

TIME & PLACE *An O.S.I.R. van pulls up outside a downtown office building in Chicago on October 27.*

DOYLE DICTATES A case log update: "After completing

fifteen sessions with Garth Lindenaur, we have discovered that there may be as many as four more intersecting past lives. We are now attempting to contact Ian Vethamany, hoping to lure him into a regressive hypnosis to understand the connection between these two men."

Doyle, Donner, and two other investigators watch out the window of the mobile van and see Vethamany walking down the street.

Doyle speaks into his comlink. "Okay, Dr. Hendricks, let's take Lindenaur back to the present in Vethamany's life and have him recount exactly what is about to happen."

Lindenaur is under hypnosis in Dressler's office.

"Garth, I'd like you to go back to October 27, 1995. It's the afternoon. You're walking on Michigan Avenue," Hendricks says.

"I'm walking toward the newsstand," Lindenaur says. "Gold went down again. If it doesn't turn around soon, I'm fried."

Back in Chicago, Vethamany walks down the sidewalk toward a newsstand. "Okay, I'm going in," Doyle says.

Still under regressive hypnosis, Lindenaur speaks as Vethamany. "Just what I need. A fresh sucker. If he bleeds green, I can climb back into the black."

As Doyle walks into the Chicago office, Vethamany approaches him, inviting him in. "Actually, Mr. Vethamany, I'm not here to make an investment," Doyle says. "You have been randomly selected to be a part of an experiment involving stress in the workplace. You will be paid if you agree to participate."

Lindenaur is still under in Dressler's office. Hendricks looks at the clock on the wall. It reads 1:55 P.M.

"Okay, take yourself a little farther into the future. What's happening?" Hendricks asks.

"I'm being arrested," Lindenaur says.

"What?"

"I knew they'd catch me. They're handcuffing me."

In the mobile lab, Axon watches the video links of Lindenaur and Hendricks in Dressler's office. Another monitor shows Doyle and Vethamany from the camera in Doyle's leather folder on Vethamany's desk.

"Donner, Axon here. Lindenaur is saying that Vethamany is going to be arrested in approximately 10 minutes," Axon says.

"We don't want Doyle there affecting events that are supposed to happen a certain way. I better warn him," Donner says. She calls Doyle's cell phone to tell him.

Doyle apologizes to Vethamany, saying that something has come up, he has to go and he'll be in touch. Doyle walks out.

As Doyle gets on the elevator, Vethamany sees two men in plain clothes step off the elevator. Vethamany frowns as he watches the two men closely. They stop at reception.

Lindenaur is still under hypnosis, describing the future to Hendricks in Dressler's office.

"The cops are leading me out through the office," Lindenaur says. "Everyone's staring. It's humiliating."

"What's happening now?" Hendricks asks.

"I'm running down the stairs. Those two guys at reception were cops. I know, they've been around asking questions before. They're after me."

"I thought they had you handcuffed," Hendricks says.

"No, that never happened. I saw them **REINCARNATION** coming. I'm getting away. I think I lost them."

TIME & PLACE *The next day, Doyle and Donner arrive in the conference room in Edmonton where Axon and Hendricks are waiting.*

"BUT THE EXPERIMENT we had planned never involved helping Vethamany escape from the police," Hendricks says.

"We didn't actually help Vethamany escape," Axon says.

"No, but if I hadn't left Vethamany's office as the police were arriving, Vethamany never would have seen them coming," Doyle says.

"According to Lindenaur's memories, Vethamany no longer gets caught by the police in the future," Hendricks says.

"Did the change in Vethamany's life have any ripple effects on Lindenaur?" Doyle asks.

"I questioned Lindenaur extensively after the session," Hendricks says. "As far as I can tell, he left Dressler's office as the same person that came in."

That afternoon, Dressler and Hendricks are conferring in Dressler's office when Lindenaur bursts in. "What the hell have you done to me?" he yells, rushing straight at Hendricks and slamming him against the wall beside the fourth-story window.

"Garth! What are you doing?" Dressler yells.

"I'm going to kill you both for screwing up my life!"

Dressler slowly approaches Lindenaur, telling him to calm down, but Lindenaur glares at her fiercely. "What are you really doing to me during these sessions?" Lindenaur demands.

"Tell us what happened to you, Garth," Dressler says.

Lindenaur releases Hendricks and starts pacing the room like a caged animal. "Annie left me," he says. "She said she finally saw me for what I am—a loser. She's right. Two hours after she walked out, I got laid off!"

Later that day, Doyle, Axon, Donner and Hendricks hold a round table in the mobile lab.

"There are too many coincidences," Donner says. "The changes in Lindenaur's life must be related to the change we effected in Vethamany's life. Because Vethamany never gets caught by the police and never atones for his crimes, Lindenaur suffers the consequences."

"And only the future can be changed because it hasn't actually happened yet," Axon says.

"Then how is Lindenaur able to see the future through Vethamany's eyes if that future hasn't happened yet?" Hendricks asks.

"Lindenaur can't really see the future," Axon surmises. "He can see *a* future. What he sees can be altered. He can see possibilities specific to Ian Vethamany's life."

"Then why Vethamany?" Donner asks. "It sounds like a relationship consistent with certain aspects of reincarnation."

"Then," Doyle asks, "how could they be living at the same time?"

TIME & PLACE *The next day, Dressler, Hendricks, and Doyle talk with Lindenaur, who now knows everything.*

"**LET ME SEE** if I get this straight," Lindenaur says. "This Vethamany guy is my past life, but he's actually alive right now? How is that possible?"

"We don't know," Doyle says.

"But you think that what happens to him can change my life? So if you can catch Vethamany and make him go to jail like he did before, then Annie will come back to me and I'll get my job back?"

"We don't know for sure, but you may be able to help us catch Vethamany," Hendricks says.

"Hell, what do I have to lose?" Lindenaur agrees.

At 4:05 P.M., Axon is in the mobile unit watching Hendricks and Lindenaur in Dressler's office. Lindenaur is under regressive hypnosis.

Meanwhile, Doyle, Donner and two investigators stand outside the van. They listen to Axon through the comlink. "You were right about Vethamany," Axon says. "He was laying low. Right now, he's on his way to First National Bank. According to Lindenaur, he's going after the contents of his safety-deposit box."

"Where is Vethamany fifteen minutes from now?" Doyle asks Axon.

Hearing instructions over his headset, Hendricks looks at the clock, which says 4:10 P.M. "Garth, take yourself ahead a little bit," Hendricks says. "A few minutes have passed since you emptied the deposit box. Where are you?"

"I'm getting into my car on level three in the parking garage. I can't believe it. I think I'm actually going to make it," Lindenaur says.

Axon relays the information through the comlink to Doyle and Donner.

Fifteen minutes later, Vethamany drives his car through the garage. The O.S.I.R. van comes around the corner and stops, blocking the path. Vethamany stops his car. Doyle and Donner get out of the van and slowly walk toward the car.

"Ian Vethamany," Doyle says, "please get out of the car. We just want to speak to you for a moment."

Vethamany recognizes Doyle from the office. Looking behind him, Vethamany realizes he can't get out that way. "Get out of the car!" Doyle demands.

Vethamany punches the gas, zooming forward. He swerves to go around the van and heads straight for Donner, who can't get out of the way fast enough.

The car hits Donner, and she slams into the windshield, rolling up and over the car. Vethamany's car screeches to a halt. Doyle rushes to Donner as the two investigators jump out of the van and grab Vethamany, who is staggering out of his car.

"I didn't mean to hurt her," Vethamany says, crying.

Doyle looks up after checking for a pulse. "She's dead," he says, stunned.

In Dressler's office, Lindenaur recounts the scene under hypnosis. " I'm sorry! I didn't mean it!" he says.

In the mobile lab, Axon stares at the screen, looking at Hendricks staring right into the camera. The clock reads 4:17 P.M. "Uh, Doyle, we may have a problem here," Axon says. "Doyle, do you read?"

TIME & PLACE *Present. As Vethamany drives his car through the parking garage, the O.S.I.R. van comes around the corner, forcing Vethamany to stop.*

"**DOYLE AND DONNER** get out and slowly move toward the van. "Ian Vethamany, please get out of the car," Doyle says. "We just want to speak to you." Vethamany panics. "Get out of the car!" Doyle yells.

Vethamany hits the gas and zooms forward, swerving to go around the van. He heads straight for

Donner. At the last second, Donner dives out of the way.

A second O.S.I.R. vehicle peels around the corner, blocking Vethamany's escape. His car screeches to a halt just before ramming the second O.S.I.R. vehicle.

"Everybody okay?" Axon asks over the comlink.

"We're fine," Doyle says. "Lindenaur was right and so were you. Thankfully, Lindenaur's version of the future can be changed."

In Dressler's office, Hendricks allows himself a small smile of relief. "Garth, when you wake up, you are not going to remember anything that has happened in the last three days," Hendricks says. "Here's what you will think happened. You came to see Dr. Dressler for regressive hypnosis therapy three days ago..."

TIME & PLACE *The next day, Doyle, Axon, Hendricks, and Donner talk in the mobile lab.*

"WE TURNED VETHAMANY over to the Chicago authorities. He's being held without bail, pending trial," Doyle says.

"He seemed extremely remorseful," Donner says. "He vowed to do everything he could to pay back the clients he stole from."

"Headquarters has officially ordered us to close all active investigation in this case," Doyle says, "but let's stick around in a covert capacity to observe the effects we may have caused."

A couple of months later, an exuberant Lindenaur leads Dressler from her office to the parking lot.

"She said the time apart made her realize she couldn't live without me," Lindenaur says, heading toward a shiny white convertible, where Annie sits in the passenger seat.

"Garth, where did you get the money for this?" Dressler asks, amazed.

"After Annie came back to me, we took one of them personal investment courses and made a bundle on gold futures! Can you believe it?"

"How did you know to invest in gold futures?" Dressler asks.

Lindenaur shrugs. "It just came to me. I dunno what I ever did to deserve this, but I ain't complaining! See ya, doc!"

He drives away waving. Dressler is left amazed.

Epilogue

Further research by the O.S.I.R. uncovered a third intersecting consciousness that Garth Lindenaur and Ian Vethamany shared: a young boy living in Australia. What could be the determinants behind this kind of existential cross-circuiting? A function perhaps of powerful random telepathic transmission, or maybe as the population of this earth plane expands, there just aren't enough souls to go around. One thing is certain: Garth and Ian were connected by a bond that drastically affected their lives past, present, and future. Perhaps we all share a similar connection.

DAN AYKROYD

The Office of Scientific Investigation and Research has logged hundreds of hours researching psychokinesis, the ability to move objects without touching them. Now PK ability would for most of us be an extraordinary gift. But for Elena Bostwick, an overworked single mother trying to balance the conflicting demands of parenthood and career, this power which she always took for granted had become unwelcome. When Elena lost control of her psychokinetic ability, it became an extreme hazard. And it came to threaten the elements in her life that she most deeply cared about, the safety and custody of her daughter, Lisa.

DAN AYKROYD

The P O W E R

 *After dinner at Elena Bostwick's house in Kelowna, British Columbia.*

Elena Bostwick, a thirty-one-year-old nurse, is on the telephone in the kitchen. Her refrigerator is decorated with photos of her with her daughter, Lisa, five. Her conversation sounds angry. "I promised I'd take my daughter to the park. That's why," she says. "Can't you organize a schedule that gives me more than one day off?"

Just then, a car pulls up outside. She ends her conversation and hangs up. She looks at the radio, concentrates, and it suddenly turns itself off. Lisa and her father, Brian, enter the house.

Elena smothers Lisa in kisses and turns to Brian, "Do you realize what time it is?" she asks. "I have to be at work at 7 tomorrow. This means Lisa has to be at day care at 6:30. Mornings are hard enough as it is. You just screwed up her whole sleep schedule."

"If you stayed home and were a proper mother," Brian answers, fuming, "then none of this scheduling crap would be a problem! Maybe she would be better off living with me." He slams the door and leaves. Furious, Elena marches into the kitchen with Lisa. Suddenly the radio starts blasting and the blender starts whirring. A look of panic clouds Lisa's face. A glass bottle explodes. Dishes stacked on shelves crash to the floor and glass starts flying. Elena grabs Lisa, pulls her to her body, shielding her, and they both fall to the floor.

TIME & PLACE *The next day, Elena goes for a therapy session with her psychiatrist, Dr. Jonathan Haynes.*

THEY ARE MID-SESSION
in Dr. Haynes' office. Elena is on the couch. "If Brian was my only problem, maybe I could hang on. But nothing much else seems to be going right. With all the cutbacks in the hospital, I have to work double shifts. On top of that I have to be a mother to Lisa, do the laundry, make the meals," she tells Dr. Haynes.

"That must be very upsetting," Dr. Haynes says.

"Brian hasn't been a part of my life for a long time. He's never made a single support payment," she says. Then quietly, almost to herself, "I'm just afraid if he finds out about it, he'll use it as ammunition to take Lisa away from me. He hates me enough to do that."

"Finds out about what?"

Elena pauses, then says, "I can move objects around without touching them. Turn things on and off. It's never been that big a deal. It's just, a couple of nights ago things went crazy. I don't know what happened. Dishes exploded. Glass was flying. Lisa could've been hurt."

"A COUPLE OF NIGHTS AGO THINGS WENT CRAZY. DISHES EXPLODED. GLASS WAS FLYING. LISA COULD'VE BEEN HURT."

"Do ... you hear voices, also?"

"Of course not. You think I'm crazy? Psychotic?"

"Elena, sometimes the mind reacts to stress in odd ways. It runs away with itself. Delusions ..."

Elena stares at an ashtray before her. The ashtray slides across the table. A nearby fan turns on, blowing papers everywhere. Haynes shrinks back. Elena looks at each object again. As she does so, they stop moving.

"Can't you just prescribe some medication? Help me calm down, keep things under control?" Elena begs.

"Elena, I do want to help you, but I've never handled anything like this before. I am aware of an organization. They can analyze this ... power, test it...."

"I work sixty-five hours a week. I take care of a little girl. I don't have time to go off to some lab and be picked and probed." Elena, dejected, storms out of Dr. Haynes' office.

Elena makes a stop at the grocery store before heading home in her car. She pulls into her driveway and gets out of her car holding the bag of groceries.

"Cookies!" Lisa shouts as she sees her mom with the grocery bag in hand. She runs forward and manages to grab a tomato jar from the bag. It falls from her hands and shatters at their feet on the driveway.

"Lisa!" Elena snaps.

"I wanted the cookies!" Lisa cries.

"But you know you can't ... it's dinnertime," Elena says angrily.

At that moment the car begins to shake violently. The windows roll up and down, wipers whip back and forth, and the engine turns over and revs. Lisa cries out in fear.

After she has calmed Lisa down, Elena, disheveled and defeated, dials a number. "Dr. Haynes. It's Elena Bostwick. That organization you told me about ..."

TIME & PLACE *The next day, two O.S.I.R. jeeps are parked outside Elena's house. Case manager Marian Smithwick makes notes, supervising an initial on-site inspection.*

SMITHWICK REPORTS INTO her tape
recorder: "Case manager Marian Smithwick. Day one. We are exploring claims of psychokinetic activity by Elena Bostwick. Preliminary interviews are under way and will follow with psychological and physiological assessments."

Meanwhile, technicians are scanning the walls of Elena Bostwick's home with electronic instruments. Investigators are interviewing people who know Elena, beginning with Dr. Jonathan Haynes.

"Ms. Bostwick came to me to discuss her problems dealing with stress and tension," Dr. Haynes says. "I did not know how to help her with her apparent psychokinetic ability, which she demonstrated in my office. Quite unnerving."

Investigators also speak with nurse Keira-Marie Todd, one of Elena's co-workers at South Okanagan Regional Hospital. "I remember an incident from a couple of months ago," Todd tells them. "Bus load of kids hit an oil patch on the freeway. We were understaffed. One of the surgeons was giving Elena a hard time. You know, wanted her to be in three places at once. She needed a break. Just wanted two minutes off her feet and a glass of water. He really laid into her. Suddenly the water cooler started bubbling, like boiling water.... Then the whole tank just exploded."

Elena's father, Joe Bostwick, tells investigators: "My daughter's always been ... special. Had this power, I guess you'd call it, since she was a kid. Don't talk about it much. We taught her better. Power like that can mess up a kid's mind real good. I thought she'd kind of forgotten about usin' it. But lately, she says it's been almost out of control."

Throughout the interviews, Elena sits separately at a kitchen table with O.S.I.R. psychologist Dr. Alexandra Corliss. Smithwick, standing with several other investigators, looks on as Elena performs psychokinetic feats. She moves marbles on the table and makes a child's toy spin.

TIME & PLACE *Same day in the O.S.I.R. mobile lab, physicist/statistician Peter Axon, Smithwick, Corliss and other investigators assess the case.*

"SEISMIC TESTS SHOW ■■:■ POWER

no anomalous geologic activity or disturbances in the area," Axon says. "If things flew around in that house, it wasn't because of any earth tremor."

Smithwick asks Dr. Corliss, "What is your impression of Ms. Bostwick?"

"Excessive workload, being a single mother," Dr. Corliss answers. "It all adds up to massive personal tension."

Axon holds up a fragment of a smashed plate. "This plate didn't break from impact. My analysis indicates it imploded. On its own."

"Let's assess her abilities under more controlled conditions," Smithwick says. "I'll contact headquarters and set up a test site."

■TIME & PLACE■ *The next day, Elena, accompanied by Dr. Corliss, enters a large room in an O.S.I.R. testing facility. Elena has left Lisa at home with Elena's father, Joe.*

E L E N A
S E E S a 10-by-10 cube within the large room. The cube's interior is completely mirrored.

Remote controlled cameras twist and turn as they are being tested.

Inside the room are a single chair and table. Two technicians in the cube ready instruments and electrodes that they will attach to Elena's body. Above Elena

"ELENA HAS EXTRAORDINARY PK ABILITY. WE HOPE TO DETERMINE THE ROOT OF HER SPONTANEOUS AND VIOLENT OUTBURSTS."

is a glassed-in observation room full of television monitors and instruments. Axon, Smithwick and other technicians are working there, preparing their instruments.

"After initial testing we felt it necessary to control Elena's environment down to the smallest detail," Smithwick records in her log. "A full range of experiments should determine the extent of the subject's power."

Dr. Corliss gently takes Elena's arm, and Elena moves toward the cube. Elena looks back to the observation room, frightened. "Don't worry," Dr. Corliss reassures her. "We'll be right here."

Smithwick speaks into her tape recorder: "File #10106. Case manager Marian Smithwick. We have completed 16 separate phases of psi testing, including physiological and psychological stimuli, altered environments and electro matrix interaction. Elena has extraordinary PK ability. We hope to determine the root of her spontaneous and violent outbursts."

In the mirrored cube, Elena sits in front of a shallow box filled with sand. Another test. The letter "E" etches itself in the sand as Elena says the letter "E." The letter "L" begins forming itself, connected to the "E." "L," Elena says, concentrating on the box of sand in front of her. She has electrodes around her arms, and a thermographic monitor measures temperatures in various parts of her body while an oscilloscope measures electrical activity within her brain. The name "ELENA" forms itself completely in the sand.

"That's very impressive, Elena," Dr. Corliss says. "But there is something else I would like you to do."

Elena, in the cube, looks on puzzled as a technician enters and puts a cup and saucer on the table. Another technician places a Plexiglas shield in front of Elena.

"What's this for?" Elena asks.

"For flying debris. So you don't get cut," Dr. Corliss answers. "We need to see you consciously create an outburst, implode the cup and saucer like you did at home, and we'll monitor your biostats. Anytime you're ready."

Elena is uneasy about this test but nods her agreement. She concentrates. Stares at the cup. It starts to rattle, to dance on the saucer. Violently. The cup and saucer shatter.

A couple of hours later, Dr. Corliss and Elena are watching the explosion on tape. "Have you always had this much control of your PK ability?" Dr. Corliss asks.

"I've never tried to do so many things before," Elena says.

"We are fairly sure the outbursts stem from various forms of subconscious stress in your life. We're going to run some more tests."

TIME & PLACE *The next day, in the O.S.I.R. lab, Elena sits in the cube, wired to a battery of sensing equipment.*

E L E N A   I S   B E H I N D the Plexiglas shield again and wears a virtual reality helmet. Another cup and saucer have been set up in front of her, and she appears to be in a hypnotic state.

"Elena, you're relaxed," Dr. Corliss says. "How do these images make you feel? Please specify for each picture."

Through the virtual reality goggles appears an image of Lisa. "Happiness," Elena says.

Next is an image of Elena and Brian in happier times. "Sadness. Um ... bitterness."

Next is an image of the hospital where Elena works. "Pressure ... Irritation ... Frustration."

The images start appearing at a faster rate. Repeating images of Lisa, Brian, the hospital, the doctor. Flash. Brian with his new sports car. Flash. Hospital corridors. Flash. Brian and his new girlfriend. Lisa.... The images increase in speed and intensity. The cup and saucer in front of Elena begin to tremble. Finally, they implode, but something else seems odd. The whole lab is vibrating.

Axon and Smithwick shrink back as dials on instruments in the control room suddenly explode. The technicians near the cube look on in surprise. Suddenly there is a shout. The glass observation window shatters, sending glass flying all over the control room and down into the lab below.

"No! Not again!" Elena cries.

An hour later, technicians are repairing smashed oscilloscopes and equipment. Elena sits with Dr. Corliss and nervously holds a cup of coffee. "Sorry I trashed your lab," she says.

"It helps us to understand why these events happen," Dr. Corliss says. "Everybody has their own reactions to stress. Your uncontrollable psychokinetic outbursts are directly linked to personal and professional stresses. It is possible your subconscious accesses your PK power and lashes out."

"So can you cure me?"

"There's really no such thing as a cure. We can help you maintain control of your power and strengthen your mind."

TIME & PLACE   *The following day in a quiet room at the O.S.I.R. lab, Dr. Corliss sits with Elena, who has assumed a meditation pose. Elena's eyes are closed.*

SMITHWICK UPDATES HER

case log: "File #10106. Elena has been undergoing stress management training, visualization techniques combined with meditation exercises supervised by Dr. Corliss. Our goal is to help her find methods by which she can maintain control of her abilities."

Smithwick and Axon monitor Elena, who is wired with electrodes and biofeeds. Dr. Corliss stands over her, clicking a penlight and putting Elena into a hypnotic state.

"Every thought is a bubble," Dr. Corliss says. "As each thought rises to the surface of your mind, it evaporates. And then another thought comes into your mind. And it too rises....

THE CUP AND SAUCER RATTLE. ELENA BREATHES, CALMING HERSELF AND STOPPING THE PHENOMENON.

"You're working the late-night shift on the emergency ward. A cardiac patient arrives in severe distress. You prepare half a milligram of digoxin. The attending physician misreads the chart and orders you to administer a triple dosage ... He insists. What do you do?"

Elena becomes tense and clenches her fists.

"It's your job or the patient's life," Dr. Corliss continues. "Your only source of income. Your daughter's welfare depends on your paycheck. Yet the patient's life is on the line."

"I would lose my job before allowing a patient to die," Elena says. Her fingers loosen as she begins to calm. The biofeedback exercises are working, allowing Elena to control the level of adrenaline in her system and prevent a PK outburst. In the cube, the virtual reality helmet shows rapid images from Elena's life. Elena is wired up to sensing instruments. Another cup and saucer have been set up in front of her. Again, Elena wears protective gear. The images change to old photos from Elena's past—high school photos, lost loves, old friends long gone.

"I remember all these faces," Elena says. "It's been so long since I saw any of them."

"Do you feel lonely? Deserted?" Dr. Corliss asks.

"I do. But it's okay. I have Lisa."

Axon and Smithwick watch the activity on their instruments. The cup and saucer begin to rattle. Elena breathes, calming herself down and stopping the phenomenon. The equipment monitors return to normal wave patterns. In the cube the cup and saucer become still. Elena smiles and takes off the helmet.

After Elena leaves the session, Smithwick makes this case log entry: "File #10106. Case manager Marian Smithwick. Day nine. After successfully completing twenty separate psychokinetic tests and stress reduction techniques, Elena Bostwick's ability to control her power is now within acceptable margins."

TIME & PLACE *Elena and Lisa are at home, sitting at the kitchen table, laughing.*

ELENA PAINTS CAT
stripes on Lisa's face while Lisa giggles and examines herself in a mirror. Suddenly, the door swings open and Brian walks in, a cigarette hanging from his mouth. The atmosphere in the room turns cold.

"Hi, Daddy!" Lisa says.

"Sweetie, why don't you go play in your room?" Elena asks. When Lisa leaves, she turns to Brian and says, "There is a doorbell. And put out that cigarette."

"There you go again, telling me what to do," Brian answers, stubbing out the cigarette.

"While you're in my house, yes."

Brian looks at her angrily for a few seconds, then says, "I'm suing for custody of Lisa."

Elena turns away, closes her eyes and breathes deeply. "Do what you want," she says.

"Huh?"

"You want to take me to court, take me to court."

Brian looks at Elena, completely puzzled by her calm response.

"I have to give Lisa a bath now," Elena says. "Close the door behind you."

Brian, stunned and speechless, watches Elena leave the kitchen. He walks to the door and leaves. Elena goes upstairs to Lisa.

"Is everything going to be all right, Mummy?" Lisa asks while Elena tucks her bedcovers in.

"Yes, sweetie, it will."

"You won't get mad and make things break anymore, will you?"

"No," Elena says, reassuringly.

Lisa turns and sees her stuffed dog atop the nearby toy chest. "Mommy, what about Loci?" she asks, concentrating on her toy friend. Just then, Loci smoothly flies through the air into Lisa's waiting arms. Does Lisa have the power, too?

Mother and daughter smile.

Epilogue

Through her work with the O.S.I.R., Elena Bostwick learned how to manage her anger and in turn control her psychokinetic outbursts. But far more important for Elena, she empowered herself to deal effectively with the kind of stresses we all face and ensured that her most precious loved one, her daughter Lisa, will always be with her.

DAN AYKROYD

FOUR   ALTERNATE LIFE FORMS

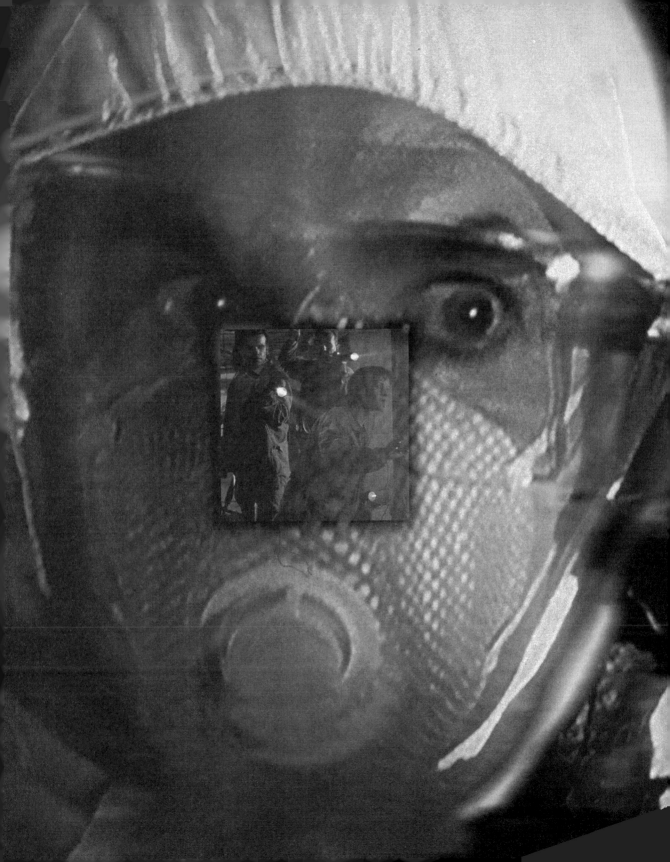

Ancient myths and man's imagination have conjured up a lexicon of monsters: the Greek minotaur, the dragons of Avalon, ocean leviathans, werewolves. We tell our children they are only made-up stories. Nothing so hideous in our world.

DAN AYKROYD

The UNDERNEATH

After a birthday party picnic at a park in Lyons, France.

Marisa's parents, Maurice and Elise, and her Uncle Armon are cleaning up when Maurice finds an unwrapped present under the table. Marisa grins and dives in, letting out a scream of joy as she sees a new tennis racquet.

"C'est bien! Thank you," Marisa says.

Her parents smile proudly. Marisa's best friend, Claire, reaches into her gym bag and pulls out her own tennis racquet and a can of balls. The two girls race down the path toward the tennis courts.

As she cleans up, Elise looks at the half-eaten cake. Suddenly, a distant blood-curdling scream pierces her like an electric shock. A second heart-wrenching scream hits them, and Maurice bolts toward it. Elise and Armon chase after him.

Maurice arrives first but doesn't see the girls. Elise and Armon run to the court looking for them.

Elise runs in first, seeing a trail of blood streaked along the court surface leading to the bodies of the girls. Armon runs in behind Elise, who becomes hysterical. He runs for Maurice but stops as he sees Maurice lying face down, red with blood.

A couple of hours later, Jacques and Patrick, two local police officers, investigate the sewer area.

"YOU'RE LUCKY YOU didn't see the bodies," Patrick says, covering his mouth and nose from the smell with his collar. "Never seen anything like it before."

Jacques looks at Patrick as a loud roar echoes toward them. Jacques grabs his radio and calls for backup.

"Run!" Patrick yells. Both cops scramble for their lives, looking back in terror as the oncoming menace gains on them. But they can't run fast enough. Patrick pulls his gun, and Jacques falls behind him, dropping his radio.

Jacques is trampled and forced down. Patrick gets off a couple of shots, but it keeps going full speed. Quickly it reaches Patrick and runs him over.

TIME & PLACE ▬▬ *Days later at the Lyons autopsy lab.*

CASE MANAGER DOYLE records his initial case log: "File #28120. We are investigating the mysterious deaths of four individuals. There was one survivor of the attacks, Officer Jacques Gaulthier. He remains in a coma. Preliminary interviews under way."

French pathologist Stephanie Lebeau leads Doyle to a cluttered office. "I found certain facts of the case highly unusual," Lebeau says, handing a file to Doyle. "The victims were, how shall I say, mauled. Torn up, not unlike the few large animal attacks I've investigated."

On O.S.I.R. archival video footage, Elise speaks to investigators, her voice shaking: "You could tell by the sound something terrible was happening," she says, her eyes widening as if she's reliving the scene. "There was so much blood. I saw Armon's face when he came back out of the sewer and I knew it. My husband ... my family was dead."

A young cop tells his experience. "I was the third man on the reconnaissance. Jacques stationed me near the mouth of the sewer. I heard that roar, then screaming and thrashing in the water. I nearly lost it when I found them. Patrick was still twitching. His eyes were open, like he didn't know his guts were floating in the water. And Jacques, he was barely breathing."

Doyle stands beside psychobiologist Lindsay Donner and zoologist L. Q. Cooper in the mobile lab, where they are operating several recording devices. O.S.I.R. security coordinator Ray Donahue and chemist Sandra Miles also stand nearby.

"One of the officers' walkie-talkies remained on call mode during the attack. I've isolated the unidentified sound from the recording made by the local police dispatch," says Donner, who plays the tape.

"It most closely resembles the warning sound of a bear," Cooper says, "so we compiled the attack sounds of all *Ursus arctos* species indigenous to this part of the world, hoping for a match, but European brown bears have been extinct in this region since the turn of the century. So I widened the net and found this."

Cooper plays another recording device that sounds similar to the first recording. He then plays the first recording at the same time as the second. They are nearly identical.

"It's a North American grizzly," Donner says.

Several investigators complete an on-site inspection while Renée St. Cyr, a 40-year-old French military commander, confers with two well-armed military men. Doyle and Donahue approach.

"Our objective is to identify and confirm the origin of the responsible element and rectify the situation," Doyle tells St. Cyr.

"I understand," she says. "I've been instructed to assist you in any way I can."

"Good," Doyle says.

Doyle sees Cooper by the entrance to the sewer and excuses himself. Cooper examines several plaster casts of large footprints.

"These impressions are inconsistent with paw prints associated with *Ursus arctos,* the bear family," Cooper says. "However, notice the four-toed spread and the scale markings indicative of a reptile."

"So we are dealing with more than one creature?" Doyle asks.

"It would seem that way. However, the tracks indicate only one animal leaving and re-entering the sewer. Add to that the length of the prints, as well as the width of the claws ... it's puzzling."

Wearing protective outerwear, Cooper, Miles, Donahue and another investigator move into the sewer. Donahue mans a portable motion detector, and the investigators take air-and-water sample readings.

"Hold it," Cooper says, shining his light on some deep scratch marks on the sewer walls and door.

Cooper takes several pictures. He stops as he sees a greenish substance clinging to the sewer wall. Miles comes over and examines the substance on the lower portion of the wall just above the water line.

"It's radioactive," Miles says. "Some kind of organic waste byproduct." Miles takes a sample of the substance.

Donahue and the team move forward. Turning the corner, they're startled by a distant roar. The investigators draw their weapons.

In the mobile lab, Doyle and Donner check views of the sewer tunnel on monitors.

"Do you have any readings?" Cooper asks through the comlink.

"Negative. Checking other feeds," Donner says.

Suddenly, a large dark shadow flashes past another surveillance camera in an empty tunnel. "There!" Donner says. "Donahue, something's moving through Tunnel 7."

"Yeah. We're picking him up on our motion detectors," Donahue says.

Surveillance audio catches another loud roar. Suddenly, struck by a vicious blow, the camera goes flying. It catches a blurred view of a hulking form before hitting the ground and shorting out.

"Retreat to sewer entrance," Doyle orders. "We need additional security before we go after it."

The O.S.I.R. team backs out of the tunnel. Doyle tells Donner to review the audio to see if there is another match. They move to the recording equipment.

A surveillance monitor shows another tunnel, but Doyle and Donner don't see it. The monitor shows two French soldiers from St. Cyr's unit splash past, rounding a corner out of sight.

In the sewer, the soldiers talk. *"C'est quoi,"* one says. The creature watches, waiting. It appears to be clinging to the side of the sewer wall. The soldiers approach. One stops. *"Quoi?"*

TIME & PLACE ■ *That evening, St. Cyr watches medics carry two body bags outside the cave to a military vehicle.*

DOYLE SPEAKS ■ ■:■ ■ UNDERNEATH INTO his recorder: "Case log update.

The deaths of two officers of Commandant St. Cyr's squad have resulted in her increasing desire to terminate this phenomenon. Requesting additional security and more scientific and technical support from headquarters."

Donner and Cooper watch the computer scan a frozen video image from the sewer encounter with the creature. The image shows a blurred claw.

"I can't conclude anything, but based on the size of that limb, we are dealing with a creature at least 7 feet tall," Cooper says.

Investigator Wilkinson enters. "Good news," he says. "The police officer who was attacked has come out of his coma." Donner leaves for the hospital.

Cooper goes to the autopsy lab to examine one of the victims. He speaks into a recorder: "I must concur with our autopsy report. Lacerations appear to be inflicted by a bearlike claw. Individual wounds are approximately 2 millimeters and range in depth from superficial to 4 centimeters. Large areas of flesh on the upper torso have been torn away. Bite pattern indicates a large, flat, rounded snout, sharp, irregular, multilayered teeth. Tearing action is consistent with the feeding behavior of alligators."

Cooper bends closer to a wound. Putting down his recorder, he picks up the tweezers and a mag-nifying glass. He gently reaches into the wound and pulls out a 2-inch-long dark fiber, which appears to be a coarse hair not belonging to the victim.

Back in the mobile lab, Cooper looks through a microscope. Doyle comes

"IT LOOKS AS IF THE FIRST TWO VICTIMS WERE ATTACKED BY A GRIZZLY AND THEN SCAVENGED BY AN AMERICAN ALLIGATOR."

over and peers through the eyepiece to see two similar hair fibers.

"The one on the left is a hair follicle from a grizzly bear," Cooper says. "The other is a fiber I extracted from one of the victim's wounds. They appear to match but I'm sending it to headquarters for further DNA analysis. Our pathologist and I agree that it looks as if the first two victims were attacked by a grizzly, left for dead, and then scavenged by an American alligator."

Doyle hands Cooper a sketch of something that can only be described as some sort of mutated combination of a grizzly bear and an alligator.

"It came from Jacques Gaulthier, our only eyewitness," says Donner, back from the hospital.

Miles walks in. "I've isolated the radioactive material from the sewer. It's an isotopic tracer commonly used in medical and biological research. This isotope could be used to highlight a particular organ on an X ray. Or to track the growth of a tumor."

"Could it be hospital waste?" Doyle asks.

"Could be, but just upstream of this part of the sewer system is a charming multinational corporation called Biodefin, which conducts cutting-edge genetic research."

Miles and Donner head for Biodefin, where they meet with an administrator. "When can we speak with Monsieur Juneau?" Donner asks.

"He'll be back next week. I'm sure he'll be able to answer any other questions you may have," the administrator says.

TIME & PLACE *Early the next morning, Doyle supervises several investigators as they install a full battery of thermography, night-vision, ultraviolet imagery, ultrasonic sensors, and laser-guided seismic accelerometers around the sewer entrance.*

DONAHUE APPROACHES DOYLE.

"We can arm search teams with high-caliber tranquilizer guns and radio-tracking darts. If we can't bring it down, we can at least try to tag it," Donahue says.

"Get the team together, and we'll go in tonight," Doyle says.

That evening, Doyle, Donahue, Cooper, Miles and two O.S.I.R. investigators enter the tunnel system carrying tranquilizer guns. Donner and Wilkinson monitor the team from the mobile lab, watching the team start to fan out.

Miles' meter starts beeping, indicating nearby radioactivity. She moves quickly through the sewer, hits a junction and rounds the corner. The beeping increases dramatically. Doyle, Cooper and Donahue join her. They stare at a large cavernlike space glowing light green. Fluid oozes from the walls.

"Stop," Miles says as Donahue starts moving forward. "There's enough toxicity in this area to melt your boots."

Donahue looks at his motion sensor, which shows activity in Tunnel 6A. "It's heading this way," he says. "One hundred meters and closing. We can intercept it at junction 4B."

"Let's bring it to us," Doyle says. He bangs on the pipes with the butt of his flashlight. The sound reverberates down the tunnels.

Suddenly a terrifying roar echoes down the tunnel toward them. Miles, Doyle and Cooper start moving toward the entrance. Heavy animal grunting zeroes in on the team waiting at the far end of the tunnel. Roaring, the beast charges directly at them. "Fire!" Doyle yells.

Doyle and several investigators blast a succession of darts into the oncoming beast. It rears backward and falls. The team watches in anticipation as the beast struggles to rise. It starts toward them. Impossible.

Doyle waves everyone toward the sewer entrance. Several investigators and Miles run out, with Doyle and Donahue right behind. A monstrous roar bellows behind them, and the creature emerges.

Tripping, Doyle falls in the clearing. Donahue and Miles struggle to help him up as the creature closes in. Suddenly, an explosion of bullets streams from the bushes. Donahue, Doyle and Miles duck and cover as the bullets fly over their heads.

When the firestorm of bullets finally ceases, St. Cyr steps from behind the bushes, followed by the team of snipers. Doyle stares at the dead creature before locking eyes with St. Cyr.

The next day, Cooper performs an autopsy on the creature and speaks into a recorder: "Hair covering is sparse over thick, scaly epidermis. Body temperature indicates warm-blooded, possibly mammalian order. Sex appears to be female. Proceeding to internal examination. Overall internal organ structure appears normal. Pulmonary, respiratory, digestive, internal reproductive organs again suggest female sex of the mammalian order."

Cooper bags a tissue sample, marking it for DNA analysis. Later, Miles, Cooper, Donner, Doyle, and Donahue conduct a round table.

"The creature was part of a genetic experiment involving an alligator and a grizzly bear," Donahue says.

"And my results suggest that this genetic hybrid was created prior to being released into the contaminated sewer system, pointing the finger squarely at Biodefin," Miles says.

"Perhaps the creature was mistakenly dumped with the toxic waste when it was believed to be dead," Cooper says.

"Let's persuade Biodefin to give us a tour of its facility," Doyle says.

Outside Biodefin, Doyle exits the van, leading Donahue, Miles and Donner toward the entrance. They walk through the lobby and into what at one time might have been an impressive lab but is now just another giant empty room.

Doyle gives a final log update: "We can only speculate on the true nature of the creature's origin. It could have been prehistoric, a revolutionary man-made genetic hybrid or a natural fluke mutation. A toxic cleanup of the sewer system has been ordered, and headquarters is proceeding with an investigation into Biodefin."

Epilogue

Perhaps the O.S.I.R.'s documentation of this event offers terrible vindication to those who believe in monsters. But even more monstrous is the absence of humanistic and moral guidance as man crosses over into the realm of outright biological creation. What else is being developed in these bio labs and for what purpose?

DAN AYKROYD

Animals are not the only carnivorous organisms in the world. Certain plants—like the bladderwort, the Venus flytrap, and the Malaysian pitcher plant—have the ability to consume meat to stay alive. The O.S.I.R. has been confronted with many strange occurrences in its 30-plus years of activity. A consolidation of plant life, seeming to come to life and attack humans for sustenance, has to be one of its most intriguing cases ever.

DAN AYKROYD

The Greenhouse EFFECT

TIME & PLACE *Jane Conacher lovingly tends to her beautiful garden in her greenhouse at her home in Beaconsfield, Quebec.*

As Jane prepares to clip back an overgrown ivy plant, she is interrupted by her husband, Cole, who is looking for the newspaper. Jane turns, and Cole kisses her on the cheek.

"Cole, I haven't picked it up off the porch yet," Jane says.

"It's the plants. They've consumed your life," Cole teases her.

"Call it sublimation of my real agenda."

Cole shakes his head. "A baby? Jane, we've been over this again and again. Greg's going off to university in a couple of years. There's finally a light at the end of the tunnel."

"Go wake Greg up," Jane tells him.

"Greg!" he calls. "Let's go! Don't tell me you're turning down a meal!"

When Greg doesn't answer, Cole goes upstairs to his room. He opens the door, hearing a faint teeming sound. Through the slanted beams of sunlight, he sees Greg, sixteen, bound by vines, ivy, and other hanging plant life growing up and around his bed.

"What the ...? Greg?" Cole moves quickly to his barely conscious son, who is held fast on his bed, the clinging vines gagging at his mouth.

Cole strains to snap the vines and pull his son free. Then, carrying Greg, he makes his way back to the hallway. Cole turns to look at the corner of the room. He kicks the bedroom door shut.

TIME & PLACE ■   Cole   and   Professor   Adrian Cadieux, of McGill University's biological sciences department,   approach   Greg's   bedroom   the   next morning.

" G R E G ' S   I N   T H E   hospital for shock and asphyxiation," Cole says. "It's like something out of a Stephen King novel."

They arrive at Greg's bedroom door and open it. Cadieux pulls on a pair of rubber examination gloves. Vines and ivy cover Greg's bed.

"My God," Cadieux says, noticing the plants moving, as though a wind is blowing swiftly across the room. Cadieux looks closely at the floor under the bed, where plants are growing out of heat vents.

Cadieux takes out a pair of clippers and tries to cut a piece of vine, but it wraps around his wrist. He drops the clippers in pain, and Cole helps free him. The two men leave hastily.

A couple of days later, several O.S.I.R. vehicles pull up to the house. Case manager Connor Doyle, physicist/statistician Peter Axon and psychobiologist Lindsay Donner get out of the vehicle and have a cursory look at the grounds of the house as they make their way to the front door.

Cole greets them. "No one goes upstairs anymore," he says. "The plants came up through the floor vents. Greg didn't have a chance."

Although Greg remains under hospital observation, Cole tells them he thinks Greg is a "tough kid" who will pull through. He asks the O.S.I.R. to conclude the investigation quickly and rid his house of "the jungle."

"We need to talk to a few other people before we actually go in and have a look," Doyle says.

Outside, Donner walks with Cadieux. "Theories? I've never seen or heard of a grouping of different botanical species infesting a local environment like that," Cadieux says.

"And the vine that grabbed your wrist?" Donner asks.

"Typical *Hedera helix*—ordinary household ivy. Nothing exotic or hybrid, but it had extraordinary strength. It cut off my circulation instantly."

TIME & PLACE ■   Later that day, Axon stands with Jane Conacher outside Greg's hospital room.

" C O U L D   T H O S E   P L A N T S   somehow have come from the greenhouse?" Axon asks.

"I don't see how that's possible," Jane says. "Everything was just as I left it. I take good care of my garden. I would know if there was any change in the plants."

They go inside Greg's room, and Jane sits down next to him. "Greg, you want to tell me what happened that night?" Axon asks.

"They attacked me."

"The plants in your room?"

"I don't have any plants," Greg says, shaking his head. "They came from somewhere else. At about 6 in the morning I felt something holding me down, almost like rope."

Back in the house, O.S.I.R. operatives conduct an on-site inspection, and Doyle gives a case log update: "As a safety precaution, the Conacher family has agreed to vacate the premises until the situation can be brought under control."

Commanding the operation, Doyle stands behind several O.S.I.R. operatives in the mobile lab while Axon, Donner and other investigators move upstairs in the house.

Axon nods to the others and opens the door. Plants are still creeping up from under the bed. They hear a scratching, cricketlike noise.

"Temperature abnormally high, Connor," Axon tells Doyle through the comlink. Doyle orders them to get a sample.

Donner pulls out a pair of plant cutters and moves to a vine. She tries to cut it, but the vine entwines her wrist. Donner is stunned yet fascinated.

Axon pulls out a canister of liquid nitrogen and sprays the frozen mixture on the vine. It goes dead and Donner gets free. "Let's get this back to the lab," Axon says, as the plants begin to shake.

Doyle, Donner and Axon enter the mobile lab. "The liquid nitrogen killed the vine instantly," Donner says. "We've been running tests on the sample all morning. Nothing yet to explain the plants'

"THE STRONGER VINES SEEM TO BLAZE A TRAIL THROUGH THE STRUCTURE, AND THE OTHER PLANTS CONSOLIDATE THE POSITION."

accelerated movement. I'd like to determine if we could be dealing with some form of genetic mutation."

They go into the chem lab. Donner nods to the botanist, who is examining a piece of the frozen vine under a microscope.

"This cutting is pretty badly damaged due to the liquid nitrogen blast it took, but we found something interesting in the stem," the botanist says.

Doyle looks into the microscope and sees a green liquid on the slide. "Organic waste, residue from some kind of foreign matter," the botanist says. "We need to send it back to the central lab for a detailed analysis."

"Put a rush on it," Doyle says.

Later that day, Axon sits at a console in the mobile lab, pulling up scans of the house, while Doyle and Donner watch from behind.

"Temperature's way up in the structure itself," Axon says, adjusting the controls. "I can't get a fix on the movement. It's all over the place."

In the house, an investigator runs a power saw through a section of the wall, cutting a square hole. The space inside the wall is swarming with plant life. Vines squirm as they're exposed to the light.

"Looks as though they're replicating exponentially," Donner says, looking at the monitors. "The stronger vines seem to blaze a trail through the structure, and then the other plants consolidate the position."

"Looks like their **THE GREENHOUSE** EFFECT focus is the walls and flooring around the bedroom," Axon says.

"Let's try and get a cutting from the bedroom again," Doyle says.

TIME & PLACE *That afternoon, a team of O.S.I.R. investigators carrying liquid nitrogen backpacks moves toward the bedroom door. They open the door and enter.*

THEY LOOK AROUND in amazement. The room is devoid
of plant life.

The next day, Axon and several other investigators set up ground-penetrating radar equipment and other subterranean-scanning devices near the greenhouse.

"We found the source," Axon tells Doyle. "We're standing on it."

Doyle records an update: "Day two. We have determined the geophysical source of the plant growth. A hive of botanical life has formed underneath the greenhouse and appears to be assimilating sections of the main house itself."

After returning to the mobile lab, the investigators hold a round table. "These plants aren't coming from the greenhouse but from underneath it," Axon says.

"The plants have a new access point into the house through the basement," Donner says.

"Any apparent reason for their sudden disappearance from the second-floor bedroom?" Doyle asks.

"It could be an indicator of some sort of group intelligence," Donner says.

"I heard a xenobiologist speak at a conference on genetics last year in Melbourne," Axon says. "He had the whole room convinced that the Venus flytrap was of extraterrestrial origin. The evidence was pretty compelling. Botanical life forms could be tenacious enough to survive a hard free fall from space."

"And cross-mutation of biological material is a brand-new field," the botanist says, "but we won't know exactly what we're dealing with until we get a substantial living cutting to examine, preferably with the root system intact."

TIME & PLACE *Later that day, Doyle, Axon and Donner walk to the door to the basement stairs of the house.*

"SCANS SHOW IT'S definitely down there," Axon says as
they open the basement door. They switch on the high-beam flashlights mounted on their suits to cut through the darkness. They illuminate hanging vines and flora everywhere.

One vine hangs in front of Donner. She jolts, then illuminates it. The plant slowly retracts back up to the basement ceiling.

The basement is totally infested. The team moves down the stairs slowly, making their way through the jungle. "The sheer mass of the plants must have cut the power coming into the house," Doyle says as they start hearing a teeming sound.

Donner moves to a vine and pulls out the cutters. She quickly cuts a sample and pulls back, expecting the worst. Nothing happens. She places the green sample in a plastic baggie.

Then the vines suddenly wrap around her ankles, flipping her onto her stomach. Donner cries out as she is dragged into the swarming green mass.

Axon and Doyle run to help her. Vines are suddenly around their wrists as well.

"Freeze them!" Doyle yells. "Aim for the base of the plants!" They blast frozen liquid nitrogen at the vines, and a storm of white gas is released.

Safely back in the mobile lab, Donner looks through the microscope. As she focuses it, she sees a million tiny, insectlike creatures swarming around the slide. Doyle and Axon also look.

"Central lab confirmed our findings," the botanist says. "The first cutting we took revealed traces of organic waste. We now know where it came from," she says, pointing to the slide.

"The parasites are using the plants as hosts," Donner says. "Their waste seems to act as a kind of super-fertilizer, causing the plants to replicate at a phenomenal rate."

"There are rare cases of subterranean botany," the botanist says. "Underground orchids have been unearthed in Western Australia. They were found to have a symbiotic relationship with root parasites who provided nourishment."

"And insect groups often have a collective mentality and a common goal," Donner says.

"So we just need to figure out what their goal is and why this hybrid species is appearing here and now," Axon says.

The next day, O.S.I.R. agents move heavy equipment into the house, and Doyle dictates a case log update: "After identifying the phenomenon, we are now experimenting with different methods of remote eradication. So far, our standard approach has come up empty."

Axon approaches Doyle. "Nothing," Axon says. "Sound-frequency modulation, temperature fluxing, environmental tampering all had zero impact. We need to destroy the hosts."

"Load up a compound pesticide and prep the sprayers," Doyle says. "Time we did a little gardening of our own."

In the basement, a light cuts through the blackness. The O.S.I.R. team in protective suits moves through the jungle with chemical tanks strapped to their backs. Doyle, Axon, and Donner are in the lead.

The team begins spraying the deadly chemical gas onto the plants, and the place erupts with movement. Vines attack the team, and Doyle sprays chemicals in all directions.

Axon is soon swarmed by plants. They tear at his suit and strangle him around his neck. Then Donner, holding a large machete blade, moves to help. She slices several vines that slacken enough to free Axon.

The amputated vines swing crazily in front of them and suddenly spray a fluorescent green liquid that hits Donner full force on the arm. Acid smoke steams off her, and she screams in pain.

Axon blasts Donner's arm with chemicals. "Everyone fall back!" Doyle orders. The others struggle to their feet, spraying as they retreat.

TIME & PLACE   *Minutes later, the team sits, still in their hazmat suits, helmets off, catching their breath in the mobile lab.*

DONNER IS STIFF with pain. A nasty laceration on one arm burns from a vine that cut through her suit.

"The chemical worked, but the application is the problem," Doyle says. "We need to find a way of dousing all the vines without having to get too close."

Then an investigator hears a warning beep from a nearby console. "Doyle, seismic sensors show rapid movement throughout the entire house."

Doyle moves to the console and looks at the monitors as the beeping grows louder. "They're expanding their position," Doyle says. "Peter, grab as many gas canisters as you can, and meet me on the south lawn. Lindsay, get the portable chem generator. Let's move."

The team assembles outside the house near a heat exhaust vent. "Donner, feed the hose into this vent," Doyle says. "Axon, start pumping the chemicals on my mark. We're going to hit it at the source."

Donner snakes the hose into the vent. Axon turns valves, releasing pesticides into the exhaust vent leading into the house.

Pesticide gas explodes out from behind the heater, and the washer and dryer in the basement, then billows out over the plants. The team hears the screaming plants inside, then silence.

An hour later, Doyle and Donner walk through the basement. "We've sprayed the whole house with pesticides and herbicides. No traces of parasites or plants anywhere in the house," Donner says.

"The question is," Doyle says, "did we kill them or drive them off? Continue wide-range scanning just to be sure."

The next day Cole and Jane Conacher enter the basement, surveying the damage with horror.

"You said you'd terminate the phenomenon, not the whole house," Cole says.

TIME & PLACE *Nine months later, the greenhouse looks exactly as before.*

A L L   T H E   P L A N T S have been replaced and recultivated. Jane enters and looks at her plants lovingly. She is pregnant.

Doyle records a final case log: "After successfully eradicating the parasite infestation from the Conacher home, we are no closer to understanding what caused the biogenetic mutation in the first place. In the past year, no further sign of this anomaly has been recorded."

Jane moves through her greenhouse happily, content. She does not seem to notice the fluorescent green ooze dripping from her ear....

Epilogue

Someday, the scientific disciplines of biology, botany and entomology may discover and confirm the anomalous relationship between flora and fauna as presented in this case. And when science can offer explanations for such anomalies, then mystery is forced to play a lesser role in determining whether there is, or is not, a Psi Factor.   **DAN AYKROYD**

What happens to us when we die? This primal question both tantalizes and terrifies us. Different belief systems choose to answer that question in a variety of ways. But, as the O.S.I.R. was forced to consider, could it be possible for a man to rise up from his grave and cheat death entirely?

DAN AYKROYD

The UNDEAD

TIME & PLACE *Dusk in a garbage-strewn alley in Hamilton, Ontario.*

A steady drizzle falls on the sidewalks, where two street kids, Darren and Melissa, search for cover from the rain. Darren pulls a cardboard box from a Dumpster and hands it to Melissa.

Melissa breaks down the box, placing the flattened cardboard between another Dumpster and some wooden crates, completing a makeshift roof. She crawls inside, spreading out a blanket from her knapsack.

Darren sticks his head inside. Holding up a discarded fast-food container, he pops a fry into his mouth.

"You're disgusting," Melissa says seductively. "Come here."

Darren raises his eyebrows coyly and moves closer, slowly rolling up his left shirt sleeve. As he pulls a ball of tinfoil out of his jacket, Melissa sighs.

"Jesus," Melissa says, noticing a limp white hand sticking out of the garbage. Pushing aside more garbage, they uncover a corpse.

130

TIME & PLACE *Later that same night in the city morgue, deputy coroner Sally Torrance pulls back the sheet covering the dead man.*

SHE DICTATES WHILE moving around the body: "Deceased is a well-developed, although undernourished, Caucasian male in his mid-30s. Although his corneas are cloudy, he appears to have blue eyes."

She presses her finger gently against his cheek. There is no blanching. She lifts a hand, noticing needle marks in the left arm. "Early rigor mortis is present in the extremities," she continues. "Extensive damage to the nails and fingertips of the victim. Numerous needle marks along the left arm. Subject could be a drug user."

Sally picks up a syringe to secure a blood sample for alcohol and drug tests. As she preps the needle, she stares at the face. She leans closer, when, without warning, the corpse's eyes fly open. Sally gasps, and the corpse grabs her wrist forcefully. Scrambling backward, Sally knocks over a tray of pans and utensils.

Slowly, the corpse sits up on the examining table, staring at Sally with blank milky-white eyes. He eases off the table and moves toward her.

A couple of hours later, Sally sits in the hall, shaken, with detective Phillip Roth.

"Phil, that John Doe you brought in here tonight was anything but dead!" Sally says.

TIME & PLACE *The O.S.I.R. mobile lab slows to a stop in the parking lot, and Doyle gives an initial log entry.*

"FILE #763139. CASE manager Connor Doyle. First team and mobile lab confirming arrival on location to investigate the alleged reanimation and disappearance of a deceased man."

Doyle and pathologist Dr. Linda Davison head toward the morgue, where they meet detective Phillip Roth and deputy coroner Sally Torrance. Phillip leads Doyle and Davison to the examining room.

"I suspect the cause of death was an overdose," Sally says. "There were extensive track marks in his arm."

Doyle notices the dry dirt still on the examining table. He scrapes some samples into a plastic bag and passes it to Donner, telling her to have chemist Sandra Miles run an analysis.

"Any idea who the 'deceased' was?" Doyle asks.

"No ID, and his description didn't match any of our missing person lists," Phillip says. "The kids who discovered the body were pretty heavy into drugs, so I don't know if I believe them, but they said they'd seen him around town."

TIME & PLACE *The next day, psychiatrist Dr. Anton Hendricks talks with Darren and Melissa in the alley.*

"ARE YOU SURE he was dead?" Hendricks asks.

"I've seen a dead body before, and that dude was gone," Darren says.

"Now I have to ask this. Were either of you on anything on the night in question?"

"Not yet," Melissa says, glaring at Darren. "Look, he sort of looked like a guy we'd seen around the streets or the shelters. Larry, or Cary, maybe?"

"Yeah, but it isn't possible," Darren says. "The guy we're talking about—we heard he died two weeks ago."

Walking to the mobile lab, Donner tells Doyle that the soil samples obtained from the morgue contain a high level of lead. Donner then leads Doyle to the surveillance area. "This is the tail end of Dr. Torrance's autopsy report on the John Doe," Donner says, playing a tape.

The investigators hear the clanging of pans as Sally crashes into them. "That's where she stated she passed out," Donner says. "Now listen."

Footsteps accompanied by raspy breathing appear to be approaching the microphone. "He must have leaned right over her," Donner says.

As the breathing sound fades, there is the sound of a door opening and closing. "So the purported corpse cannot only walk, but it can speak," Doyle says. "Did you play this back to the witnesses?"

"OUR INVESTIGATION HAS LED TO THE DISCOVERY OF ONE MALE INDIVIDUAL WHO HAS BEEN POSITIVELY IDENTIFIED AS THE MISSING CORPSE."

Donner nods. "Nobody recognized the voice. Our John Doe is still a John Doe."

The next day, Doyle, Donner and Phillip walk through the alley where the body was found, and Doyle speaks into his recorder: "Case log update. Environmental assessment completed. No abnormal readings were found that could account for the alleged phenomenon. Have directed Hendricks to undertake a door-to-door of the surrounding area in an effort to identify the missing body."

Across town, Hendricks walks into a homeless shelter with Darren and Melissa. Aubrey Le Selles, a tall, distinguished Haitian man, walks up to them.

"Darren, Melissa. Long time no see."

"Hey Aubrey, meet Anton," Darren says.

Darren and Melissa move over to chat with some of the drifters standing in line.

"So, what can I do you for?" Aubrey asks. Hendricks pulls out the police crime-scene photo and shows it to Aubrey.

"I'm trying to locate a friend. He's missing. I tried talking to the police, but they haven't been able to help," Hendricks says.

"Hey, I don't want to tell you this, man, but your friend looks dead."

"It's not the best light. He look familiar to you?" Hendricks asks.

"Maybe, but I can't be sure. We get a lot of folks through here."

Hendricks sees several Haitian voodoo items on the wall, including chicken feet, a straw doll, and a wooden cross with a ball of feathers and a knotted cord attached to it.

Hendricks looks over to see a Haitian woman, Adelina Le Selles, back in the kitchen stirring a large vat. Hendricks walks slowly through the shelter, past the haunted, sunken faces. He then rejoins Melissa and Darren in the soup line.

Just then, someone moves into the shelter, staggering toward the soup line. Aubrey looks up at the figure, who collapses onto him like a drunk. The two fall to the floor.

Hendricks pulls the figure off Aubrey. The figure turns to look at him. It's pale and drawn, staring blankly with cloudy white eyes. Melissa screams and backs away.

"It's him!" she yells. "Cary!" The figure looks at Hendricks with wide, panicked eyes.

An hour later, an O.S.I.R. vehicle drops off Doyle and Davison at the shelter. Doyle gives a case log update as they enter the building: "Our investigation has led to the discovery of one male individual who has been positively identified by two witnesses as the missing corpse."

Davison walks to an area where two investigators stay with Cary. Doyle joins Hendricks, who is speaking with Melissa and Darren.

"The subject was identified by Darren and Melissa as the body they found in the alley, but he doesn't appear to recognize them. He's like a frightened animal, disoriented, confused," Hendricks says.

At the back of the room, Davison checks Cary's heart rate. Doyle and Hendricks join her.

"He appears to be suffering from profound dehydration, malnutrition, and cathexia, but he's definitely alive," Davison says.

"Don't be afraid," Doyle says. "We're here to help. Do you understand me?" Cary nods.

"Do you know your name?" Doyle asks.

Cary pauses, looks around and shakes his head.

"Family. Do you have a family?"

"I don't know, I don't know!" Cary says. "Who are you people? What is happening to me?"

The team leads Cary out of the shelter to take him to the lab. Once there, Cary lies hooked up to an IV and monitoring equipment.

Donner walks up to Doyle. "Connor, I think this is our man," she says. "Voice-print analysis matches the subject with the voice heard on Dr. Torrance's autopsy tape." Donner leads Doyle to a microscope in the testing area.

"Take a look," she says. "Miles was able to determine a match between the soil left on the morgue's examination table and a sample taken from our subject's clothing."

"And the location of the soil?" Doyle asks.

"You'll like this."

TIME & PLACE *Later that day, Doyle, Donner and Hendricks lead Cary through a graveyard.*

" W E   W A N T   T O help you discover who you are," Hendricks says as Cary nods apprehensively.

They slowly walk into the sea of tombstones. "Forty years ago, Leaside Cemetery was built over an industrial complex. The lead levels were a 100-percent match," Donner says.

"Hard to argue with that," Doyle says.

Cary, far ahead of the team, suddenly makes a sharp left turn and starts running. Then he stops at the foot of a grave. The team falls in behind him, reading the headstone: Cary Edwin Hicks, Feb. 20, 1962–Sept. 2, 1996.

Doyle crouches down. At his feet is a small hole. He peers down and sees that the hole is about three feet deep. "It looks like this hole was dug up from the inside," Doyle tells the group.

"Are you Cary Hicks?" Hendricks asks Cary.

"I ... I don't know, but I know this place, and it scares me," Cary pleads.

An hour later, a back hoe scoops up a final mound of dirt, revealing a wooden coffin. "Who wants to do the honors?" Doyle offers. None of the investigators respond. With a sigh, Doyle clambers down into the grave. He taps the lid of the coffin.

"No echo. There's something inside," Doyle says, taking a small crowbar from Davison. He pries open the lid and sees the coffin half-filled with dirt. Doyle tentatively pushes the dirt aside, but there is no body. He turns the lid of the coffin over to find scratch marks deep in the wood.

TIME & PLACE *Later that afternoon, Sally hands Davison and Doyle several files at the morgue.*

DOYLE PULLS A file titled "Hicks, Cary Edwin." Inside are autopsy photos of the same Cary Hicks.

"This autopsy is dated September 2," Sally says.

"And," adds Davison, "the cemetery confirms his burial on September 5."

"But according to your testimony, this same man was brought to you on September 15, nearly two weeks after he was buried," Doyle says.

Hendricks leads Cary to the homeless shelter while Doyle dictates a case log update: "1600 hours. We've decided to return the subject, Cary Hicks, to what seems to be his natural environment. I'm hoping this will trigger something in his memory, allowing him to remember what happened to him."

They enter Aubrey's Kitchen. The investigators watch Cary move through the shelter. Cary looks around until he notices Adelina watching him from the kitchen. His eyes widen for an instant as she stares him down.

A roundtable is in process in the mobile lab, where investigator Nicholson passes out some file folders and leaves the room. The screen in the room displays the original morgue photo of Cary Hicks, another photo of Cary from the crime, and a current photo of Cary's face, gaunt, drawn, and eyes, milky-white.

"Background checks list Cary as a drifter. He was buried in Leaside Cemetery on September 5," Davison says. "It's the same man who was pronounced dead not once, but twice. Although his system is now clean, he used narcotics. Perhaps he overdosed on some designer drug and was mistaken for dead."

"Assuming our subject is Cary Hicks and he was buried alive, how do we explain his apparent escape from the coffin?" Doyle asks.

Donner spreads out photos of the coffin on the boardroom table. "The missing panel was found inside the coffin, under the dirt. Cary could have used a molelike action to pull soil inside and, in effect, tunnel out of the grave. Improbable, but not impossible," Donner says.

"Anton, your report mentioned zombification. Can you elaborate?" Doyle asks.

"The term is a bit dramatic," Hendricks begins. "It is believed that zombies are people who've been poisoned and appear to be dead. After release from their grave, they are left without memories and have little will to resist the control of others."

"What causes a zombie to be a zombie?" Donner asks.

"The primary active component is tetrodotoxin, or TTX, a poison obtained from the puffer fish," Davison explains. "It paralyzes a person's neuromuscular functions, making it difficult to detect signs of breathing or a pulse."

Hendricks adds, "Followers of voodoo claim this toxin is diluted by mixing it with certain plants. The victim recovers from his deathlike state, but the person remains in some type of deathlike trance."

"So who might be responsible for administering this potion or drug, and why?" Doyle asks.

"In voodoo practice," Hendricks explains, "the bokor is a witch doctor who chooses the victim, usually to be their slave."

As Doyle nods, Nicholson steps back into the room, warning the investigators of a situation developing at the shelter. The team follows Doyle out. They reach the shelter to find several homeless people looking at a body lying under a blanket on a couch.

"He was lying there all morning," Aubrey says. "I thought he was just sleeping, but ..."

Doyle removes the blanket, seeing Darren lying dead, his eyes staring blankly. Cary stares helplessly from Darren to Doyle.

Medics place Darren in a body bag. Aubrey stands beside Cary. Behind them, Aubrey's sister, Adelina, works in the kitchen.

Doyle gives a final log entry: "Case manager Connor Doyle. Our autopsy of Darren Talbot revealed cause of death to be an apparent drug overdose. Although we discovered evidence of voodoo practice at Aubrey's Kitchen, subsequent investigation found no conclusive findings that Aubrey or his sister was responsible for the poisoning, apparent death and subsequent reanimation of Cary Hicks."

Leaside Cemetery. Underneath the earth, Darren lies peacefully, quiet. His eyes flutter open, he realizes where he is and ...

Epilogue

In the 1800s, some coffins were fitted with alarm bells in case the deceased awoke after burial. Was Cary Hicks the target of a cult using voodoo pharmacology, was he affected by a designer drug with an unexpected side effect, or was he merely the victim of a premature pronouncement of death? Perhaps in some instances the medical requisites for the death certificate may not always mean that a life has ended with finality. **DAN AYKROYD**

There is a legend about giant apelike creatures roaming the woods of the Pacific Northwest, walking upright and exhibiting a high degree of intelligence. Sightings, photographs, film and video footage, as well as footprint molds and hair samples, all comprise compelling evidence indicating that the Sasquatch could really exist. A man-beast—not quite simian and not quite human. Something strangely in between.

DAN AYKROYD

Forbidden NORTH

TIME & PLACE *Deep in the forest, in Fraser Valley, British Columbia, just before dusk, a group of men is cutting down trees when a grim-looking man, Renquist, tells them to head back down to camp.*

The five workmen shut down loaders and chain saws, but Renquist still hears the buzz of a chain saw in the distance. He finds Jacquard digging a chain saw into a massive tree. Sawdust and gas exhaust fill the air.

Jacquard finally notices Renquist and shuts down the chain saw. "We're headin' back," Renquist says.

"I'll be there just as soon as I fell this sucker," Jacquard says, firing up the chain saw again. Renquist heads back.

Jacquard can't make any headway through the tree. Then, suddenly his chain saw makes a severely distressed sound and self-destructs. The chain flies off the blade, and the motor dies. Jacquard bends down to look into the hole he's made in the tree and sees a metal spike coming through the trunk.

Hearing a "whoop whoop" sound, Jacquard turns, slowly moving toward the sound. Suddenly he's caught in a leg trap hanging upside down, both legs snared in rope, about six feet off the ground.

"Guys! Hey! Help me!" he screams, but the workers are gone. Then something catches his eye. A huge, hairy man-beast is moving straight for him.

TIME & PLACE *Three hours later, Renquist and several construction workers move through the woods looking for Jacquard.*

JOHN JACOB MOSES, a young Chehalis Indian,
walks with Renquist. Someone up ahead calls to them: "Boss, over here!"

They come across Jacquard's figure hanging limply from the tree, still ensnared in the trap. Moses fearfully approaches the body, poking his torso. Jacquard's eyes fly open. He lets out a yell.

"Ahh! Don't kill me you son of a —" Jacquard yells. Then he looks around him, seeing the crew. A workman pulls out a knife and cuts Jacquard down.

Shaken, Jacquard begins talking a mile a minute. "I saw it!" he says. "I saw it right here. It came right up to me and ..."

"Jacko, slow down. You saw what?" Renquist asks.

"The Bigfoot. Real as life."

Moses inspects the trap and the ground underneath it. "Mr. Renquist, you better see this," he says, pointing out Bigfoot tracks in the dirt.

Then everyone hears the "whoop whoop" sound. "Over there, about a hundred meters," Moses says. The group turns to see a huge humanoid creature moving away through the trees.

TIME & PLACE *The next day, several O.S.I.R. vehicles pull up on a dirt road through a phalanx of environmentalist protesters near the work camp.*

DOYLE SPEAKS INTO his recorder: "Case file #260140.
Case manager Connor Doyle. We have arrived at a remote road-building site to investigate several claimed sightings of a humanoid animal in the area. Our objective is identification and observation of the creature."

Doyle steps out of one of the vehicles with physicist/statistian Peter Axon and zoologist L. Q. Cooper. "They're just building a road to access a hydrodam project," Axon says.

"Advance security reports say the conflict is intense but peaceful," Doyle says.

Doyle and Cooper walk through the rustic compound with Renquist. "The protesters arrived about a month after we did," Renquist explains. "Chained themselves to the trucks when we first tried to get in here. Haven't gone away since and I don't expect them to. Now they're spikin' the trees."

"Some of the environmentalists like to put iron spikes in the trunks to stop chain saws," Cooper tells Doyle.

"What exactly did you see when you went looking for Jacquard?" Doyle asks.

"A big animal walking upright through the trees," Renquist says. "It coulda been anything. I didn't get a good look at it."

At 1:30 that afternoon, Axon and Cooper, along with a few other investigators, inspect the area where Jacquard was trapped. The trap is an elaborate rope/sling device. "Looks like this trap was laid by someone who knew these woods pretty well," Axon says.

"And had a size 28 shoe," Cooper says, examining huge Bigfoot tracks in the dirt. The other investigators take photographs. Cooper measures the prints.

"I've studied Bigfoot tracks from all over the Pacific Northwest, and I've never seen this before," Cooper says. "Two distinct sets of tracks in one place. Looks like there could be more than one creature out here."

Later that afternoon, Doyle and Axon walk through the encamped protesters with Mullen, a man in his thirties who is leading the protesters. "I'm not buying it," Mullen says. "The Bigfoot is just a hoax cooked up by the construction company to scare us off."

"Or perhaps something cooked up by you to scare off the road crew," Doyle says.

"Look, I would never risk our movement's credibility like that. We're going to win this battle through protest and raising awareness. Hearts and minds, professor."

"The foreman, Renquist, claims your people planted iron spikes in trees to destroy their equipment," Axon says.

"We want to stop this ecosystem from being destroyed, not hurt anyone," Mullen says. "They were pretty extreme."

"What about someone outside your organization?" Doyle asks.

"There were two wing nuts we tossed out three weeks ago," Mullen says.

That evening, Doyle and Cooper stand at the campsite with two other investigators. A portable camping stove still has water boiling on it.

"Seems Brad and Nancy are pretty adept at living off the land," Cooper says.

"They couldn't have gone far. Everything's unpacked," Doyle says, examining the stove.

Then they hear a man's voice in the distance. Brad Harper, a man in his early 20s, stands on a large rock about 50 meters away. He's got a bow loaded with an arrow aimed right at Doyle.

"Stay right where you are," Brad says.

"We want to talk, that's all," Doyle says.

"We've got nothing to say to you," Brad says, as Nancy Byatt walks up to Brad.

"Relax, Brad. They're just Bigfoot hunters," Nancy says. Brad relaxes the bow, and he and Nancy join them.

"What exactly are you doing out here?" Doyle asks.

"Those Hydro Nazis are trying to destroy this forest. We're going to stop them by any means necessary," Nancy says.

TIME & PLACE *The next day, the investigators hold a round-table discussion in the mobile lab and look at photographs of the Bigfoot tracks from the trap site.*

"WE HAVE ENOUGH circumstantial evidence to move forward under the assumption that there is something or someone deeper in the woods," Doyle says.

"We lifted casts of two sets of prints, both too large for any animal indigenous to this area and definitely not from the bear family," Cooper says. "Closer to, well, a primate in bone structure. But these tracks differ in detail. Both are somewhat similar to other Bigfoot prints trackers have found over the years."

"We also collated every bit of Bigfoot information gathered over the last fifty years," Axon says.

"Seems there are only two rules about this creature: One, it's a hominid of unknown species, and two, it always operates alone."

"It could be a male-and-female pairing or a mother and her offspring," Cooper says.

That night, Doyle and Cooper move through the woods with other investigators. Doyle speaks to Axon through his comlink. "What's your position?" Doyle asks.

"We're about one hundred meters west of you and closing. Nothing on the scans so far," Axon says.

As Doyle and Cooper move forward, Cooper notices motion ahead through his scanner. "Human?" Doyle asks.

"Maybe. Two, three meters in height. Can't get a fix."

Doyle and Cooper move ahead, reaching a moaning woman. Cooper bends down. "I'll get a medical team," Axon says, leaving.

"It's all right. We're going to get you some help," Cooper tells the woman, Nancy Byatt, whose face has been severely scratched, as if by a wild animal.

"I saw it, I saw it," she says faintly.

TIME & PLACE *That night in the mobile lab, the team watches footage from Nancy's camcorder on the green screen, and Doyle gives a case log update.*

"**AFTER COMING ACROSS** an injured environmentalist in the nearby woods, we have secured video footage that may help reveal what is roaming the forests in this area," Doyle says. "The witness, Nancy Byatt, remains in catatonic shock in our medical lab."

The footage on the screen shows a huge, hairy creature moving off in the distance in the woods. Then the camera is knocked onto the ground, but it keeps filming as Nancy's screams fill the air. There are deep growling and the sounds of a struggle. Then a huge foot lumbers past a corner of the twisted frame.

"Any sign of her friend?" Doyle asks.

"Nothing," Axon says. "Either he's gone or he knows these woods better than your average bear."

"Our psychologist writes that in Nancy's current state of shock, regressing her would be dangerous," Doyle says. "We have to wait for her to come around, get over whatever she saw."

"What might help is an aerial survey of the area," Axon says. "It will give us a better idea of the terrain and what's on it."

That night in his cabin, Renquist hears crashing and banging coming from somewhere in the camp. Renquist bolts out of the cabin, and Moses joins him, holding a flashlight.

They move toward the supply shed, which has nearly been demolished by something. A dark humanoid shape moves at the periphery of Renquist's flashlight beam and stalks off into the woods.

The next morning, Axon and Renquist look inside the toolshed. Tools are mashed, and heavy equipment and oil drums are thrown aside. "This is going to push my schedule back at least another month," Renquist says. "Damn Green Movement punks."

"Wait a minute, protesters did this?" Axon asks, picking up a chain saw, its blade completely bent.

Just then Jacquard, nervous and angry, walks up. "We gotta hunt it down," he says. "It's coming into the compound at night, now. Just a matter of time before it decides to rip us apart."

"You guys aren't hunting anything," Axon says. "You don't have a hunting license. This is our investigation. Let us handle it."

That day, Doyle talks with Mullen, who is packing up his things because regional police are forcing everyone out. "For the last time, we had nothing to do with any of it," Mullen says.

"To the police, you have a motive since you want the construction to stop," Doyle says as two cops approach Mullen and drag him away.

TIME & PLACE *That afternoon, investigators in the mobile lab watch a tape of Doyle interviewing John Jacob Moses.*

"THE STORIES SAY that Sasquatch lives in the hidden ground, the sacred ground where the Chehalis can't go," Moses says. "He makes sure the forest will survive. He's supposed to be the spirit of a great Chehalis warrior, full of strength and wisdom."

"Do you believe these stories?" Doyle asks.

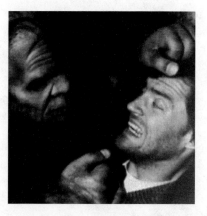

A DARK HUMANOID SHAPE MOVES AT THE PERIPHERY OF RENQUIST'S FLASHLIGHT BEAM AND STALKS OFF INTO THE WOODS.

"Look, I've got two kids to feed. I need this job," Moses says. "Maybe I'm not the most noble Indian in my tribe, but at least I'm a good father. Those stories are just that—stories. But now and then I get the feeling that sometimes a story exists because maybe it's true."

The image freezes, and Doyle turns to the team.

"How old is this Chehalis legend?" Cooper asks.

"Ancient," Doyle says. "The Chehalis aren't the only North American tribe with a Bigfoot legend. Every culture seems to have a mythical creature that acts as the missing link between man and his protohuman ancestors."

Axon stands, moving to an aerial survey of the region. "The aerial and environmental assessments show limited animal life to sustain a creature as large as the one we're talking about."

"If the Bigfoot is as large as we suspect, then it would depopulate this entire area if it only ate meat," Cooper says. "It's probably an omnivore. Eats anything and everything."

"What about the creatures' movements?" Doyle asks.

"There are a million places they could hide or roam freely without being detected, but these patterns here indicate where the foliage is less dense," Axon says. "Could be a good place to start looking."

TIME & PLACE *The team, plus numerous investigators carrying scanners and dart guns, moves through the woods at 2 p.m.*

north," Cooper

says. They follow the prints and find a huge, hairy form. The humanoid form lies motionless on the ground, dead from several wounds to its abdomen.

Cooper examines the body before pulling out a small dissecting knife. He cuts into the creature's stomach, peeling back a layer of hair. "Human," he says, peeling back more hair, revealing an elaborate costume.

Cooper uses the knife to remove the mask covering the body's face. It's Brad Harper. Dead. "Great. His tactics got him killed," Cooper says.

"What threw all that heavy equipment around, and what attacked Nancy?" Doyle asks.

"Whatever it was," Cooper says, "it was bigger than him."

As the team examines the body, a giant humanoid figure stands in the distance, backlit by the fading sun and shrouded in mist. The real Sasquatch finally turns, disappearing into the woods.

The next day, a regressed Nancy speaks in the mobile lab.

"It was Brad's idea," she says. "He thought if we could make a video and leak it to the media, they would back off. I was filming Brad and this—this animal burst in from the right. Hit me across the face. I blacked out."

Meanwhile, Doyle gives a final case log entry: "After Nancy Byatt emerged from her state of shock, we were able to learn what we had suspected since we first encountered her and Brad Harper in the woods. Harper's fatal injuries appear consistent with an attack by some predatory creature, most likely a grizzly bear. Ironically, due to a prolonged delay in the completion schedule, construction has ceased indefinitely. As to the evidence suggesting a second larger creature, no further traces were found."

John Jacob Moses watches the woods as he breaks camp. Out of the corner of his eye, he sees something ... or nothing at all.

Epilogue

As nature retreats before man, new insects and even mammals continue to be discovered. In 1995, a hitherto unknown species of deer was found in an isolated area of Vietnam. Findings like this clearly mean we should not cease our search for elusive, mysterious and possibly very genuine primal creatures. Perhaps the Sasquatch is another unknown animal species whose existence is only waiting to be verified. **DAN AYKROYD**

One of the joys of living on this planet is to watch shooting stars streak across our heavens, meteorites from the depths of space burning up our atmosphere. Some have collided with earth and caused massive destruction. There are those who believe a giant meteor contributed to the Ice Age and the extinction of the dinosaurs. As the O.S.I.R. investigated the horrifying deaths of a NASA scientific team, it had to determine if the meteorite in this case brought with it an unwanted hitchhiker. **DAN AYKROYD**

The INFESTATION

TIME & PLACE *Near a crater in the middle of the day at Ozark Mountain Plateau, Arkansas.*

A squad of U.S. National Guardsmen heads single file through the forest. Squad leader Lieutenant Jack Vaughn speaks into a military mobile radio.

"New orders, Lieutenant?" asks Corporal Gardner, the radioman.

"Nah, same as when we started out," Vaughn says. "Locate the lost fly fishermen and bring them home."

Sergeant Phillips, a burly 40-year-old man, calls to Vaughn, who rushes over. As he arrives, the faces of the rest of the squad register sheer horror. Bodies from a NASA scientific team are sprawled everywhere, bloody and torn. A terrible stillness fills the air. Vaughn moves up to Phillips.

"Looks like they were attacked by some kind of animal," Phillips says. "They're all dead."

From far away, Vaughn hears a faint buzzing. Lifting a fist in the air, he opens his hand wide, and the squad members unshoulder their weapons and fan out.

As Phillips moves through the trees, M-16 at hand, he hears a high-pitched buzzing whipping through the trees. Phillips wheels around, trying to locate the source. It appears to be coming from the ground itself. Suddenly something zooms through the underbrush, rapidly closing in on Phillips. It leaps up at him. He turns to see it, but it's too late.

Vaughn hears Phillips' scream followed by rapid bursts of gunfire. Vaughn turns and comes across the bloody sergeant. A neck wound drains the life from him, and the buzzing sound increases.

"Lieutenant," Phillips murmurs. Vaughn looks at him and orders the squad to fall back.

The squad dissolves into chaos as Vaughn tries to grab frightened soldiers and move them back from the site. An intense buzzing fills the air.

The next night in the middle of the woods, Vaughn walks through a few wrecked tents. Bodies of five family members lie nearby.

"Yes sir, same story." Vaughn speaks into a radio. "Five victims, all dead. We've begun evacuation of the entire park. Sir, I am aware of the threat. I lost one of my men on that ridge last night."

TIME & PLACE *That evening, two O.S.I.R. vans pull up.*

CASE MANAGER CONNOR Doyle, physicist/statistician Peter Axon, psychobiologist Lindsay Donner and psychiatrist Dr. Anton Hendricks get out as Doyle summarizes his initial log entry: "File #33130. Case manager Connor Doyle. We have been asked by federal authorities to investigate the mysterious deaths of a team of NASA scientists and a member of the Arkansas National Guard in the Ozark Mountains. This mission follows hard on the heels of our tracking the orbital entry and impact of a meteorite in the same general area."

Vaughn greets Doyle and tells him about the latest attack. "It was about 12 hours ago. So far the body count is up at 13."

Investigators examine the victims as Doyle tells Donner that the NASA team was there for inspection of a meteorite and data collection.

"Seems like light duty for NASA," Donner says.

"Let's just say that this particular meteorite has government intelligence watching us closely," Doyle says.

"According to military sources, Vaughn was under direct orders not to tell his men what they were looking for," Donner says.

"Then it was a high-security military operation," Hendricks says. "Connor, I'd like to conduct some preliminary autopsies."

Investigators interview Corporal John Paul Gardner of the U.S. National Guard. "My family's lived in these hills nearly a century. Know 'em like the back of my hand. But what we found was out there. Something tore those people to pieces. Killed Phillips in three seconds."

Hendricks and Donner move past a sentry guard into a large canvas tent, where twelve corpses lie covered on Army-issue cots. Hendricks pulls back the sheet on one of the corpses.

Donner notices severe trauma to the neck, guessing cause of death as massive blood loss.

"Odd," Hendricks says, inspecting the body. "These entry marks around the neck are smooth. There's something lodged in the trachea."

Donner holds the scientist's head back as Hendricks reaches into a wound and pulls out a piece of organic matter. Then Hendricks looks at the face of the dead man for a moment. The corpse's face stares wide-eyed into oblivion. Hendricks' brow furrows.

"Dear God," Hendricks says.

"Anton? You knew this man?"

"Dr. Frederick Walsh. I met him at a symposium on genetic botany in London last year. His specialty was xenobiology."

"So what was an expert in unknown life forms doing looking for a meteorite?"

Outside, investigators zoologist L. Q. Cooper, Russell and Scanlon inspect the area where the NASA team was found.

"Most of us are just weekenders, called up to do a little service twelve times a year," Vaughn says. "I couldn't tell them what to expect. Had specific orders to keep the objective hush hush."

"What did they tell you?" Doyle asks.

"That there was a top-level science team lost in the bush. Find them, bring them out. Take a fully armed squad with me."

As Vaughn leaves, Doyle hears Donner over his comlink. "Connor, some new information," she says. "Seems like NASA was out there looking for something a little livelier than a meteor. They had a team of geneticists with them. Air Force Space Command and NORAD both confirm tracking the meteor's entry and impact, but they're being too quiet about NASA's involvement."

Thanking Donner, Doyle moves through the forest with Axon, Russell and Scanlon following. They carry portable environmental-scanning equipment and motion-detecting sensors.

Through the fog, the team sees a massive crater with the remains of the meteor deep in its recesses. Scanlon and Russell fan out and begin waving their instruments around it, collecting data.

SOMETHING CHASES RUSSELL THROUGH THE UNDERBRUSH. THEN IT LEAPS UP AT HER. SHE TURNS, SCREAMING IN HORROR.

In the mobile lab, Hendricks and Donner watch the monitors closely, seeing the team's progress.

As Doyle and Scanlon examine part of the meteor's remains, Axon finds a nest of large egg-shaped objects, about the size of grapefruit.

"I've got a bad feeling about this," Vaughn says.

"It appears to be an embryonic shell," Cooper says. "Shape and consistency is unlike anything I've seen before." Cooper puts on a protective glove and picks up an egg.

Scanlon and Russell move along the perimeter of the site, motion detectors in hand. One sensor lets out a warning beep. "We have movement," Scanlon says. "Five hundred meters southeast and closing."

Scanlon and Russell look at their sensors, noticing that the beeping is growing louder and faster. Scanlon turns on a thermal-imaging camera while Hendricks and Donner watch thermal images of the forest appear on a video screen.

"Life-form readings. Closing fast," Axon says. "Trying to get a thermal lock on it."

As a red hot creature the size of a small dog leaps past, an intense buzzing comes out over the speakers.

"Peter, something big just went through the scan," Donner says.

"Fall back! Repeat, fall back!" Doyle orders.

Something chases down Russell through the underbrush. Then it leaps up at her. She turns, screaming in horror.

In the mobile lab, the thermal scan goes black.

A shape moves quickly past Axon, who ducks instinctively. "Oh, God. Team, move out! Evasive action, now!"

"Peter, what happened?" Donner asks.

"Scanlon and Russell are dead."

TIME & PLACE   *Later that night, technicians run through data in the mobile lab as Doyle gives a case update.*

"WHILE PERFORMING ENVIRONMENTAL

scans of the impact site, our team was attacked by some strange malevolent life form," Doyle begins. "Two investigators, Kevin Scanlon and Karen Russell, died as a result. We have retrieved their remains, and they will be returned to their families. I have requested that protocol in this case be expedited due to the deadly threat this phenomenon poses.

"We have a job to do," Doyle says. "Scanlon and Russell knew that. Now let's get back to work. Lindsay, prepare a report of the on-site footage."

Donner sits down at a console. On one monitor are the thermal images Scanlon recorded moments before he died. On another is Russell's on-board video, which is shaky as she runs through the forest. A huge dark shadow moves over her.

"Freeze it right there," Donner says.

On the first monitor, thermal images of the forest end with a scream and a red hot shape moving past the frame.

"Back it up. Now, freeze that," Donner says.

The shape on the monitor is indistinct, yet huge and insectlike with tendrils. Doyle moves over to the console. "Dump this footage onto tape and send to the A/V lab at headquarters," he says. "See if they can enhance it."

In the chem lab, Cooper stands at the isolation chamber, his hands reaching in through rubber access gloves. Inside the chamber is the large egg taken from the nest.

"We picked up nominal radiation signatures from the site. Typical with astrogeologic matter. The sample from the meteorite itself is a classic aerolite, composed mainly of silicates with some iron deposits."

"What about the organic matter Dr. Hendricks found in the victim's wound?" Doyle asks.

"Some sort of barb left behind from the physical attack. It's like an organic feeder tube."

"And it's related to this ... embryo?"

"Seems likely. I believe it to be made up of similar organic matter common to heterotroph parasites."

"Anything from the physiological assessments?" Doyle asks Hendricks.

"Nothing unusual among the survivors," Hendricks says. "Some post-traumatic stress, typical across-the-board disorders."

"Move on to regressive hypnosis," Doyle orders. "Start with Peter. Put him under."

TIME & PLACE   *That night, Hendricks hypnotizes Axon. Doyle and Donner watch from behind a glass partition.*

"PETER, I WANT you to go back to yesterday, to where the meteor came down," Hendricks says.

"Yes. We're near the impact site. Soldiers are securing the perimeter. Russell and Scanlon are running environmentals."

"Then what, Peter?"

Axon flashes back, seeing images in his mind of Scanlon and Russell being killed. "I'm delaying too long. I want the scan readings. Maybe it's a new life form ... Oh, God! Russell, she's screaming."

"Is she hurt?" Hendricks asks.

"It's got her by the neck—the blood. She's dead, and Scanlon ... It's moving right past me!"

"Peter, freeze the image of this creature in your mind and describe it in specific detail," Hendricks says.

As Axon speaks, a sketch artist draws what he describes. "Wingless insectoid. Obvious exoskeleton with what looks like 10 pairs of legs along the thorax. Legs are covered in some kind of tendrils, bristles really, and tipped with small hooks. The mouth, peculiar-shaped mandible, is about 6 inches across."

Just then, Cooper calls Doyle from across the lab. "I've been detecting rhythmic vibrations coming from within the embryo," Cooper says as the egg begins to vibrate and shake. "Surface tension and interior temperature are climbing."

Suddenly the egg cracks open, and an insect the size of a grapefruit leaps out at Donner, smacking violently against the Plexiglas. As the insect leaps around the chamber, as though looking for a target, the chamber shakes.

"Flood the chamber, and put it to sleep." Doyle says.

"*Siphonaptera minorus,*" Cooper says, incredulous. "Believe it or not, it's a close genetic cousin to a flea."

"How big can it get?" Doyle asks.

"Insects of this class usually grow to twenty, sometimes thirty times their birth weight," Cooper says.

Hendricks holds the artist's sketch from Axon's description. It's a larger, deadlier-looking version of the one in the chamber.

"We found several dozen eggs out there, in the nests we found," Doyle says. "What's the possible rate of reproduction?"

"Normally 10 adult females can produce 100,000 eggs in under thirty days," Cooper says.

"We need to go back in for some firsthand data," Doyle says. "The infestation source has been identified; now we need to rectify the situation."

TIME & PLACE ■ *That night, Doyle, Axon, Cooper, Gardner and Vaughn march along a path through the woods toward the thick fog shrouding the meteor site.*

DOYLE SPEAKS INTO a recorder: "Case log update. Having determined that the life form we are looking for may be a mutated or possibly an extraterrestrial insect, we are returning to the impact site to gather as much firsthand information as possible."

The O.S.I.R. team carries odd-shaped rifles slung over their shoulders. Tubes snake from the rifles to canisters strapped on their backs. A few carry powerful xenon flashlights. Everyone wears comlink headsets with mounted video feeds.

Donner, along with other operatives, sits at a console, watching their progress via the monitors.

"Those crackerjack freon guns you got aren't gonna do you any good when they come at you," Gardner says.

"We'll take our chances," Doyle says.

The site remains as it was before, except for dozens of egg nests wedged up against the meteorite. Axon moves closer to the eggs. Xenon lights illuminate the scene.

"They're multiplying rapidly," Cooper says.

Cooper and Axon are examining the nest when Vaughn calls over to them to see the dead body of a giant full-grown insect. Its armorlike shell glistens in the night.

"Its mate probably killed it, which means more reproduction is under way," Cooper says.

As Cooper and Axon lift the insect, a buzzing begins to grow from a distance. On Doyle's command, they drop the insect. The soldiers and the O.S.I.R. team hustle through the woods.

In front of Axon, a giant insect blocks his path. Transfixed, Axon stares at the creature.

Donner watches, aghast, from the mobile unit. She alerts Little Rock National Guard, which says that reinforcements are en route.

Suddenly, an insect lunges at Axon. Doyle blasts it with his freon rifle, and the creature is knocked out of the air, falling stiffly to the ground.

The team, led by Doyle, slowly moves through a blockade of insects. Axon grabs the dead carcass of the freoned insect, dragging it with him. "I'll take this in the name of science," Axon says.

Back in the mobile lab, Axon and Donner stand over the frozen carcass of the insect. "Ran every long-range scan we could. No traces of chemicals, no tox levels or radiation that could explain this level of mutation," Axon says.

"Maybe it's some extraterrestrial effect from the meteor," Donner says. "Or maybe the impact opened up an access route for subterranean life forms."

"Either way, we'll always have this little souvenir to remember them by," Doyle says.

The next morning, Doyle speaks into his headset: "Final case log entry. After discovering the magnitude of the infestation, authorities have ordered the total and complete termination of the life forms encountered. The region has been evacuated, and widespread air strikes are being implemented."

Doyle looks at the monitors, seeing planes flying over a section of the woods. After a moment, the forest ignites in a massive ball of fiery napalm. Sitting unnoticed in the non-napalmed underbrush, an egg quivers slightly before cracking open.

Epilogue

Where did these deadly creatures come from? Were they cosmic stowaways? Were they a mutated form of insect affected by radiation from the fallen space rock? Or were they a grotesque and deadly prehistoric species unearthed by the meteorite's collision? Well, if the last is true, then who knows what else may rest beneath the surface of our soil, waiting to grow under the light of our nurturing sun?

DAN AYKROYD

FIVE   P O S S E S S I O N S   A R E   E V E R Y T H I N G

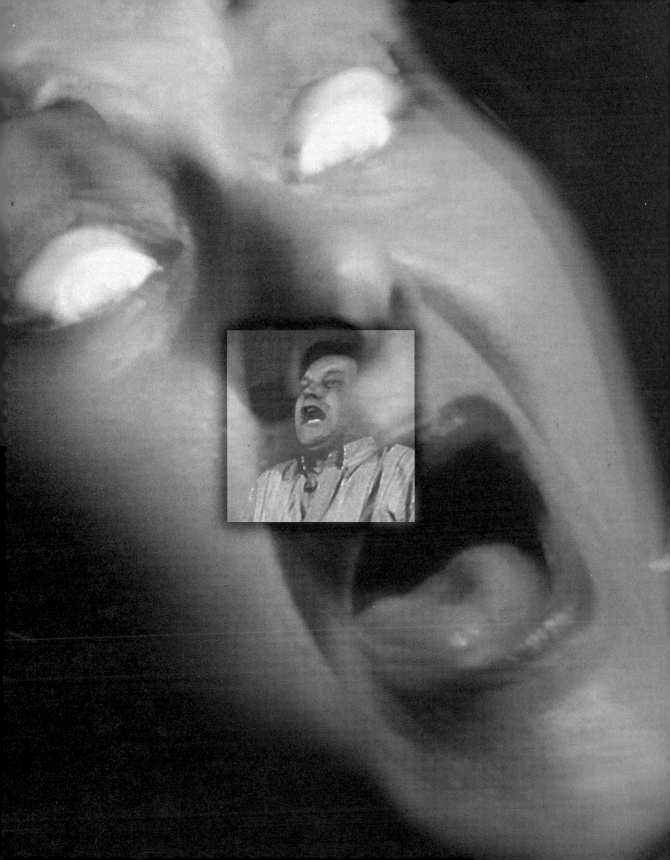

After thousands of years of attempting to comprehend the battle for the soul, we still seek answers as to why malevolent entities consume unwilling individuals. In the case involving Rabbi Rothstein's synagogue, the O.S.I.R. was compelled to employ Judaism's mystic sacred rituals in the fight between good and evil.

DAN AYKROYD

The TRANSIENT

TIME & PLACE *Saturday morning at a synagogue in Toronto, Ontario.*

A few mourning members of the congregation rise as Rabbi Reuben Rothstein leads the Kaddish, the prayer for the dead. A woman enters the synagogue, slowly walking toward the podium.

As she walks by the congregation, worshippers begin to asphyxiate as if the air is being sucked out of their lungs. As the woman nears the podium, a member of the congregation rises to intercept her. With a quick blow, the worshipper is thrown across the rows, and he lands in a heap several feet away.

Rothstein stops his recitation and turns to see the woman standing in front of him.

"Bevakasha. Mimcha azon nahee Rabbee" (Please help me, rabbi), she says.

"Rita? What is the meaning of this?" the rabbi asks.

Responding in a different voice, she says, "Chote margish et nigsho kav ve cha asa." (Sinner, thou shalt feel the might of my wrath.)

She grabs Rothstein by the throat, and he begins to choke. Blood starts to trickle from his nose. Four members of the congregation rush at her and try to pull her away from Rothstein. Although she struggles violently, they wrestle her to the ground.

After regaining his breath, Rothstein stands and moves over to where the woman is pinned to the ground, growling and writhing. Rothstein looks at her, then presses firmly on her neck. After a few seconds, the woman passes out, unconscious.

The men carry the woman into the anteroom, where the rabbi begs Cantor Carl Lowenbaum not to jump to conclusions.

"I know what I saw," Lowenbaum says. "In the middle of the prayer for the dead, she attacks all of us! Reuben, she's a dybbuk!"

"Save the old superstitions for your grandchildren, Carl. Demons do not visit us in the 20th century."

"You must perform the ritual of the Baal Shem," Lowenbaum insists. "Cast out the evil in her."

Later that day, Doyle, Constantine, Hendricks and Peter Axon walk into the synagogue. Doyle speaks into his recorder: "Case #64131. We are now investigating the reported appearance of an ancient and powerful phenomenon, know as a dybbuk, a Hebrew term for demon."

Rothstein and Lowenbaum greet them as they enter, and the rabbi invites the scientists to look around. The investigators go into the anteroom. Hendricks sits on the table next to the woman while an O.S.I.R. physician examines her.

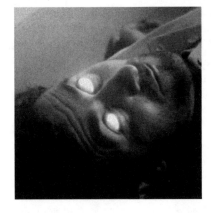

"Her name is Rita Naimand, a member of our congregation, although we haven't seen her at synagogue since her husband died three years ago," Rothstein says. "She and her late husband worked at the Royal Ontario Museum. Research on early Aramaic writings, ancient scrolls, that sort of thing."

"TRYING TO RESTRAIN HER WAS LIKE FIGHTING 10 MEN. THE STRANGE THING IS SHE KEPT SAYING, 'HELP ME.'"

"How long has she been unconscious?" Hendricks asks.

"Three, four hours. Hasn't moved a muscle, though it isn't quite unconsciousness. It's as if she's in some trancelike state."

"You reported kinetic activity surrounding the attack. Bio-physical distress among the victims, superhuman strength," Constantine says.

"Yes, and no logical explanation. That's why I contacted you."

TIME & PLACE *That evening, O.S.I.R. team case manager Connor Doyle, anthropologist Natasha Constantine, physicist/statistician Peter Axon and psychiatrist Dr. Anton Hendricks interview Carl Lowenbaum.*

" I SAW JOSH Weiss as he was thrown across the room," Lowenbaum says. "I looked over to see this woman standing in front of Reuben. Suddenly she had him by the throat. Trying to restrain her was like fighting 10 men. It took four of us to hold her down. The strange thing is she kept saying, 'Help me.'"

"Naimand is still only semiconscious, making it impossible to collect physical or psychological data. And according to her co-workers at the museum, she has no close relatives," Constantine says. "We're trying to track down any family."

"What was she working on?" Doyle asks.

"I recognized the texts on Eastern European Kaballah, but the ancient Aramaic scrolls, they were beyond my ability to translate," Constantine answers.

"What have you learned about this 'dybbuk myth' from the rabbi?" Doyle asks.

"For thousands of years, Jewish scholars have written of the dybbukim, lost souls who seek to possess another's body. They tell of the evil eye that takes a man's soul. The dybbuk will search out the perfect host."

"Which is?" Doyle asks.

"Traditionally, a young girl," Constantine responds.

Doyle, Constantine, Axon and Hendricks confer in the O.S.I.R. mobile lab. "The psychological assessments are all normal. DEP testing of the witnesses revealed honest accounts of the incident," Hendricks says. "Rabbi Rothstein sustained a localized second-degree burn on his neck."

"If she is host to some unnatural, possibly predatory force," Doyle says, "I don't want to risk taking her to a public hospital. Let's see what we can do for her here."

The next day, Axon waves a portable scanning device around the anteroom. Rita Naimand remains motionless on the table.

"How odd," Hendricks says. "Her eyes are open, and she seems to be aware of us, but ..."

Just then, the scanner lets out a tiny warning beep. "It's coming from her," Axon says, moving the scanner toward Rita. As he does, she begins to stir. "Her temperature just shot up to 110 degrees Fahrenheit, and I'm reading hazardous toxins emanating from the subject. Climbing to the red zone. It's getting real unhealthy in here," Axon says, jumping back as Rita begins to thrash violently.

"Mavit yee kach Eesha zoo" (Death shall take this woman), Rita says.

Roaring wind fills the room, and the table starts to shake. Doyle and Constantine rush in.

Hendricks and the physicians manage to hold her still long enough so a physician can inject a sedative. After a few tense moments, she collapses again. "The tox levels were redlining. Now I've got normal baselines," Axon says.

"Tell Rothstein we're ready to observe his ritual," Doyle says.

TIME & PLACE *Axon watches several monitors from the mobile lab as he captures the ritual via remote camera.*

IN THE SHUTTERED anteroom, Doyle, Constantine, Hendricks, Rothstein, and Lowenbaum face Rita Naimand. Rothstein, wearing a yarmulke and talis, opens the ancient text.

"In the name of the lord, Shaddai, who created heaven and earth ... in the name of the lord God of Israel ... In thy name, God of mercy ... save this soul before us ... Kein Ayin Ha Rah."

Rita Naimand begins to tremble. Rothstein raises a hollowed-out ram's horn, the ceremonial Shofar, and puts it to his lips. He blows into it, producing a deep, mournful sound.

"Connor, kinetic activity climbing. I'm reading increasing energy levels, but I can't identify them," Axon says. "Body temperature is rising fast."

Shaking, Rita opens her eyes. A visible flicker of glow flares to a blinding light. Suddenly there is an explosive sound, then silence.

Axon watches the static monitors and hears the awful silence. He stands and checks their biostats. Heading to the synagogue, Axon instructs another technician to keep his eye on the monitors.

Heading inside, Axon notices two O.S.I.R. operatives lying on the ground asphyxiating near an open door at the side of the synagogue. He bends to check them, then whirls around to see Rabbi Rothstein, who no longer has evidence of the burn on his throat.

His face devoid of emotion, Rothstein grabs Axon by the throat, yelling, "Ata tish lach la rasha. Tevater ulnish macha ul shmee." (You will repent, sinner. Give up thy soul in my name.)

Rothstein's touch causes Peter's skin to smolder. Axon gasps and flinches in pain. Then Rothstein lets go and moves away. Axon falls to the ground, trying to breathe again. He weakly looks up as the rabbi walks away.

In the anteroom, the entire team lies motionless on the ground, out cold. Doyle slowly comes to, trying to get his bearings. Rita lies on the table. Doyle checks her pulse. She's dead. Doyle looks around, seeing burn marks on the text Rothstein was holding.

Soon after, O.S.I.R. agents help injured operatives and members of the synagogue out of the

IN THE ANTEROOM THE ENTIRE TEAM LIES MOTIONLESS ON THE GROUND. DOYLE COMES TO AND CHECKS RITA'S PULSE. SHE'S DEAD.

building. Hendricks sits near an O.S.I.R. vehicle with Axon, who has a burn mark on his neck. Doyle approaches them.

"Are you all right, Connor?" Hendricks asks.

"Just a few bruises. Is anyone else hurt?" Constantine and Hendricks nod. Doyle looks at Axon.

"He grabbed me and said something in Hebrew," Axon explains, touching his neck. As Hendricks helps Axon to his feet, Constantine comes out of the mobile lab. "We still have the rabbi's biostat signals," she says.

"So he can't have gone farther than 200 meters. Put a monitor in each of the vehicles. We can track him by triangulating his signal with one of the monitors here at the lab," Doyle says.

"Police and paramedics are on the way for Ms. Naimand," Constantine says.

"Divide into teams of two. Anton, you're with me. Natasha, you're with Peter. The rest split into two-man teams and cover the radius of the signal. The quicker we find him the better."

Riding in the van, Axon asks Constantine if she thinks the dybbuk can change hosts at will. "From what I could find out, the dybbuk migrates only when its host is dead," she says.

From the other van, Doyle and Hendricks radio to Axon. "Peter, our signal is breaking up. Do you have him on your monitor?"

"Yeah, I still got him. He seems to be heading toward the lake."

"Wait a second, stop," Constantine says. "I see something."

Constantine and Axon's vehicle stops at a corner, and they get out. Constantine picks up the rabbi's prayer shawl. Doyle tells them to wait for him.

TIME & PLACE *Moments later, Constantine and Axon along with another investigator move carefully around a garbage-strewn alleyway.*

CONSTANTINE ENTERS THE alley alone.

Hearing a clatter, she whirls around to see Reuben Rothstein hiding like a trapped animal behind garbage cans. "Rabbi?"

"Stay back," he says, weakly. "I don't know how long I can control it."

Constantine radios that she's located the rabbi. Doyle and Hendricks hear her in their car through the comlink, and Doyle instructs her to back away.

Keeping her distance, Constantine tells Rothstein that help is coming. As he explains that it's too late, Axon walks up. Trembling, Rothstein starts reciting the prayer for the dead. He then leaps at Constantine and throws her across the alley. She lands painfully. Rothstein runs.

"This is beta 2. Have lost subject on Inglis. He may be heading east. We're pursuing on foot," Axon says, moving to Constantine.

"I'm okay," she says.

As Constantine and Axon walk down the street, Constantine sees something ahead. A taxicab is stopped in the middle of the street, and a crowd has gathered. Rothstein lies in the middle of the road, blood streaming from his head. Constantine and Axon move in.

Constantine bends down to Rothstein, who isn't moving. His eyes stare straight ahead. "It's ... gone," Rothstein says. Constantine turns to Doyle. Rothstein is dead.

Doyle pulls up and stands near Axon. Jack Thompson, an eyewitness, comes over and tells them he saw the whole thing. "The cab hit him dead on. Knocked the poor guy about 15 feet across the street. The cabby jumped out and ran to the guy, and so did I."

"Sir, may we examine you?" Hendricks asks. Thompson agrees. Hendricks inserts a thermometer into Thompson's ear. A normal temperature shows that he's okay.

"Where's the driver now?" Doyle asks.

A policeman approaches, saying that the cabby's gone. "He said he was going for an ambulance. I told him to stay put and he sucker-punched me."

Constantine reads the driver's name from his license posted in the cab. "Antony Valenzuela. I'll access the data banks for his address."

Axon examines the ground around Rothstein's body. "Looks like the same carbon traces present that we found in the synagogue," he says, as Constantine comes up with the cabby's address.

"Let's go," Doyle says.

"How do we know Valenzuela will run home?" Axon asks.

"Dybbukim seek out a pure soul. That's why it possessed the rabbi," Constantine says.

"Valenzuela has two young daughters."

En route in the van, Constantine listens to the police frequency. "Seems Valenzuela spotted the SWAT team as it got into position," she says. "He has at least two hostages."

The O.S.I.R. team arrives to find a lobby full of police and SWAT officers. SWAT Captain Turner intercepts them, saying he had to send in a team to dislodge him.

"But you knew we were en route," Doyle says.

"I had no choice. He's got his kids in there. Shots were fired."

Walking down the hallway inside, three SWAT officers slowly approach a doorway. The senior SWAT member, McCally, moves in front of the door. The SWAT team silently counts to three and busts in.

Valenzuela wheels from the window, gun in hand, and tries to get a shot off. McCally nails him in a quick burst of gunfire, and Valenzuela slumps to the floor. McCally kicks the gun away from his hand. It skitters across the floor toward a partially open closet door.

SWAT members go to the two young hostages in the corner, where they had been cowering. As McCally approaches the dying man, Valenzuela's head turns toward the closet door, which swings open ever so slightly.

Medics soon arrive to wheel away Valenzuela's body. Constantine approaches Doyle. "He took three bullets in the upper torso," she says.

"The children seem all right," Hendricks says, walking up. "They didn't make eye contact with Valenzuela at the time of death."

Doyle walks to one of the O.S.I.R. vehicles to record a log entry: "In the aftermath of the hostage situation, we have yet to isolate another living host of the transient demon. We still have no method of dealing with the phenomenon except to prevent transference at the time of the host's death. This file remains open."

That night, a young girl sits quietly in the closet. For a quick moment, her eyes appear to glow.

Epilogue

Where is it today, this demonic entity capable of moving from living host to living host? Does it dwell in someone walking the streets of your city or town? This case remains open, and the search continues for this powerful and dangerous supernatural threat. **DAN AYKROYD**

Demonic possession—occupation of an individual's soul by the devil—is a primitive belief. Yet despite centuries of social advancement many still appeal to demonic lore in explaining some disturbing and frightening events. Paul Tanner, software developer, gourmet cook, proud owner with his wife, Kelly, of a restored Victorian-era San Francisco house, is very much your modern man, but when the foundations of his life were shaken by wrenching visions fueled through an image of the devil, everyone assumed that this force had set out to capture his soul. Was Paul Tanner battling an evil influence over the control of his spirit? This was the question facing the O.S.I.R. in case number 67102.

DAN AYKROYD

Possession

TIME & PLACE *Dinnertime at Paul and Kelly Tanner's San Francisco home.*

Paul dangles a piece of raw beef in front of his cat as his wife, Kelly, and their friend Frank Kelterbourne wander into the kitchen with some wine glasses.

"Our new friend here likes my cooking," Paul says. "Care to try some?"

"I think I'll wait till it's cooked," Kelly says.

As Paul tosses the meat into the wok, the phone rings. He answers it, and Kelly and Frank leave the kitchen. "Hello? Hey, Jeff. Yeah, I know. I'll deal with it first thing in the morning. Tonight? But head office said the numbers were fine!"

As he's talking, he notices a small spider crawling out from a nearby drawer. It transforms into a massive tarantula. Paul screams. Suddenly, blood begins gushing from the telephone's mouthpiece. Paul drops the phone. He looks inside the wok only to see a handful of squirming maggots.

Paul backs up against the wall. Feeling something pressing against him, he turns in shock as a demon appears out of the wall. Frantic, he finds a crucifix in a drawer and points it at the wall. In a blast of light, the demon leaps from the wall and into Paul's face.

Hearing Paul's screams, Kelly and Frank rush to the kitchen, where Paul is hunched low on the ground, quivering in fear. "There!" Paul yells.

Kelly looks up at the wall but sees nothing. She gingerly moves forward. Paul looks at her without recognition, and Frank pulls her away protectively. "Paul, what's wrong with you?" Kelly asks.

"The beast is within," Paul says, dropping the crucifix.

TIME & PLACE *Later that evening, Father Martin comes to the house to meet with Kelly, who's asked for his help.*

"MRS. TANNER, I am not very experienced in these matters. There has been no time to prepare," Father Martin says. Paul hisses while Frank tries to hold him down.

"Almighty Father, grant strength to your servants to fight valiantly against the Evil One," Father Martin says. "I command you, O evil spirit, through God, the Father Almighty, and Jesus Christ, his son, and through the Holy Spirit — that you depart from this his vessel, Paul Tanner, whom you hold captive. Exi! Exi!"

After a fearsome struggle within Paul, the rite seems to take. Paul calms, slumping over semiconscious. Father Martin leads Kelly to the corner of the room. "Mrs. Tanner, this is unlike anything I've seen before. But, I will do all I can to free his soul. I must discuss this matter with my superiors. I think I know another way to help."

TIME & PLACE *The next night, technicians from O.S.I.R., using a variety of hand-held monitoring instruments, scan the living room for airborne chemicals and radiation.*

CASE MANAGER CONNOR Doyle supervises, speaking into his headset mouthpiece. "Case manager Connor Doyle. File #67102. Day one. Tanner residence. Initial sweeps report no anomalous energy fields. Radiation levels are within acceptable ranges. No unusual environmental conditions."

Criminologist Ray Donahue enters. "Perimeter secured, Connor. Witnesses have signed the releases and are ready for preliminary interviews."

"Then let's get started," Doyle says.

The investigators watch separate videotaped interviews of Frank Kelterbourne and Kelly Tanner.

"Known Paul and Kelly for maybe six months — since the company transferred me up here," Frank begins. "They'd invited me over for dinner. Things seemed normal, I guess. Then Paul just went berserk. Screaming. Tearing at things. I mean, I didn't recognize him. It was frightening. And you know who I really feel sorry for? Kelly. This is destroying her."

Kelly elaborates: "The first time it happened, there was no warning. I tried to ignore it, but it kept happening. I mean, I couldn't admit that maybe he was; you know ... possessed. It was just so horrible. Paul was fine one minute, and the next he's saying, 'The beast is within.' Out of nowhere, it's in him, taking him over. I brought him to the hospital, but our doctor ran a bunch of tests and found nothing. I'm scared. It's like Paul's turned into someone else. I had no choice but to turn to Father Martin."

Another videotape shows Father Martin. "I am not an official exorcist in the eyes of the church, but when you enter the room and the devil is there, yes, you typically feel a presence. But in the case of Paul Tanner, I could not directly sense this evil. After trying to exorcise the demon, I asked the Archdiocese for further assistance. We decided to contact your office for help."

The investigators also interview Paul Tanner. "I don't remember any of it. I wake up and have this empty feeling, like I've just done something horrible. It's like I don't know who I am anymore, like I have no control," Paul says.

Inside the O.S.I.R. mobile lab, psychologist Dr. Alexandra Corliss shines a sharp, focused white light into Paul's left eye, putting him into a regressive hypnotic state. Even under hypnosis, Paul appears uneasy.

Corliss' penlight blinks out, and a bank of video monitors play out Paul's brain waves, EKG, respiratory rates, galvanic skin response and pulse while a technician watches the monitors.

"Paul, you're relaxing, relaxing," Corliss says. "I want you to take yourself back. It's May 16th, 8 p.m. Where are you?"

"My house. The living room. With three demons," Paul says.

"SO WHY THE PSYCHOTIC EPISODES?" DOYLE ASKS FATHER MARTIN. "DO YOU BELIEVE TANNER IS POSSESSED?"

"What do they want?"

"My soul. They want to take me!"

Paul flashes back, seeing blood coming out of the phone. Then, demon versions of Kelly, Frank and Father Martin laugh at him. Insects and blood line the walls. "Get away from me!" Paul yells.

"I don't like this," Corliss says. "Paul, come back." Corliss snaps her fingers. Paul fights off the visions and breathes normally. Corliss watches the levels on the biostat graphs steady and return to normal.

Meanwhile, technicians set up video cameras to capture the phenomenon, and Doyle speaks into his recorder: "File #67102. Day two. Environmental assessment complete. Data pouch containing air, water and soil samples being sent to headquarters for further analysis. Thus far, all baseline results are normal. Proceeding with on-site surveillance of the Tanner house."

Psychobiologist Lindsay Donner, chemist Sandra Miles and other investigators brainstorm.

"His account of the episode is a delusional reverse of the other witnesses," Corliss says.

"He has no history of mental illness. What's he reacting to?" Doyle asks.

"Background archival and field checks reveal nothing unusual," Donner says.

"What else is going on here? What about his job? His relationships?" Doyle asks.

"Tanner's heading up a bid for a large software contract," Donner says. "It's not going well. He could be a nervous breakdown waiting to happen."

"It doesn't mesh with his psychological profile. He's absorbed by his work but not overwhelmed by it," Corliss says.

"So why the psychotic episodes? It's almost like a post-trauma disorder," Doyle says, asking if Father Martin believes Tanner is possessed.

"He says he's never seen anything like this before," Donner says.

Ray Donahue enters, telling everyone to follow him. They go to a bank of monitors depicting various surveillance angles of the Tanner house. One shows Paul beginning another episode. Paul screams. Another monitor shows Kelly and Frank reacting to the scream. Paul foams and rants, knocking over furniture. Donahue and other investigators restrain Paul. Kelly cowers from him, sheltered by Frank.

"Stay away from me!" Paul yells.

Corliss preps a syringe with a sedative, finally managing to inject Paul. He slumps in Donahue's arms.

"I'll station a man to keep an eye on him for the night," Donahue says.

Doyle, Corliss, Donahue and the two security operatives take the unconscious Paul away. Kelly sits on the couch, trying to stop her trembling hands.

Suddenly she sees a votive candle at the end of the hall start flickering, turning into a huge wall of flame. Demonic faces are visible through the flames. Kelly's eyes widen in fear. "No. Oh my God! No!" Kelly screams.

The wall of fire moves toward her, almost enveloping her. She screams and thrashes in panic.

■TIME & PLACE■ *Doyle gives a case file update in the mobile lab the next day.*

"DR. CORLISS' MEDICAL examination of the Tanners shows that Paul Tanner suffered a subluxation of his left shoulder during the struggle with the team. For their own safety, they have been sedated and are being kept under round-the-clock watch. Blood work from the couple is being sent to the O.S.I.R. labs."

Doyle, Corliss and Donner watch the monitors contemplatively. "Classical possessions rarely involve more than one subject," Donner says. "Could it be a form of schizophrenia?"

"Not likely," Corliss says. "We've basically ruled out psychological stress as the source. So any possible transference of Paul's behavior onto Kelly doesn't track."

The next day, Donner interviews a neighbor at a house across the street. "Sure, I've heard things from the Tanner house late at night—screams, things breaking. That is one marriage from hell."

"How about strange lights? Fumes?" Donner asks.

"People screaming, okay? Hasn't been this nutty around here since the quake of '89. Knocked down nearly all the chimneys on this block."

"Do you know the Tanners' next door neighbors? I haven't been able to contact them."

"Couldn't say. They keep to themselves. If you do talk to them, ask them to mow their lawn for a change."

At the Tanners' house, Donahue and Donner search the dark basement with flashlights. "What are we looking for?" Donahue asks.

"The neighbor mentioned shifting from tremors," Donner says.

"Still doesn't explain what's going on."

"You feel a breeze, Donahue?"

"Yeah, from over there."

Donner's flashlight illuminates a crack in the basement wall. They crouch down to examine it. Suddenly a cat leaps out at them from the gap, scratching Donahue's hand. The cat scurries away, and Donner examines Donahue's cut hand.

In the living room, Doyle, Frank and the Tanners hear a scream.

"Stay here," Doyle says, moving to the basement, where he finds Donahue lying on the floor twitching, fighting the possession.

"Stay back!" Donahue says. "I can feel it on my skin. Oh, God ... the sound!"

Corliss enters with two O.S.I.R. operatives who gingerly edge toward Donahue.

"It's... got me too. Stay back," Donahue repeats.

With his last gasp of self-control, Donahue handcuffs himself to the furnace and tosses the keys to Doyle. Doyle, Donner and Corliss run outside.

"Perimeter secured," Doyle says into his comlink. "Reducing status to Code Yellow. Extreme caution advised. I don't want any one of us inside that house for more than five minutes at a time."

The team gathers near the O.S.I.R. chem lab, and Doyle speaks into his recorder. "Case log update. 1740 hours. Still no evidence to suggest how this phenomenon is being transferred. Blood results are in from headquarters."

Sandra Miles comes out of the mobile unit, pops a disk into a computer and hits a few keys. A blown-up image of the blood samples appears. "Damn. Nothing. No traces of any foreign substances," she says.

"Wait a minute," Corliss says. "What did Donahue say after he went down?"

"Something about colors," Doyle says.

"He said, 'Sounds crimson. Tastes red,'" Donner says.

"Could be synesthesia," Corliss says.

Sandra runs an ultraviolet filter on the samples. She hits a few keys, and the blood sample turns neon purple. "Lysergic acid diethylamide," Sandra says. "LSD."

Exactly. Sometimes when you're on it, your senses can blur," Corliss says. "You hear colors and taste sounds."

"Why didn't we pick up the drug before?" Doyle asks.

"Must have metabolized completely before our full tox screen caught it," Sandra says, hitting another key on the computer.

"See, the Tanners have it also."

"We relied on the family doctor's report for our initial analysis," Corliss says. "They must have run a very basic drug test and missed it too."

"So they were having bad trips. All we need is to determine the mode of transference," Doyle says.

"Could've happened a dozen different ways. Most common is absorption through the skin."

"We should check all surfaces in the house," Donner says.

Doyle and two O.S.I.R. technicians in protective suits move through the room with scanners, UV filters attached to headset video cams and UV spotlights. A neon purple tint bathes the room as the camera tracks past food and plant life. The cat comes in, reading as glowing hot white on the camera.

In the mobile lab, Corliss, Donner and Donahue, who is now recovered, watch the cat on the monitor. "The cat's toxic?" Donahue asks.

"All three subjects came in contact with it prior to their aberrant behavior," Donner says.

"Looks like we found our mode of transference," Doyle says into the comlink.

"But how did the cat come in contact with the chemical?" Donahue asks.

Back inside, two technicians maneuver a borescope through the crack between the two houses. Donner looks on with Doyle.

"Homes on this block share the same roofs, piping and other structural elements," Donner says. "Shifts in the foundations from earthquakes and tremors made for some kind of crawl space, big enough for a cat anyway."

On the monitor, static blooms into an image, revealing a dark room housing jars of chemicals and dripping feeder tubes.

"What do you make of that, Donner?" Doyle asks.

"Seems to be a lab of some sort."

Doyle gives his final case log: "The cat apparently found its way into an illegal drug lab and was exposed to highly concentrated dosages of the chemical in its raw liquid state. Anyone who came in contact with the cat's fur was contaminated with LSD. The illegal drug manufacturers were arrested and charged. The Tanners have remained together and report no further incidents of aberrant behavior. Case manager Connor Doyle closing file #67102."

Epilogue

So the devil Paul and Kelly Tanner fought was not a demon of ancient superstition, but one created by pharmaceutical technology. Fear and paranoia, however, often coupled with a strong religious element, are relatively common responses to psychotropic drugs. A remarkable example may be the hysteria of the Salem witch-hunts of 1692 which some historians propose was caused by the ingestion of ergot fungus, the derivative of LSD. Scientific investigation offered the Tanners a conventional explanation of the events in their home. But to Paul and Kelly, that there was a rational cause did not make their visions any less terrifying or real.

DAN AYKROYD

Any archaeologist who is about to unseal and enter an ancient burial site does so with a degree of caution and perhaps even trepidation. For archaeologists are especially aware of the sudden and untimely deaths that befell most of those who entered and, some say, defiled Egyptian king Tutankhamen's final resting place. These events are the basis for the legend of the curse of the mummy's tomb. Could the power of an ancient curse reach into the present?

DAN AYKROYD

T h e
C U R S E

TIME & PLACE *In the middle of the day outside a tomb in El Anfushi Bay in Alexandria, Egypt.*

Archaeologist Fredrick Roberts, the team leader, and his Bedouin assistant carry an ancient vase covered in protective plastic. They arrive at a truck, where dozens of other wrapped ancient metal artifacts are stacked.

Geena Fakhry, an Alexandrian woman, stands nearby. As Fredrick slides the vase off the stretcher, Geena moves over to join Hran Jamal, a Middle Eastern man.

"Hran!" Fredrick yells. "You and Geena can deliver this load to the warehouse. I want the cleaning and cataloguing to start tomorrow." Geena smiles, and Hran gives a thumbs-up as they climb into the cab. Fredrick turns back up toward the entrance of the tomb. There, Rosetta Saad notes the hieroglyphics above the tomb entrance.

"How's the translation coming?" Fredrick asks.

"Slowly, but I've almost got it."

Fredrick nods and moves into the tomb, which is lit from above by a string of lights. Ranja Chowdry and Diana Salisbury carefully wrap the few remaining artifacts in plastic. As Fredrick approaches, Diana staggers slightly and sits against the far wall, holding a gold plate. She looks up at him, her face pale and drawn.

"This heat is unbearable. Here," Fredrick says, passing her a canteen. Fredrick then points to a jackal statue.

"The god of mummification, guardian of the tomb," Ranja says.

Fredrick takes an air sprayer from Diana and blasts the Anubis, stirring a cloud of dust. Ranja begins coughing, and Fredrick sneezes.

As the air clears, Rosetta moves into the tomb. "Fredrick, the hieroglyphic at the tomb entrance says, 'All those who disturb this tomb will die,'" she says.

"What's a tomb without a curse?" Fredrick jokes.

Diana begins coughing. She doubles over and falls, sending up another cloud of dirt and dust. Fredrick moves to her. Also doubled over, Ranja clutches her head. She falls to the ground, and a trickle of blood drips out of one nostril.

Diana's moans turn to screams as something evil takes over her body. Fredrick hoists her while Rosetta assists Ranja, whose coughing takes over her body. As she falls to the ground, she pulls down the string of electric lights into an explosion of sparks.

TIME & PLACE *The same day, the truck, driven by Geena and Hran, pulls into the warehouse complex.*

HRAN AND GEENA set down the last wrapped artifact on a
wooden crate. "We have done wrong, removing these artifacts," Geena says. "The gods will not be happy with us for this desecration of the tomb."

Hran and Geena arrive back at the tomb that evening. Inside the tent, a table has been set for a small party. Exotic fruits, nuts and bottles of wine stand at attention, but the tent is empty.

"Something's wrong," Geena says, moving quickly out of the tent and toward the tomb entrance. Hran hustles to keep up with Geena, who nearly trips over a shape lying on the ground.

"Oh no!" says Geena, who turns over the body of the Bedouin assistant. A small trickle of dry blood runs out of a nostril. Hran moves over to two more figures lying near the entrance to the tomb. He moves closer to find Ranja and Diana, eyes open, dead.

Hran moves to enter the tomb, but Geena stops him. As she leans forward, peering into the darkness, a face lurches up at them. Hran chokes back a scream. It's Fredrick, his pale face a mask of pain. "Help me, please," Fredrick says.

They pull him out and lean him against a rock. As Hran starts inside, Fredrick grabs his arm. "Don't go in there," Fredrick says. "It's cursed."

TIME & PLACE *The next day, two O.S.I.R. vehicles arrive at the tents near the tomb and O.S.I.R. case manager Connor Doyle speaks into his recorder.*

"INITIAL LOG ENTRY. Case manager Connor Doyle.
Have arrived at dig site in Lower Egypt to continue investigation into the mysterious deaths connected with the excavation of a recently discovered tomb. The dig leader, Professor Fredrick Roberts, remains in serious condition and is being monitored. The mobile lab has been airlifted in and is on-site."

Doyle, psychobiologist Lindsay Donner and pathologist Dr. Linda Davison head into a large O.S.I.R.-issue canvas tent erected by three investigators. They watch video footage of Jared Gigorri from the University of Cairo's archaeology department. "A farmer who owns the land discovered the tomb after its entrance became exposed after a mudslide," Gigorri says. "I appointed one of my colleagues, Professor Ranja Chowdry, to work with the American, Fredrick Roberts, on the excavation."

Ranjit Anwar, the medical examiner, tells his findings. "The fact that all the deaths happened so suddenly and violently led me to believe it was food poisoning, you know, Pharaoh's revenge," Anwar begins. "But the cause of death was massive parenchymal hemorrhaging, bleeding inside the brain itself. The brain tissue had also been ravaged in each of the victims. However, my autopsies could find no evidence of a virus, nor was there any hemorrhaging in other areas of the bodies."

Donner and Doyle stand with Hran and Geena. "Our test results are all relative," Donner says, choosing her words carefully. "As we eliminate each possibility for the cause of the phenomenon, what we are left with should be the responsible factor."

"You're wasting your time. I'm telling you, it's a curse. A death curse on all those who violate the tomb," Geena warns.

"I FOUND NO EVIDENCE OF INTERNALIZED BLEEDING. IF IT'S A VIRUS, I'VE NEVER SEEN ONE ATTACK IN THIS WAY."

"You may be skeptical, Hran, but you did mention a dream," Donner says.

"The god, Anubis, told me the curse was at work, and that death will come to all those who disturb the sacred objects within. But it was only a dream," Hran says, skeptical.

Geena says she had the same dream. "We must return the artifacts to their rightful place and seal the entrance," she says.

Inside a tent, the pale Fredrick sits on a cot. "His condition has stabilized," Davison tells Doyle. "Glad to hear it," Doyle says.

Fredrick sits up as a strange look comes over his face. He begins choking and convulsing, falling back onto the cot. Davison moves to assist him, but as she turns him over, she finds him dead, a single trickle of blood seeping out of one nostril. Davison looks up at Doyle, distraught.

A couple of hours later, Davison hands Doyle some autopsy photos showing that Fredrick suffered intense intercranial hemorrhaging. "Are we talking about something like yellow fever, or even ebola?" Doyle asks.

"It's possible, but I found no other evidence of internalized bleeding. It was all localized in the brain. If it's a virus, I've never seen one attack in this way," Davison says.

Two investigators wearing environmental safety suits feed cable into the plastic-sheeting-sealed entrance to the tomb. Doyle moves beside anthropologist Natasha Constantine. In the mobile lab, investigators man various pieces of monitoring equipment, and Doyle orders them to guide the probe into the tomb.

"Any evidence of hazardous materials or toxic gases?" Doyle asks.

Investigator chemist Sandra Miles shakes her head.

"The drawings are consistent with the eleventh or twelfth dynasty," Constantine says. "That's anywhere from 3,000 to 4,000 years old."

The probe enters the antechamber. "Odd. Professor Roberts' report makes no mention of a burial chamber," Constantine says.

"Or a sarcophagus," Doyle adds. "Prepare to activate ground-penetrating radar. Perhaps the burial chamber entrance was filled in by the mudslide."

"The overall area is approximately 3 by 5 meters, but there is no evidence of any other hallways, passages or chambers. Specifically, no burial chamber," Constantine says.

"So," Doyle wonders, "what is this tomb housing?"

The probe stops on the Anubis statue.

TIME & PLACE *That night, Geena and Hran show Doyle and Donner the warehouse where they took the artifacts.*

"**THEY WERE ALL** standing by for the dig team to finish the cleaning process and initiate cataloguing," Geena explains.

They head along a long corridor, passing dozens of wooden crates and plastic-wrapped artifacts. Hran stops short.

"I can't go any further," he says, squinting as he sees a figure appear in a doorway at the other end of the warehouse. "Who's there?" Hran nervously asks as he backs away, trying to make out the figure. "No! No! Anubis, forgive me!" Hran yells.

He turns and begins running through the darkened warehouse. Looking over his shoulder, he sees the jackal-headed figure point a bright light at him. Its beam hits Hran square in the eyes. Hran screams and falls, hitting his head soundly on the floor.

Doyle, Donner and Geena run to his side. As Donner attends to Hran, Doyle looks at the figure as it steps up. Donner checks Hran for a pulse. "He's dead."

Donner and Geena watch as Hran is zipped up in a body bag. Doyle speaks into his recorder: "Case log update. While performing a routine walk-through, this case suffered its eighth casualty, Hran Jamal. Dr. Davison is conducting an autopsy on the victim."

Doyle enters the mobile lab and walks to the conference room where Davison, Donner, Constantine and Miles look at a blueprint diagram of the tomb's hallway and antechamber. Beside the diagram is an enlarged photo of the hieroglyphic statement with the lower portion only half visible because it's broken away. English translations of the hieroglyphics are written underneath.

"Because of the rock deterioration, some of it's been a guessing game," Constantine says.

"And can you explain the purpose of the tomb?" Doyle asks.

"Not at this time, but the fact there was no reported mummy or sarcophagus is not that unusual," Constantine says.

Doyle asks Davison the results of Hran's autopsy. "Once again, intercranial hemorrhaging, but his brain cells showed none of the tissue destruction I found in the other victims," Davison says.

"Let's send a team into the tomb. At the same time, initiate analysis of the artifacts at the warehouse," Doyle orders.

In the warehouse, Davison and Miles, dressed in environmental protection suits, move through the plastic sheeting, removing the lids of several crates. They begin taking photographs and readings of the environment in the crates.

Meanwhile, Donner leads three investigators in environmental safety suits through the tomb. They take environmental readings as well as air, dust and soil samples. "I'm going to secure some surface samples directly from the remaining artifacts. Then we'll seal them and deliver them for disinfection," Donner says.

Doyle watches Donner on a video monitor in the mobile lab. "Affirmative," he says. "Maintain monitoring for another hour."

Donner scrapes residue off the statue into a container. She nods to the other investigators, who begin wrapping the Anubis statue in plastic.

Later in the mobile lab, Donner examines a dust sample under a microscope. "You ever see a dust particle that looks like that?" she asks an investigator, who peers at it and shakes his head. "I'm going to isolate it on a culture medium," she says, grabbing a petri dish.

In the warehouse, Davison directs two investigators to put down the Anubis statue. A suited investigator nods and enters a secure area. He opens the plastic and begins spraying the statue with a gas disinfectant.

Doyle and Constantine sit in the mobile lab's conference room. The curse's hieroglyphics are drawn across the top of a paper, with the English translation beneath it. On the next line are the partial hieroglyphics of the completion of the curse. Constantine moves from an open historical text to the paper.

"Okay," Constantine says. "This symbol can only be one of three words. She quickly references a page in a text, then fills in the rest of two partially completed symbols.

"I should have caught this hours ago," Constantine says as she writes the completed phrase: Death lies within and shall not be released.

"Released? Release what?" Doyle asks as Donner sticks her head in.

"Doyle, I want you to have a look at an irregular dust sample I collected," Donner says.

Doyle bends down to look, and Donner says that the particle's shape and texture are unique. Doyle takes his eye away from the eyepiece and stands sharply. "What particle?" he asks.

Confused, Donner bends down to look through the eyepiece. She flicks a switch, revealing a blow-up on the screen. The petri dish gel is alive with thousands of microorganisms.

"Is it contained?" Doyle asks. Donner checks the petri dish and nods. "How did the bacteria originate?" Doyle asks.

"It's almost inconceivable, but if the particle was some type of spore, germination could be triggered by the heat and moisture generated by the isolating gel," Donner says, adding that the spore would have been dormant for centuries.

Donner looks back to the monitor as the bacteria dissolve into the gel and disappear.

"It must have a extremely short life span once activated," Donner says.

"Which explains why we weren't able to find any bacterial residue in the victims. I think we've found the 'curse,'" Doyle says.

TIME & PLACE *Back at the warehouse, Miles takes an eyedropper of a chemical, holds it over the*

statue, and carefully releases a **■ ■:■:■** C U R S E
drop and some residue clinging
to the artifact. A particle cloud rises upward toward
her face.

S U D D E N L Y ,   D O Y L E ' S   H A N D   comes out
of nowhere, covering Miles' nose and mouth and pulling her and Davison away from the plate artifact
and into the disinfecting area.

"What's going on?" Davison asks.

"We'll explain later. The main thing is you're okay," Donner says. The team returns to the mobile
lab and looks at photos of enlargements of the spores.

"Once inhaled, the spores target the brain and become a deadly form of bacteria," Davison says.

"The tomb wasn't a burial chamber designed to keep grave robbers out, but a jail of sorts to keep
the spores inside," Constantine says.

"But Hran never entered the tomb. How did he die the same way?" Doyle asks.

"I ran further tests and discovered he was taking warfarin for his heart condition," Davison says.
"A side effect is a proneness to extensive, localized bleeding. Triggered when he fell and hit his head."

"What about Fredrick?" Doyle asks.

"He had a severe allergy condition, meaning his nasal passages were more resistant to foreign
particles, but that only delayed the inevitable," Davison says.

Dressed in environmental safety suits, several investigators return the wrapped artifacts,
including the Anubis statue, to the tomb, and Doyle gives a final case log entry:

"All disinfection and eradication techniques have been unable to terminate the deadly spores. To
prevent any further exposure to this unknown and extremely lethal sporulated bacteria, I've had all
artifacts returned to the tomb and have ordered it to be sealed. Closing file #324114. Connor Doyle,
out."

Epilogue

*Some myths, like mushrooms, grow in darkness. It is only under the light of
scientific scrutiny that we are able to separate superstitious and fantastic
causes of fatalities from ones that are actually biophysical in nature. Curse or
no curse, the message seems to be clear: Leave the dead to rest in their places
of peace.*   D A N   A Y K R O Y D

Scotophobia—fear of the dark. In this age, fear of the dark seems a primitive neurosis, a throwback to a time of superstition and unreason. I mean, really, isn't darkness just the absence of light? But what if absence of light becomes more, what if it becomes a darkness "visible," an almost living, growing absolute form, threatening to consume our homes, our town, our world?

DAN AYKROYD

Creeping DARKNESS

TIME & PLACE *Nighttime at the Richler villa in Jujuy, Argentina, in the highlands.*

Six-year-old Diego Richler tiptoes down a flight of stairs toward the living room, his eyes full of wonder, while his parents, Miguel and Claudia, are enjoying a glass of wine in the kitchen. Miguel hears a muffled bang.

"What?" Claudia asks. "You've had too much wine, Miguel."

"Somebody's out there," Miguel says, reaching for his nine iron in the closet. Clutching the golf club, he eases into the hall, Claudia close behind. Another bang freezes them in their tracks. They move quietly toward the living room, hearing giggling. Their eyes widen in surprise when they see Diego laughing in front of a cone of impenetrable darkness.

Diego throws a toy car at the blackness. It disappears, swallowed up by the black. From somewhere within the darkness comes a muffled bang as the toy hits the ground. Diego reaches for another toy as Claudia and Miguel are barely able to believe their eyes.

"Miguel! What is it?" Claudia whispers.

"I don't know."

The darkness, 3 feet in diameter at the floor, increases to 7 feet at the ceiling. Miguel gingerly penetrates the blackness with his club. The tip disappears into the mass for a moment. Diego sticks his hand into the blackness.

"Diego!" Claudia screams.

Miguel snatches Diego, and the family backs away from the dark shape. Claudia rushes from the room with Diego to call the police.

TIME & PLACE *The next day, case manager Curtis Rollins sits in the front seat of an unmarked van traveling to Jujuy.*

PHYSICIST PETER AXON, psychiatrist Dr.

Anton Hendricks and anthropologist Natasha Constantine sit in the back of the van, looking through preliminary police reports.

"The advance video footage Professor Alvarez sent us doesn't reveal much," Rollins says, putting a videocassette into the VCR. Amateur video of the Richler living room shows the blackness rising from the floor like a solid black cone.

"The professor who shot this footage didn't offer any theories?" Constantine asks.

"Alvarez reached only one definite conclusion," Rollins says. "It appears to be growing."

Two vans flanked by a military escort pull up to the Richlers'. The O.S.I.R. team climbs out, seeing the entire villa cordoned off by police tape. Professor Alejandro Alvarez greets Rollins and Axon.

"Professor, we've been reviewing the footage you videotaped. Is there anything you could add to your initial report?" Axon asks.

"Only that we came back disturbed and shaken. This is so inexplicable. It's a total lack of photo-reflection unlike anything I've ever seen."

A couple of hours later, the investigators interview Miguel Richler. "It made no sound," Miguel says. "Just a dark wall spreading up from the floor. Anything that went into the darkness was gone without a trace. Why has this happened to my home?"

Claudia speaks next: "I was so afraid that Diego would be swallowed up by it. Never in my life have I seen such a thing. Total blackness."

TIME & PLACE *Later that day, Rollins, Axon, Constantine and Hendricks sit in the mobile lab unit.*

"THEIR STORIES SEEM to match. They all describe

a growing wall of blackness, impenetrable by light," Constantine starts. Axon adds that testing reveals no toxicity or bio-contamination in the witnesses.

"As a safety precaution, the Richlers will be moved from their house indefinitely," Rollins says. "The Argentine government has requested identification and termination of the phenomenon."

That night, Rollins, Axon and two technicians in full hazmat gear activate various environmental detection devices. One technician flips on a video camcorder as the team enters the house. Constantine and O.S.I.R. technicians study monitors of the team's video.

"We're on the ground floor, proceeding to the event site," Rollins says. "There are no irregular readings."

The team enters the living room, placing lights in three corners. The blackness has grown. The cone, about 8 feet in diameter at the bottom, extends through the ceiling. Axon moves closer to it with a xenon flashlight, but no light penetrates it.

"The scans are picking up minimal readings," Axon says. "Displacement margins are inconclusive. No registerable chemical components. No measurable mass, but it does seem to be growing. If this is a hoax, it's a damn good one."

Hendricks, Axon and Constantine sit with Rollins in the mobile lab the next day.

"The family's convinced their story is true. Elevated anxiety levels are natural under the circumstances," Hendricks says. "Their physical examinations are within typical ranges."

"Could they be hiding anything from us?" Constantine asks.

"I don't think so. The DEP tests would have revealed something," Hendricks answers.

Laying several photographs on the table, Axon reports that results from geodetic surveys, and geothermic and geomagnetic environmental scans in a 100-kilometer radius all indicate a large, growing, unidentified mass in the area of the Richlers' villa.

"Curtis, I recommend sending in a remote probe to get some direct data from within the mass itself," Axon says.

"THE ULTIMATE THREAT THIS PHENOMENON POSES OVERRIDES ANY OF OUR PERSONAL SAFETY," ROLLINS SAYS.

Rollins agrees. "Set it up for 1600 hours. The Argentine government is anxious to see some progress."

In a few hours, Axon operates the remote control probe with a joystick, and the wheeled probe hums down the hallway inside the villa.

"Anything happen yet?" Hendricks asks.

"No trace of hazmat, tox traces or abnormal energy-field concentrations. Nothing even slightly unkosher," Axon says.

As the probe moves inside the darkness, the monitor turns black. Static slices across the screen intermittently. Technicians adjust the equipment as a low electronic hum rises to a piercing shriek. Suddenly, there's silence.

"Probe systems down. We've lost telemetry. I can't bring it back," Axon says. "It's gone."

That night, Rollins and the team sit at the conference table. On the green screen is a blueprint of the villa, blackness growing in the center.

"This region does have a history of geophysical and environmental phenomena," Constantine says. "None related in any way to this particular anomaly."

Axon suggests taking a team in.

"Into the mass?" Hendricks asks. "Peter, we just lost a probe in there."

"I'll go alone then," Axon says. "Try to get some conclusive readings. I'll suit up. According to all readings, it shouldn't be a problem."

Constantine objects. "There are no readings, Peter. It's too risky. We should just send in another probe."

"The ultimate threat this phenomenon poses overrides any of our personal safety," Rollins says. "You're sure about this, Axon?" Axon nods, putting on a full yellow hazmat suit.

Axon is rigged with bio-monitoring feeds. He carries a portable hazmat scanner with him. He waves to Constantine and moves off.

Bright lights, running off a generator outside, have been set up around the cone of darkness. The power in the house has been turned off. Axon moves toward the living room.

Rollins speaks over the comlink. "Axon, do you copy?"

"Ten-four. I copy loud and clear."

"Visuals are good. We'll keep your vitals on-line. Any elevated readings, and you're out of there," Rollins says.

The darkness, now 15 feet in diameter at the bottom, fills half the room. As Axon enters, the video image in the mobile unit becomes murky and barely discernible. Axon enters the blackness.

Rollins, Constantine and Hendricks watch Axon's grainy image on the monitor. Static jolts the screen.

"What do you see?" Rollins asks Axon through the comlink.

"Nothing. No depth perception. Light waves aren't registering in the environment at all."

"Just keep your bio cables clear. Follow them to get out of there."

"I can't read the instruments. I can't even see myself. I'm coming out. Sorry, Curtis."

Constantine lets out a small sigh of relief. A technician turns from a monitor console to Rollins. "Sir, I think you should see this. An uplink transmission is being rerouted to us from headquarters via satellite."

A map of Asia and a highlighted area near the East China Sea appear on the screen. The image rotates 180 degrees to show Jujuy as its polar opposite. "They've found the same phenomenon in China," Constantine says.

"Same configuration as ours," Rollins says.

"Curtis, are we talking about an outbreak?"

"No. Not exactly," Rollins replies. "Perhaps something worse. The new occurrence is here in Ningbo, Zhejiang province."

A technician hits some keys, superimposing lines of longitude and latitude superimposed over a 3-D image of earth. "Ningbo is Jujuy's exact polar opposite," Rollins continues. "That opens up the possibility that instead of two separate occurrences, we could be dealing with one very large, very dangerous phenomenon."

Rollins speaks into the comlink. "File #77011. Based on the fact the anomaly in China and the local phenomenon are located at polar opposites, a Bravo team has been dispatched to study the second occurrence. They will link their investigation to ours."

A technician alerts Rollins to a digital transmission from the Bravo team leader at the Ningbo site. A burst of static wipes in a digitized image of O.S.I.R. operative Gerrard.

"Established operations here," Gerrard says. "Data seem to be identical to alpha site. Phenomenon growing at the same rate, 22.6 centimeters per hour, and increasing exponentially."

Axon turns to a computer showing a map of China. The blackness has spread considerably. Hendricks looks on. "According to our numbers," Axon says, "Jujuy will be consumed within seven days."

"Our projections match, alpha," Gerrard says. "Seven days to 88 percent of Ningbo region in darkness." Gerrard fades out.

"We can't let this phenomenon spread. There would be no sustainable plant life," Axon says.

Suddenly, an old woman, Micaela Farinango, stares into the camera. A translator changes her words from Spanish to English. "It is the time of Pacha Pura Cana. Long before the time of man, he first came from the stars and bored right through the living heart of our world, creating stone and fire, night and day, light and dark."

"What is Pacha Pura Cana?" Constantine asks.

The woman responds: "Power. As old as the sun itself, but sent to us to steal the sun away. To bring darkness to the land." The image freezes.

TIME & PLACE *That night, Constantine checks her notes in the mobile lab unit.*

"IN THE LOCAL Quechua dialect, Pacha means earth and Pura Cana means darkness," she says.

"But there's no evidence that what this woman is talking about has anything to do with the phenomenon," Axon says.

"Sometimes you find answers in places you wouldn't expect," Constantine says. "We shouldn't discount the folklore angle. I mean, the Spaniards were writing about this as far back as 1600. They thought it had to do with eclipses because Pacha Pura Cana was also known as the god of darkness. Maybe there's more to these legends than just fiction."

"Tasha, it is intriguing, but at the current rate of expansion, we don't have time to chase down ancient myths. Run more tests. If all procedures fail, we go with the linear accelerator," Rollins says. Constantine and Axon exchange a worried glance. They know the linear accelerator is a dangerous piece of equipment.

The next morning, Rollins speaks into his tape recorder: "File # 77011. Case log update. We've tried various eradication procedures—temperature decrease, oxygen removal and microwave bombardment—without success. We are now attempting to alter the environment with ELF transmissions."

Two O.S.I.R. technicians and Axon study their equipment. "Steady at 3,900 angstroms," Axon says. "No reaction so far." The curve on the oscilloscope swells, and a technician adjusts the controls.

"It's been hours," Axon says. "Still no change in the phenomenon." Axon looks at Rollins, who orders evacuation of the surrounding area.

"I know it's risky, but I don't have a choice," Rollins says. "We have to try every option. As long as the civilians are clear ..."

In the mobile lab, a static-filled image of Gerrard appears on a monitor. "The situation's getting tense," Gerrard says. "Chinese authorities are dealing with it as a military emergency. They've closed the area and expelled all foreign journalists. We're working under extremely close supervision, so there's no time to lose."

TIME & PLACE *Dressed in full hazmat gear, Axon and two technicians wheel the linear accelerator to the lip of the front door of the house.*

"COMMENCE COUNTDOWN SEQUENCE," Rollins says. "How long do we have, Peter?"

Axon checks readouts on his equipment. "Three minutes till linear acceleration."

"Affirmative at three minutes," Gerrard says. "Standing by."

In the house, the LED on the linear accelerator blinks 02:45:00, 02:44:00, 02:43:00 ...

Everyone waits tensely in the mobile lab, eyes locked on the monitors. Several long seconds pass. Then, dials, oscilloscopes and everything else that was monitoring the missing probe start pulsing and beeping.

A technician checks the readouts. "Hold countdown PLA., we've got a problem." A burst of static emanates from the probe monitor. Everybody turns to watch.

"Hold on," Rollins says. "Remote probe is back on-line."

Axon manipulates the probe's joystick. The monitor camera pans across the living room, showing the toy that Diego threw into the darkness.

Live feed from Ningbo communicates Gerrard's excitement over something. "Come in, alpha," Gerrard says. "Visuals confirm the phenomenon has disappeared."

Axon orders technicians to shut down the accelerator, and Rollins confirms that linear acceleration has not been run. Monitors in the lab show surveillance images inside the house. Rollins, Constantine, and Hendricks step out of the van to join Axon and the technicians as they stare at the house as the creeping blackness dissipates.

As it stands empty, abandoned, the villa displays a "For Sale" sign. Micaela Tupa-Amaru stares at the house before turning to walk away.

Rollins speaks into the tape recorder: "File #77110. Case manager Curtis Rollins. Final log entry. Theories as to the origin of the phenomenon range from it being a bizarre geological anomaly to the possibility of extraterrestrial phenomena. One theory speculates a rare, nongravitational black hole originating inside the earth's core. But we have found no conclusive evidence as to how the manifestation actually occurred. Curtis Rollins, out."

Epilogue

Man-made or truly supernatural? What was this growing blackness? Well, the O.S.I.R. never could determine the exact cause of this amazing phenomenon. Was this merely an isolated event? Or an introduction of something to come? Perhaps those of us who are afraid of the dark have good reason to be.

DAN AYKROYD

The SETI project, the search for extraterrestrial intelligence—a worldwide network of radio dishes designed to receive any communication from outer-space cultures if they exist. Now despite the absence to date of any such messages and the repeated non-acknowledgment of actual contact by our North American military, we are continually confronted with reports of craft sightings, communications and abductions associated with a variety of sentient, extraterrestrial beings. When the O.S.I.R. was asked to investigate lights in Crescent County, Iowa, it found the bewildered residents' agitated state as challenging as the phenomenon it had set out to analyze.

DAN AYKROYD

U F O
E N C O U N T E R

TIME & PLACE *Late at night on a two-lane road through farmland in Crescent County, Iowa, a half-moon barely illuminating the landscape.*

Followed by his older brother Chad, seventeen, Adam Keelor, fifteen, trots along the edge of the road carrying the remains of a case of beer.

"If Dad finds out we were skinny-dipping, we're dead," Adam yells back.

"You're telling me it wasn't worth it? Sally and Janine?" The two boys start laughing and decide that if they hurry they'll be home by breakfast.

"Let's cut through the Layton ranch," Chad suggests. "That'll get us home in twenty minutes." Ignoring Adam's hesitation, Chad squeezes through a barbed wire fence. "It's 3 o'clock in the morning. How's Layton ever gonna know?" Chad yells.

Adam looks around nervously, then hustles to join his brother. Moving through rows of spring corn, Adam and Chad hear a pulsing murmur. They stop and look around as the sound intensifies. A bright light suddenly sweeps across the field, disappearing as quickly as it appeared.

Another blast of bright light swoops across the field, now closer to the boys. Chad pulls Adam, who's mesmerized. "Something's coming! Let's go!" Chad yells.

Adam snaps out of it, turning to follow Chad. The lights are right behind them; the noise is deafening. A sudden wind springs up, flattening the corn to the ground. Chad trips and falls, and Adam ends up on top of him. They scramble to their feet.

Suddenly, electrical arcs encircle the boys. They shudder and collapse, unconscious.

The following week in a different field, a crowd of about twenty townsfolk gather at the edge of a road overlooking farmland. Men, women and families stare silently at the sky. Sheriff Jesse Weckel approaches one of the townspeople, Fred Hilliard. "All right, Fred, what's going on here?" he asks.

"I think you know, Jesse, after those kids got taken last week," Hilliard says.

"Fred, we're still not sure what happened last week. Now I want all of you to move on out of here."

But Fred's not listening. He stares out at the sky, and Weckel turns to follow his gaze. As swirling bright lights approach, the townsfolk murmur with excitement.

Weckel's eyes widen as one of the UFOs illuminates him for a brief moment. He climbs in his 4x4, preparing to chase them down when blackness takes over and the glowing lights disappear.

TIME & PLACE *The next day in downtown Crescent, a small midwest town of 1,000, case manager Connor Doyle pulls up to the police station with O.S.I.R. anthropologist Natasha Constantine.*

DOYLE GIVES HIS first report: "File #52111. Case manager Connor Doyle. We are investigating possible UFO sightings and a claimed alien abduction in Crescent County, Iowa."

In his office, Weckel drinks some old coffee from a mug. "Yes, there were multiple sightings," he answers Constantine. "You'll be hard-pressed to find someone in this town who hasn't seen those lights."

"Our contacts at the FAA confirmed that nothing was scheduled to fly over your airspace during the times of the sightings," Doyle says. "So we only have visual confirmation."

"Not if you factor in the boys," Weckel says. "It was what happened to them that got the town all lit up."

"Your report says the doctor who examined them feels they underwent something traumatic," Constantine says.

"They told everyone they got abducted by aliens, and they have the scars to prove it," Weckel says.

Fred Hilliard, a service station operator, gives the first interview: "Yeah, I've been out there waiting since those boys first got probed. I figured if those things came back, we'd better be ready to defend our young. About a week later, they came again. Circled around the field, but there were too many of us for them to try a landing."

Investigators also speak with rancher Kurtis Layton. "If there was anything going on out on my land, I slept right through it. Maybe it was a flock of geese or car lights reflecting from the highway. Or maybe just a couple of kids up to something."

Adam and Chad Keelor stand with their shirts off, exposing red burns on their chest and arms. "We were cutting across this field when it happened," Adam says. "This flying saucer came out of nowhere. We tried to run, but it was too fast."

Dr. Neil Petersen, a general practitioner, says the sheriff carried the boys in at 5 A.M. "They had symptoms of dehydration and disorientation. Both had injuries and pupil-response time consistent with a serious concussion. First- and second-degree burns on the feet and hands. Then there's the gouge on Chad's shoulder. He said the aliens had taken a sample."

Investigators set up equipment near the two-lane road. Doyle speaks into his recorder: "Case log update. I've decided to expedite protocol and focus our attention on a 10-square-mile perimeter. It is hoped a thorough on-site inspection in conjunction with a physiological assessment of the subjects will help determine what happened here."

Doyle walks over to O.S.I.R. aeronautics engineer Sandor Winkler, who sits with a laptop. "I've charted all reported UFO sightings to date," Winkler says, unrolling a topographic printout on the conference table. "They could have been anywhere within this 20-mile square area."

"No water towers, no power lines, nothing in the area that could have been perceived as a UFO," Axon says. "No anomalous energy fields, no odd geophysical elements."

In another part of the mobile lab, O.S.I.R. psychiatrist Dr. Anton Hendricks examines Jesse Weckel. Weckel has his shirt off and a pressure cuff on his arm.

"Have you had any insomnia? Shortness of breath, migraine headaches?" Hendricks asks.

"Yeah. All of the above," Weckel answers.

"How's your night vision? Any dimness or clouding of peripheral sight?"

"A bit. Anything wrong with me, Doc?" Weckel asks.

"Yes. You are overworked and underpaid."

Later, through tinted glass, Doyle observes Hendricks performing a physical examination of Chad and Adam Keelor.

"It felt like something was pushing us down. The lights were blinding. The air smelt funny, like after a thunderstorm," Adam explains.

"And then they knocked us out," Chad says. "Zapped us, I guess."

"And you're sure you received these wounds during your ordeal that evening?" Hendricks asks.

"It wasn't no ordeal, man," Chad says. "We were abducted by aliens. Don't you get it?"

TIME & PLACE *Later in the mobile lab, Doyle walks to the conference room speaking into his recorder.*

"DR. HENDRICKS HAS completed a physiological and psychological assessment of the immediate witnesses to this phenomenon. All have responded positively to digitally enhanced polygraph testing. With two exceptions." Doyle clicks off the recorder.

Doyle, physicist/statistician Peter Axon, and Constantine watch the screen that displays images from the physiological examination of Chad and Adam. "Both boys registered high cardiovascular and neurological responses during questioning," Hendricks says. "They're hiding something. They do not respond well to authority figures. I'd learn more if I could regress them to a hypnotic state, but they refuse to cooperate."

"Anything further from your scans of the area?" Doyle asks Winkler.

"Minor traces of pesticide. We've sent soil samples to headquarters for further analysis."

"Reduce the perimeter and prepare full surveillance of the area," Doyle orders. "I want to know if anything comes within 5 miles of this field."

The mobile lab's long-range sensors operate into the early morning hours as the radar dish turns. Doyle sips coffee while Winkler and other investigators man tracking stations. It's 1:40 A.M.

Constantine sits at a console with Axon, who hangs up a phone he's been speaking into and turns to Doyle.

"Des Moines air traffic has clear skies over our general area. No scheduled flights tonight," Axon says.

Then they hear a small warning beep. Winkler leans up to the screen, reporting long-range bogies coming in from the northwest at 5 miles. "There are two," Winkler says, "coming in low, 20 feet off the deck."

"We have a target lock," Axon says. "Confirm two bogies zeroing in on our position. Fast." A night-vision monitor shows faint lights in the distance.

Without warning, the radar screens go down. The blips disappear. Axon flicks switches to no avail.

"But we still have visuals," Doyle says. "Launch the aerial probe. I want identification ASAP."

"Probe is airborne," Winkler says. "Hold on, I've lost remote scans." Throughout the lab, sensing monitors go black. Outside, the aerial probe explodes in the night sky. One by one, the monitors go down.

"The probe's disappeared," Constantine says.

"What the hell is happening out there?" Doyle asks, moving to the night-vision monitor to watch the bright lights circle and dance and suddenly disappear.

TIME & PLACE *The next day, Axon, Constantine and a farm worker walk through Layton's field trying to retrieve the remote aerial probe lost during the night.*

"OVER THERE," AXON says, waving his tracking device. "About 20 yards." The remains of the probe lie in a heap in the field. They approach it, inspecting the damage.

Suddenly the worker doubles over in horrible paroxysms of coughing. Constantine and Axon drop the probe, helping him sit down.

"Sounds like a bronchial infection," Axon says, examining his eyes and skin. "How long have you had this?"

"Too long," the worker says. "Many of us are sick, but we must work for our families."

"We should get him back to the lab to run some tests," Constantine says. Leaving the remains of the probe behind, they help the worker back across the field.

TIME & PLACE *Later in the mobile lab, med techs examine a red-blistered, festering boil-covered field worker. Other field workers are being examined too.*

"HOW ARE THEY?" Doyle asks.

"Luis has a severe chest infection," Hendricks says. "His friends, well, we found large amounts of chemical-based toxins in their systems. I haven't seen anything like this since Kurdistan."

"Could it have come from the field?" Doyle asks.

"Possibly. Luis doesn't know where it could have come from but did say that most of the farmhands he works with have the same illness."

"But they're all working illegally, so no one will speak up," Doyle says. "Tasha, grab Peter. I want you to go on a covert sub-operation to the exact location of the sightings. Let's see if they can make a positive ID of any UFOs using remote-sensing equipment."

SUDDENLY AXON STOPS.

"Tasha! Don't move," he yells, circling her. He notices a low tripwire running along the border of the field.

Axon waves a scanner near the wire. "High-energy field emissions," Axon says as he takes a stick and throws it at the wire. Sparks fly as high-voltage electricity fries the stick.

"And it's barbed too," Constantine says. "Not very neighborly, Mr. Layton."

"Wait a minute," Constantine continues. "Didn't Chad say something like 'The air smelled funny, like after a thunderstorm?'"

Axon and Hendricks communicate via radio from the mobile lab unit. "Ozone. There must be 200 volts running through it. Those kids would have got a hell of a shock," Axon says.

"That would explain the irregular heart rate. The barbed wire could also account for Chad's wounds, but it doesn't explain the boys' reluctance to cooperate," Hendricks says.

AXON CONFIRMS A VISUAL ON TWO UFOS LOW ON THE HORIZON. "ABOUT 20 FEET OFF THE DECK AND CLOSING FAST!"

Constantine, having spoken with the girls the Keelor brothers were with on the night of the abduction, fills in the investigators. "Turns out they all indulged in a little home-made jungle juice," she says. "As a devout Baptist, Mr. Keelor wouldn't be too pleased. They didn't want Dad to find out."

A warning beep suddenly emanates from a scanner. "I have a target lock," Winkler says from the lab.

Doyle warns Axon that double bogies are headed in his direction, and Axon confirms a visual on two UFOs low on the horizon. "About 20 feet off the deck and closing fast!" Axon says.

Over the comlink comes a low throbbing whoosh; then static partially distorts the radio link.

Just as Doyle asks Axon to identify the UFO, another whoosh comes over the comlink. Investigators tap quickly at keyboards. Monitors respond, showing the field under surveillance from different angles. Two UFOs appear on the screens.

Suddenly the data freeze. Sandor hits a button and superimposes a schematic of a helicopter on top of the thermographic image. "I've got a lock," Sandor says. "We have an ID match on the UFOs. Helicopters. Bell Jet Rangers—two of them."

"Why didn't we ID them before?" Doyle asks.

"They appear to be modified for night-flying and stealth runs," Sandor says.

"But what are they doing here?" Hendricks wonders aloud.

In the field, a helicopter zooms in low, lights flaring off the crops. Axon and Constantine run, breathing heavily. "Lab one, do you copy? Do you copy?" Axon tries reaching the lab, but the helicopters are jamming the transmissions.

As Axon and Constantine run, they are hit by a flaring light and a fine mist.

In the lab, Sandor sits at the console tracking the choppers on the screen. "Looks like the UFOs are emitting some kind of liquid," Sandor says.

"They're crop-dusting," Axon says.

"At this time of night?" Hendricks asks.

Doyle exits the mobile lab. Sheriff Weckel intercepts him as he pulls up in his 4x4. "Looks like we've found your UFOs," Doyle says. "Let's go."

Doyle climbs into the 4x4, which starts racing down the country road parallel to the field. Two helicopters fly along the field next to them.

Weckel turns to Doyle. "We're about to run out of road in a hurry," Weckel says as he brings the 4x4 skidding to a stop. The choppers continue ahead into the darkness.

Winkler types furiously at the radar-station console. Using infrared laser technology, the screen soon reveals a topographic aerial point of view of a three-dimensional image of each helicopter.

"Heading due southeast, about 4 kilometers away," Winkler reports. Doyle and Weckel listen through a headset.

"Copters," Weckel says. "Who'd have thought? I'll have two squad cars meet us at the landing field."

Parked near two modified choppers are several sheriffs' department vehicles and O.S.I.R. vehicles. Weckel's deputies lead two pilots in handcuffs. Weckel turns to Doyle, who stands with Axon, Miles, Hendricks, Sandor and Constantine.

"I just put out an arrest warrant for Kurt Layton, the man who owns that land," Weckel says.

"Turns out they were spraying toxaphene, a banned pesticide they smuggled in from Mexico," Constantine says.

"He put stealth modifications in the helicopters, flew in low and jammed all radio transmissions to cover the operation. These guys were good," Winkler adds.

"But why go to all this trouble just to dust crops?" Weckel asks.

"His acreage was dying, and his corn was infested with earworms, which are resistant to most pesticides, except toxaphene."

"Now," Doyle says to Weckel, "you can tell the boys and the rest of the town what they really saw."

Doyle speaks into his tape recorder: "Final case log entry. Kurt Layton has been arrested and charged with illegal use of aircraft and emission of deadly chemicals. The farm workers were all treated for various ailments caused by the pesticides. Case manager Connor Doyle, out."

Epilogue

Sometimes the most extraordinary occurrences have the simplest explanations. These teenagers weren't abducted by aliens in UFOs. No, this was human greed coupled with a blatant and criminal disregard for the health, welfare and stability of an honest, hard-working community. No E.T. or flying saucers here.

DAN AYKROYD

One of the intriguing North American myths is the quest by Ponce de León for the fountain of eternal youth. Today, scientific researchers seek genetic keys that could unlock a human life span of 150 years or more. For Doug Kilmartin, his was exactly the opposite discovery. Nothing less than a fountain of aging and decay.

DAN AYKROYD

Two Lost Old MEN

TIME & PLACE *Afternoon at a campsite in Anderson National Park, British Columbia.*

A thin trail of white smoke spirals upward from the embers of a dying camp-fire. Conservation officers Beverly Damico and Ted Larkin stomp on the embers. The site appears deserted. Larkin asks Damico if anyone issued open fire permits for the area, and Damico says no. Just then, someone bursts through the trees.

"Help, please help me!" he cries. "Back there in the woods. Everything's dead. A dead zone! We went in and ..."

"Slow down," Larkin says. "Is this your campsite?"

"Yes. We're tree planters. Three of us. We're university students and ..."

"Okay, sir, one thing at a time," Larkin says. "We found an open fire here. That's a big no-no. Let's see your ID and camping permit."

Bewildered, the man nods, reaching for his wallet. Larkin takes it as Damico brings the man some water.

"You're Douglas Kilmartin?" Larkin asks, looking at the driver's license.

"Yes."

"This ID says you're twenty-one years old."

Kilmartin slowly lifts his hands in front of his face. They are frail and wrinkled. Shocked, he drops the cup of water and wrenches the side-view mirror on the ATV round to face him. "Oh no. What's happened to me?"

A couple of hours later, Larkin and a few other rangers move through the bushes. "I found him! Over here," Damico says.

Damico cradles the head of another man, about seventy years old. He's ragged and torn, barely conscious.

"This is the guy Kilmartin described. Barry Strother, according to his ID. Also twenty-one years old," Damico says.

TIME & PLACE *The next day, case manager Connor Doyle speaks into his recorder in the parking Lot of Saint Agatha's Hospital.*

"FILE #86126. INITIAL log entry. After

being contacted by provincial police, we are launching an investigation into an alleged anomaly. Two men claim to have aged nearly 50 years following an encounter with an unexplained zero-growth zone in the Canadian northern wilderness."

Beverly Damico talks to investigators. "When we got Kilmartin to the hospital, he was hysterical. Tells us there's somebody still out there. Said they'd found a place in the woods, nothing growing, a dead zone. And he thinks she's still there."

Ted Larkin, also of the forestry service, elaborates: "And then it gets really weird. None of this was making sense so we had the OPP run a check on both their names, and it turns out the second guy we found, Strother, had a little run-in with the law when he was younger. A break-and-enter five years ago when he was sixteen. And the guy looks seventy. But the thing is, his fingerprints. They actually match the ones in the Strother kid's file."

Investigators also speak with Dr. Martin Dornan, who examined Strother and Kilmartin. "They were both in shock. Kilmartin, for a man in his seventies, is in pretty good shape. Strother, much less so. But for two men who're twenty-one, as they claim, they're in trouble."

TIME & PLACE *Later that afternoon, Doyle leads psychobiologist Lindsay Donner and physicist/ statistician Peter Axon down a trail. Donner listens through her headset.*

"COPY. DONNER OUT," she says, turning to

Doyle. "Provincial police say there's still no sign of the missing woman, a Katherine Fitzgerald."

"What's the status of the two subjects?" Axon asks.

"Kilmartin's condition has stabilized so we'll be able to talk to him this afternoon," Doyle says. "But Strother is still drifting in and out of consciousness. And we have no choice, really, but to treat him as if he's as old as he appears. Kilmartin's effective age is about seventy. Strother's, eighty-five."

The team stops as everyone sees an unusual sandbar area in the middle of the forest. Axon hands Doyle some photographs taken from the helicopter.

"It's oval-shaped, covering about 8,000 square meters," Doyle says. "Desolation in the middle of a living forest."

Two O.S.I.R. investigators in hazmat gear move meticulously along the periphery of the zone taking readings. Axon crouches down at the edge of the dead earth. He pulls out a still camera and snaps some photos.

A bird flutters across the periphery, settling on the dead earth. It disappears behind a dune. Intrigued, Axon and several investigators move around to get a better angle of the bird. Its skeleton lies in the dead earth.

Later in the mobile lab, monitors show the bird's skeleton. Doyle watches the videotape with Axon, psychiatrist Dr. Anton Hendricks and Donner, who is timing it with a stopwatch. "Just 12.3 seconds from point of entry to discovery of the skeleton," Donner says.

Aerial photographs depict a barren swath amid rugged forest. The scant remains of a human skeleton lie on the sand.

The next day, Hendricks interviews Kilmartin, who is hooked up to electrodes for DEP testing. "Doug, let's start back at Tuesday," Hendricks says.

"Me, Barry and Katie were flown in with a bunch of new seedlings to plant. So we set up camp, had breakfast and started work."

"And then what happened?" Hendricks asks.

"I'm not sure. We were planting, and we found a place. The dead zone. I think I walked in, but ..."

"Did you all go in?"

"No, I mean ... I'm sorry. It's so hard to concentrate these days, you know."

"It's all right, Doug. We'll try again shortly," Hendricks says.

TIME & PLACE *Guided by a remote control unit from the mobile lab, the terrestrial probe unit moves toward a skeleton in the forest.*

"WITH ANY LUCK, the dental records should give us an ID," Doyle says.

The next day, the team of investigators watches the main screen, showing enlargements of Douglas Kilmartin's, Katherine Fitzgerald's and Barry Strother's driver's licenses.

"The skeleton is Katherine Fitzgerald, age 21. Cause of death unknown," Doyle says.

"We've eliminated several obvious explanations for the lack of vegetation. No radiation traces anywhere near the zone. The site itself has no past connection with any toxic substances," Axon says.

"Kilmartin vividly recalls everything that happened until he encountered the anomaly—then it's almost blank. This is consistent with the repression of a traumatic experience," Hendricks says.

"Could there be a straightforward medical explanation like progeria—accelerated aging?" Doyle asks.

"Not in this case," Hendricks says. "It's an extremely rare genetic disorder and it invariably begins in early childhood."

"Let's keep digging," Doyle says. Hendricks reports that Kilmartin is responding well to counseling.

TIME & PLACE *At Saint Agatha's Hospital.*

DONNER ▦▦▦▦▦▦▦▦▦▦ MEN SEES SARAH

Kilmartin walk up to the nurse's station requesting to see her son.

Donner introduces herself to Sarah, who stands just inside the door, stone-faced. Donner stands in the doorway behind her. Across the room, Kilmartin tries to smile. "Mom, you made it," he says.

"I don't know this man," Sarah says. "He isn't my son. Look at him." She turns to leave, and Kilmartin recalls the day Gypsy stole Old Man Telford's salmon. Sarah stops short, horrified.

The next day, Hendricks sits across from Kilmartin, who is already under hypnosis. "Take me back to Tuesday morning," Hendricks says.

"I'm planting in the woods. Barry and Katie have gone ahead." Kilmartin flashes back, seeing Strother and Fitzgerald push through the undergrowth.

"What do you see now?" Hendricks asks.

As Kilmartin moves into a clearing, he sees Katie go into an area of desolation. "Guys, check this place out," Katie says.

"Is Katie in the zone?" Hendricks asks.

"Yes. She wants us to follow her in, but I'm not so sure. It's really freaky. They're just laughing, like I'm being paranoid. So I go in."

Young Kilmartin and Strother walk slowly forward. Katie turns to young Strother. Her appearance stops him short: She's aging before his eyes. Young Strother tries to hide his shock. Then he winces at a stab of back pain. Holding one hand to his lower back, he turns, and now he too is aging.

YOUNG STROTHER TRIES TO HIDE HIS SHOCK. HOLDING ONE HAND TO HIS LOWER BACK, HE TURNS, AND NOW HE TOO IS AGING.

Katie faces the two boys. Kilmartin and Strother slowly back away from her as she swiftly morphs into a decaying corpse, then a skeleton. Strother turns in horror to Kilmartin.

"Let's get out of here!" Kilmartin yells. The two old men try to run out of the zone. They make it to the edge of the trees. Strother falls to his knees, exhausted. Kilmartin keeps running.

▦ TIME & PLACE ▦ *Later that day, the terrestrial probe unit traces slowly across the zone in the forest.*

INVESTIGATORS MONITOR ITS

progress from a distance, and Doyle speaks into his recorder: "Case file update. We're proceeding with environmental analysis and surveillance to attempt to establish the precise nature and characteristics of the phenomenon. Additionally, our medical team is searching for possible ways of reversing the effects."

In the hospital, a nurse draws blood from Strother's finger. The sample is transported to the mobile lab, where a technician puts it onto a slide and places it under a microscope.

"I've been reviewing some of the preliminary interviews," Donner, in another part of the lab, says. She pulls up an interview of Chief Dan Leonard, a Native American in his thirties.

"I remember hearing the stories when I was a kid. Rumors about a place where nothing lives," Leonard says.

"Do any of the stories tell of people who went in and came back out again?" Donner asks.

"No. Just lots of stories about people from our tribe who just disappeared. Legends say some of them got eaten by wild animals. Some of them fell into raging rivers and drowned. Look, I've lived here my whole life and never seen this so-called dead zone."

Later in the lab, Doyle, Axon, Donner and Hendricks congregate. "This much we already know," Axon says. "Horizontally, the zone is covering an area just under 8,000 square meters. We mapped it by helicopter and charted the height at which the disintegration began."

"Elliptical, which could suggest some sort of energy-patterned phenomenon," Donner says.

"But the configuration appears unstable. We're seeing slight fluctuations," Axon says.

"What if we were to chart these fluctuations over a period of hours?" Donner asks.

"AFTER PERFORMING 87 EXPERIMENTS, IN MY ASSESSMENT, WE'VE EXHAUSTED ALL MEANS OF PROVIDING A SCIENTIFIC EXPLANATION."

Doyle holds up his hand, listening into his comlink. "The hospital just contacted us," he says. "It's Strother."

In the hospital, Strother lies on his back, eyes open, staring out unmoving. Dr. Dornan checks for a pulse. Behind, Hendricks stands with Kilmartin, who is trembling and distraught. Dr. Dornan looks up and shakes his head. Strother's dead.

TIME & PLACE *Two metal poles have been planted in the sand, on opposite sides of the zone. A blue electrical charge arcs from one to the other.*

DOYLE GIVES A LOG update: "2200 hours. We have introduced a variety of technologies into the environment in an attempt to cause a detectable disturbance. None of these attempts has been able to produce a significant result. After performing eighty-seven experiments, in my assessment, we've now exhausted all means of providing a scientific explanation."

The team assembles for a round table in the mobile unit, where the zone appears on the wall monitor. "The phenomenon could be extraterrestrial. That's why it won't react to earth-based technology," Donner says.

"Or it could be an as-yet-unspecified geophysical phenomenon that subatomically accelerates all forms of living matter," Axon says. "It could be some form of rare and mutated vortex that absorbs concentrated life-form energy. This would be consistent with the results of the physiological assessments."

The next day, an O.S.I.R. investigator loads some bags into the trunk of a waiting car at the hospital. Hendricks comes up to the car, where Kilmartin sits in the passenger seat beside Sarah.

"Look after yourself. We'll be in touch," Hendricks says. Kilmartin nods, summoning a smile.

As Doyle and Donner watch Kilmartin leave, an incoming transmission from O.S.I.R. headquarters comes in over Doyle's comlink, and they go to the mobile lab.

Elsinger appears on the viewing screen, addressing Doyle. "Government officials have asked us to design and implement a method of sealing off the hazard permanently," Elsinger says. "Effective immediately."

"But sir, we're just beginning to make some headway as to understanding the phenomenon," Doyle says. "We need to know exactly what this phenomenon is."

O.S.I.R. Director of Operations Frank Elsinger apologizes, explaining that the mandate is final. The screen goes blank. Doyle gives a final log entry: "Following consultations with headquarters, local government officials and the assigned team, it was decided to construct a giant cage of steel rebar to cover the entire area of the hazard. Once the cage has been lowered into place by helicopter, concrete will be poured over it until a massive block of solid rock takes form."

Epilogue

Geophysical anomaly, paranormal manifestation or alien bioforce? The answer lies hidden forever in a concrete vault, no longer a threat. At last report, Doug Kilmartin was working at a crisis center, counseling trauma victims and living each day to its fullest. **DAN AYKROYD**

In our planet's history, some civilizations have disappeared mysteriously—the lost tribes of Israel and the Essenes, for example. North America has its lost peoples too. Sir Walter Raleigh's Virginia Colony and, some 300 years earlier, the Anasazi, a culturally advanced Indian people of the American Southwest, suddenly abandoned their ancestral homeland. In the course of investigating violent deaths in a cavern somewhere in New Mexico, did the O.S.I.R. uncover a clue regarding the fate of the Anasazi tribe? **DAN AYKROYD**

A n a s a z i C A V E

TIME & PLACE *Daytime in the sandy desert of Chaco Canyon, New Mexico.*

Proceeding down the canyon, Darren, an archaeologist, and Simon, an anthropologist, reach a spot where mud slides have eroded the cliff. They walk toward the remains of a single ancient Anasazi hut and a large tent where men are camping. Another archaeologist, Paul, hurries out of the hut, calling them over.

Darren, Simon and his dog, Sonny, join Paul, and they enter the hut. Paul shows the men the back wall of the hut where he has been excavating. Paul knocks on the wall, which sounds hollow. "There's something back there," Paul says.

Darren, the leader of the group, steps in and takes the pick. As he breaks a small hole through to the other side of the wall, a loud sucking sound accompanies a whoosh of air that sweeps into the hole.

The dog barks at the hole, and Darren peers in to see a substantial space. Paul pulls away a piece of the edge of the opening and examines it.

"Darren, it's man-made," Paul says excitedly as the dog barks wildly.

After a couple of hours, the opening is big enough to climb through. Inside, the two archaeologists examine the wall. Simon climbs in, and the men walk down a long corridor shining their flashlights on the walls, which are covered with ancient designs.

"The triangular-bodied figures with the crescent-shaped halos floating above their heads are unmistakably Anasazi," Simon says. "This will win us our tenure for sure."

Darren comes upon a huge empty chamber. The archway entrance is marked with more Anasazi drawings. Two of the pictures appear to be guards holding weapons. A corridor on the far side of the chamber continues on. Beyond a slightly bluish light emanating from the corridor, there is pitch blackness.

Upon entering the chamber, Darren immediately starts to choke. He falls to the floor and begins convulsing. Paul runs to him, but he too is immediately overcome by the same phenomenon. Clutching his throat, he screams in agony. As Simon comes to help, Paul tells him to stay back before collapsing on the ground.

Frozen in horror, Simon watches the archaeologists writhe and die in agony.

TIME & PLACE *The next morning, three Disease Control Center specialists in hazmat gear stand at the entrance to the chamber, and Doyle speaks into a recorder.*

FILE #288128. CASE manager Connor Doyle,
initial case log. Commence briefing of the team regarding an apparently fatal phenomenon in a cave in northern New Mexico."

Two of the three DCC agents prepare to enter the chamber. They are connected to the third member by a long cable.

Later in the mobile lab, Doyle, physicist/statistician Peter Axon and anthropologist Natasha Constantine watch the tape, which Doyle pauses. "Two archaeologists died in the cave," Doyle says. "Witness Simon Bonito believes the inner chamber is directly responsible for the deaths. He managed to remove the bodies of his two friends without setting foot inside. Despite Bonito's warnings, two DCC members also entered the chamber."

Doyle presses "play" again, and the tape shows the two DCC agents entering the empty chamber. After a few steps, both scream in pain and collapse. "No chemical or biological agent currently known to man could penetrate that suit," Axon says.

They follow Doyle to the doorway of the lab and start walking toward the base of the cliff. "The Anasazi are the ancestors of the modern-day Pueblo tribe," Constantine says. "A mile south of here are the ruins of an ancient Anasazi village."

At the cliff, investigators set up equipment. Doyle greets DCC agent Arthur Quigley, anthropologist Simon Bonito and George Featherstone of the Native American Tribal Council.

That night, Constantine sits across from Simon in the mobile lab. "There is an expansive network of sophisticated roads converging on the village from dozens of outlying communities, yet the Anasazi had no vehicles or weight-bearing animals. There may have been a ritual pilgrimage to the village," Simon says.

"Tell me about the cave," Constantine says.

"We were very excited when we discovered the lone hut. It was a major find. Then when we uncovered the cave opening inside ... well, it was awesome," Simon says, pausing. "But I can't get the sight of them writhing in agony out of my mind. I've never felt so helpless."

Investigators also interview agent Quigley of the national Disease Control Center. "According to the autopsy report, all four men suffered massive internal hemorrhaging as well as severe rupturing of the major organs," Quigley begins. "There were no antibodies to known viral agents present. No apparent external cause of injury. I've never seen anything like it."

That night in the mobile lab, Axon operates the environment-monitoring probe unit with a joystick as it explores the 25 feet of the cave's corridor leading up to the large chamber.

"No hazardous materials, toxic traces or abnormal energy fields. Everything within normal range," Axon says. "Nearing the mouth of the chamber. Unusual atmospheric readings," he continues. "I'm getting an increasing amount of air pressure coming from deep within the cave."

The probe enters the huge chamber, and the investigators lose their signal.

"Increase the signal transmission power," Doyle orders. When Axon does, he regains control, but Doyle wants to pull the probe out and examine it.

In the mobile lab, Doyle, Axon, Constantine and some other investigators have a round table.

"IF YOU ASSUME THE PUEBLOS ARE RIGHT AND THERE IS A GUARDIAN SPIRIT IN THE CAVE, WHAT IS IT GUARDING?"

"Something disrupted the monitoring equipment, possibly the same phenomenon that caused the probe to malfunction," Axon says.

"Run a full diagnostic analysis on the equipment before we rule out mechanical failure," Doyle says.

"I spoke to a number of Pueblo people," Constantine says. "The Pueblos believe that ancient spirits may guard the remains of the Anasazi dwellings."

"If you assume the Pueblos are right and there is a guardian spirit in the cave, what is it guarding?" Axon asks.

TIME & PLACE   *That night, smoke billows out of the cave's corridor.*

A LIGHT BRIGHTENS the corridor, and a silhouette appears. Emerging from the smoke, it shows itself as a beautifully exotic Indian girl from an ancient time.

Suddenly, Simon Bonito is standing in the chamber. Shocked and horrified, he looks around as if surprised by his location. The chamber is now filled with skeletons and rotting corpses.

In the tent, Simon wakes up with a start. Covered in sweat and breathing hard, he's confused by his nightmare.

"I know it was just a dream, but it was the most unusual sensation—too strong to resist," Simon later tells Doyle, Axon and Constantine. "I felt compelled to walk into the chamber."

"I wouldn't do that just yet," Axon says. "The cave entrance and corridor are safe, but we've sealed the entrance to the inner chamber until we understand what happened in there."

. The next day, Doyle, Constantine, Axon and Simon enter the corridor. Axon leads Doyle to a section of the interior wall that had originally blockaded the entrance to the cave.

Constantine and Simon move on to the drawings. "Your last name, Bonito. Isn't that the Pueblo name of the ancient village that occupied the canyon not too far from here?" Constantine asks.

"Yes. There are hundreds of us in the Taos phone book," Simon says.

"Then you're Pueblo?"

"My family is of Pueblo descent." He walks away in the direction of the chamber, and Constantine follows.

"Over here," Doyle suddenly calls.

They walk back to the entrance, where Axon points out the top of the wall. "The wall appears to be constructed of a primitive mortar," Axon says. "The dirt is packed into the cracks between the bricks."

"Not unusual," Constantine says.

"It is, if you consider that this is the inside of the wall," Axon says.

Simon, apparently not interested in the discovery, turns back and looks at the entrance to the chamber. They are all struck by a blast of air. Startled, they turn, realizing that Simon is not with them. At the entrance to the chamber, Simon has ripped down the plastic seal.

"Stop him!" Doyle yells, but it's too late.

In a strange trancelike state, Simon steps into the chamber. He is all the way inside by the time an investigator reaches the entrance. Reacting instinctively and concerned for Simon's life, the investigator sticks his hand in to grab Simon and pull him back. "No!" Axon yells.

The investigator starts to choke. He stumbles further into the chamber and collapses to the ground, convulsing. Simon snaps out of his trance, realizes where he is standing and finally leaves the chamber.. He looks around, startled. The investigator's eyes are open and he's staring up, dead.

Later, Doyle, Axon, Constantine and other investigators discuss the situation. "The additional shielding of the probe's communications systems seemed to work since we were able to send the probe back into the chamber," Axon says. "We had it introduce samples of human blood and tissue to the chamber environment. Nothing occurred, and no unusual residue of any kind was found when the samples were extracted."

TIME & PLACE *After dark, the probe moves throught the chamber toward the corridor on the other side.*

B E Y O N D   T H E   B L U I S H glow in the corridor is unending blackness. Doyle and Axon watch from the mobile lab. "What's down there?" Doyle asks.

"There's no definition on the scans," Axon says, adjusting the controls. "Hold on. The probe is registering infinite space in front of it."

"That makes no sense. Are we getting more interference?" Doyle asks.

"All systems are functioning correctly. That's the reading I'm getting."

The probe stops in front of the bluish void, but Doyle tells Axon to make it continue. It enters the darkness and disappears. Then, a shriek pierces the air, and the monitors go black. "I can't believe it," Axon says. "We've lost another probe."

That night, Doyle, Axon and Constantine sit in the conference room with the radar survey of the cliff area displayed on a screen behind them. "The probe must have fallen into a deep cavern," Axon says.

Constantine offers another explanation: "There are many theories as to why so many Anasazi abandoned their cultural homeland," she says. "One is that a powerful new religion took shape east of here and drew them away."

Constantine puts a videotape into the VCR. She clicks it on, and the investigators see footage of her interviewing George Featherstone.

"There is a story that is sometimes told to children at night," Featherstone begins. "It's about how in ancient times there was a god in the mountain. When the ancient ones became divided, those that remained in the homeland could no longer defend themselves against their enemies. That was when the god of the mountain offered them a choice. If they would follow, he would lead them back to a time when they could live in peace and harmony. To prevent evil-doers from following, he left a guardian at the doorway. The guardian would beckon the good people who had been led astray and destroy those who threatened the peaceful Anasazi way of life."

Constantine turns off the VCR.

"Are you suggesting that somewhere in the depths of the cave is some kind of dimensional portal that can transport people from one time or place to another?" Axon asks.

"Based on Mr. Featherstone's story, I'm suggesting the phenomenon we're dealing with may be the spirit that guards the portal."

TIME & PLACE *Later that night, two investigators standing guard at the cave see Simon coming toward them.*

H E   R E A C H E S   T H E M ,   smiles and nods, trying to walk past, but they say the site is off-limits. "We have orders. No one is permitted inside," an investigator says.

Simon looks at the opening in desperation. Then he nods at the investigator and turns, apparently to go, but he only takes a step before he turns back and tries to rush past the investigators, shoving one to the ground.

The investigators chase Simon down, restraining him before he can get inside. Simon struggles. Finally, he screams in desperation as they drag him away.

"I don't know what came over me. I just couldn't resist the urge," Simon later tells Doyle, Axon and Constantine. "I feel like the answer is in that chamber."

"The answer to what?" Doyle asks.

"I don't know. I mean, why would a spirit beckon me? I've never believed in things like that. If you ask Mr. Featherstone, he'll probably tell you I'm not even Pueblo."

Axon pulls Doyle aside and convinces him to ask headquarters if they can put Simon in the chamber.

Later, Simon sits by a fire with Featherstone, who asks him why he thinks he is drawn to the cave. "I don't know. I guess I've never really felt like I belonged anywhere," Simon says.

"Is that why you abandoned your family?" Featherstone asks.

"I didn't abandon my family. I decided to live in the real world."

"Ah, the present. Then why do you spend all your time searching in the past? The answers you seek are not with our ancestors, the Anasazi. They are right here, right now."

"How do you know?" Simon asks.

"I know who you are, Simon Bonito. It's a shame you don't," Featherstone says, tossing a handful of sand into the fire.

The next morning, Axon checks the biofeedback and video camera rigging on Simon as Doyle gives a case log update: "Headquarters agrees that, despite the unusual nature of the experiment, we should proceed."

Doyle wishes Simon good luck as he prepares to enter the chamber. Simon steps inside, walking to the edge of the corridor. "What do you see?" Axon asks.

"Just darkness," Simon says, slowly slipping into a trancelike state.

"Brain-wave patterns slowing," Axon says, reading the monitors.

"There's a light," Simon says. From the lab, Constantine checks the monitor but sees no light.

"It's getting very bright," Simon says. Slowly, a beautiful, exotic-looking Indian girl appears in the light. "There's a girl." She beckons Simon to come to her.

"His brain-wave patterns indicate he's entering a dreamlike state," Constantine says.

"Can you speak to her?" Doyle asks Simon.

"I don't have to," Simon answers, starting down the corridor.

"Simon!" Doyle yells.

Slowly, Simon is enveloped by the bluish light in the corridor, and finally he disappears. Doyle turns to Axon. "He's gone," Axon says.

Later that day, investigators prepare explosives to seal the mouth of the cave. Doyle, Axon, Constantine and Featherstone watch as Doyle gives the final case log: "In the interest of public safety and at the request of the government and the Native American Tribal Council, we have decided to seal the cave entrance until another method of investigation into this phenomenon presents itself."

The investigators rigging the explosives clear out, and Axon hits a remote. BOOM! Tons of rock and dirt fill in the cave opening. Rock and dirt slide down the face of the cliff and re-bury the probe.

Six weeks later, Sonny leads George Featherstone to a peculiar clump of rocks. Sonny barks incessantly until Featherstone starts moving the rocks. Featherstone uncovers part of the O.S.I.R. probe, pitted and rusted. Doyle reports that the probe may have been pushed to the surface by the explosion. However, analysis of the probe indicates that it is two hundred years old.

Epilogue

There are many O.S.I.R. case files relating to the mysterious and dangerous occurrences associated with sacred tribal ground. In most of these cases, as in this one, the determinations were uniform: There are some places that are better left alone.   **DAN AYKROYD**

The Bermuda Triangle has long been associated with lost crews and vessels. Since Columbus first traveled this route, hundreds of ships and planes have also reported encounters with an unexplained phenomenon and dozens of craft have vanished in these waters off the coasts of Florida, Bermuda and Puerto Rico. What is the true nature of this strange triangular zone? In the following case, the O.S.I.R. was engaged to confront an unusual series of events in this famous and mysterious area of the world. **DAN AYKROYD**

Devil's TRIANGLE

TIME & PLACE *Morning, on the long dock that gives seafaring customers access to supplies and fuel at Jones Marina on the island of Bermuda.*

As Bailey Veloz, a tanned and athletic woman in her early thirties, lifts a pair of binoculars to her eyes, marina owner Wilton Jones walks up.

"Who did Joey take out for a cruise this time?" Jones asks.

"Sonny Brasco," Veloz says.

"*The* Sonny Brasco?"

"He's a new client of my husband's."

"Bailey, every time you come here on holiday, he takes some criminal out on the boat while you take the plane. Hardly seems fair."

Bailey scans the waters through her binoculars, zeroing in on a medium-sized cabin cruiser—the *Seaspray*—slowly approaching.

"There they are, but I don't see anyone on deck."

Bailey passes the binoculars to Jones, who looks through them. "Hold on," Jones says. "They're flying a distress flag."

"WHY DIDN'T YOU look for us?" Joey asks. "We were lost out there for so long."

"Joey, you left Miami five days ago."

Jones comes up from the cabin saying that no one else is on board.

"Sonny's gone, abandoned ship," Joey says. "We were out there for *three weeks!*"

TIME & PLACE Later that day, Bailey sits by Joey's bed in the hospital while an older man, Dr. Whitney, stands nearby.

JOEY SLOWLY OPENS his eyes. "Hey, babe, glad to see you," he says. "Did you find Sonny?"

"Coast Guard's been combing the area for nearly 12 hours," Bailey says, shaking her head. "Nothing. Joey, you said you were lost. Why didn't you radio for help?"

"All our instruments went dead. We were out there for at least two and a half weeks."

"Honey, I was there when you guys left five days ago," Bailey says.

"That's impossible. We ran out of food on day seven. And then ... We saw things out there that I can't explain, and then Sonny panicked," Joey says. "He took off in a life raft before I could stop him."

TIME & PLACE Several O.S.I.R. vehicles pull up near Jones Marina the next morning, and case manager Connor Doyle, physicist/statistician Peter Axon and psychobiologist Lindsay Donner get out.

DOYLE GIVES AN initial case log entry: "Case manager Connor Doyle. We have arrived in Bermuda to investigate claims of an unusual marine phenomenon. As a matter of historical record, this is not the first time the O.S.I.R. has investigated anomalous activity in this region."

"Glad to be back here, Doyle?" Axon asks. He turns to Donner, saying that Doyle is the resident expert on Bermuda.

"Six times I've led teams out there, and six times we came back with nothing," Doyle says. "Don't expect this time to be any different."

Marina operator Wilton Jones gives the first interview: "The weather offices reported clear skies and calm winds all along the route they were sailing. According to their port of origin, they last checked in by radio with Miami four days after they set sail. They reported calm seas and said everything was fine. The next day we found them drifting offshore."

Joseph Veloz stands in his hospital room sipping coffee.

"We had clear sailing all the way past the Bahamas," he says. "Four days out of the Caicos Passage, we hit some kind of zone, some place where time and weather and the laws of nature didn't apply. Before I could stop him, Sonny was gone."

"NO STRUCTURAL DAMAGE visible

beneath the water line," Axon says. "Jones says the only thing he found was dead instrumentation. Every piece of communication is inoperable, but there's no sign of damage. It's like the instruments just stopped working."

"Remove all the electronic-based equipment from the ship, and get it to the lab," Doyle tells an investigator.

"According to his story, their watches stopped on day four when they encountered some kind of dense weather system," Doyle continues. "Then it apparently knocked out all their instrumentation."

"If they lost instrumentation, how could they know how much time was passing? He claimed they had no indicators. No sun. No moon. No stars," Axon says.

"Joey mentioned an old clock in the main cabin. For some reason, it kept working," Doyle says, opening the face of the clock. "No electronic parts. Interesting."

Later that day, Donner interviews Joey under deep hypnosis in the dimly lit hospital room. "Joey, where are you now?" she asks.

"I'm with Sonny on the *Seaspray*. We left from Miami, and we're going to meet Bailey in Bermuda," he says, flashing back.

"Do you remember what happened?" Donner asks.

"I thought it was a storm, but it wasn't any kind of storm I'd ever seen," Joey says. "It was as dark as though someone had thrown a switch. Then we were dead in the water—no power, no instrumentation. We drifted for weeks, and then one day, Sonny just couldn't stand the waiting anymore."

Joey flashes back, seeing Sonny rowing in the distance, further into the blackness.

Doyle and Donner talk after the interview. "Were you able to pinpoint the exact time the *Seaspray* left port in Miami?" Doyle asks.

"Confirmed by the Coast Guard. We also confirmed the presence of the other man on the boat," Donner says.

They walk over to Axon, who stands by a bank of monitors. "Bailey Veloz made this videotape the day they set sail from South Beach," Axon says, pushing "play."

The tape shows Sonny Brasco tentatively stepping onto the *Seaspray*. As the *Seaspray* pulls into the harbor, the two men wave to the on-shore camera. "Bon voyage!" Bailey yells.

Axon freezes the tape. "Check out the date," he says

"August 6, 1996," Doyle says. "Five days before they arrived in Bermuda."

"And our physicians confirm that Joey Veloz was exposed to the elements for nearly three weeks," Doyle says.

Axon freezes the tape on Sonny Brasco. "According to the Dade County D.A.'s office, Sonny's a mid-level supplier for a major Colombian drug cartel," Donner says. "Was in the process of turning state's evidence when he disappeared on Joey's boat."

"Let me guess. Everyone in the Bogotá phone book would want him dead," Doyle says.

"And maybe Joey was given the job. He is connected to some very high-level criminal elements," Axon says.

"So he cooks up a Bermuda Triangle hoax to cover up a murder," Doyle says.

The next morning, Doyle gives a case log update in the mobile unit: "After completing our initial assessment we have reason to believe that the *Seaspray* could have encountered some type of paranormal event, yet there remains a strong possibility of this being a hoax perpetrated to cover up a murder."

On a large monitor are aerial survey maps of the Bermuda coastal waters. A cloud, not unlike a hurricane, swirls in the center.

"These aerial survey maps were taken yesterday 100 miles off the Bermudan coast," Axon says.

"It looks like a tropical depression," Doyle says.

"According to weather offices, it isn't. They record clear skies along the entire Puerto Rican trench. Here's why," Axon says, hitting a button. The image on the screen changes to clear skies over the same location.

"Gone, just like that," Doyle says.

"It has no pattern we can detect. It only appeared on our aerial survey once," Axon says.

"Why was the one clock we found on the *Seaspray* still functioning?" Doyle asks.

"The main difference between it and the rest of the equipment is that it is made of brass components," Axon says. "My guess is there was some sort of electromagnetic interference that hit the other instruments. The clock is paramagnetic, made from copper and zinc components. The rest of the instruments on board were ferromagnetic. That is, they had iron-based components."

"If Joey's story is true, then the lost man could still be out there, alive," Doyle says.

TIME & PLACE *That afternoon, Axon, Donner and other investigators load various monitoring equipment onto the* Seaspray *while Donner records a case update.*

" I H A V E D E C I D E D to move the next phase of the investigation to the location of the phenomenon itself," Doyle says. "The team has prepared a floating mobile lab aboard the same vessel and will go to the exact coordinates of the events."

Doyle turns from the deck of the *Seaspray* to face Joey, who moves near the boat on shore.

"You think I killed Sonny, don't you? You think I'd just let you take my boat out there to prove I fed him to the sharks? He bailed. He abandoned me. He deserves whatever happened to him," Joey says.

"Maybe he's still out there," Doyle says. "If your friend is still alive, we'll find him."

The *Seaspray* cuts through the Atlantic Ocean. Donner moves up with two mugs of coffee, handing one to Doyle.

"Look, I have to ask you," Donner begins, "what made you lead all six investigations out here? Why you?"

"Back when I was in the Navy, I was on operations out here when we encountered an area of the sea where the laws of physics didn't apply. We lost navigational control and then hit something. My ship began going down. I sounded general quarters and began evacuation. Most of the men got off the ship, but by the time Air-Sea Rescue found us, only myself and my executive officer were still alive."

As Axon and other investigators man consoles in the *Seaspray* lab, Doyle comes in, saying they're nearing the outer limit of the zone.

"We've encased all of our instrumentation in copper-based shielding," Axon says. "It should keep everything safe from outside electrical or magnetic charges."

A couple of days later, Doyle records an update. "We have patrolled the coordinates of the alleged anomaly for 48 hours without incident," he says. "We have released submersible probes and extended sonar and radar ranges to the maximum gain. So far, nothing consequential has turned up."

Doyle sits looking over a map of the area when Axon enters.

"You'd think I'd learn," Doyle says. "There's nothing out here but bad luck and deep water."

"You have any idea what we could be facing? You've seen this phenomenon before, haven't you?" Axon asks.

"That was a long time ago, and I didn't see much. It was pretty dark that night."

Then Donner comes up the stairs. "Doyle, we've got something."

They follow her, and Axon sits down at a console and points at a monitor. Doyle leans in over Donner's shoulder.

"Compass started acting strange as soon as it appeared on radar," Donner says.

"How far off is it?" Doyle asks.

BEHIND THE RAFT THE BLACK MASS APPROACHES. SONNY BRASCO IS INSIDE, BARELY ALIVE.

"Half a mile and closing," Axon says.

A dark mass appears on the radar screen. Doyle tells Axon to keep tracking it, and Doyle and Donner go upstairs to scan the dark horizon with binoculars. Donner sees something on the port side of the boat.

"Radar's picking up something really big, and it's nearly on top of us," Axon says over the comlink.

The team stares out to sea, mesmerized by a dark, roiling mass of clouds looming ahead.

"Doyle, our radar's beginning to fade from some kind of interference," Axon says.

"Ahead full," Doyle says. "We are now operating under Code-Red status. Man your stations and begin recording data."

The team disperses with a growing sense of purpose. Those on the deck look around in wonder as the boat moves into the mass.

The sky is black, and a wind blows. An odd glow illuminates the faces of the crew. Then the monitoring equipment starts malfunctioning and shorting out.

Suddenly Axon regards the instruments with alarm. They stop working. "Doyle, we're being bombarded by electromagnetic fields," he says. "Instrumentation is going dead. Switching over to shielded instruments."

Doyle glances at his watch, which has stopped.

"Backup systems are operational," Axon continues. "Data recording is being maintained," Axon says, noticing a blip on the radar.

"Doyle, we've got something half a click to the port bow. Doyle? Do you copy?" Axon realizes the comlinks don't work because they're unshielded.

Up on deck, Doyle and Donner scan the water around them, still illuminated by the odd light. Axon comes up, calling Doyle and Donner back down. They study the shielded radar.

"Can you identify it?" Doyle asks.

"Small craft," Axon says. "It's floating at the center of the phenomenon."

As the ship speeds over dark waters, Donner sees through her binoculars a small life raft floating. Donner and Axon look at the radar.

"We've got another problem," Axon says, noting that the mass is rapidly contracting, closing in around them.

"Oh, God," Doyle says.

Behind the raft, the black mass approaches. Sonny Brasco is barely alive inside. The ship closes in on the life raft. The rushing black mass finally overtakes the ship, passing through Doyle. As it does, he yells out in frustration, "No!"

In the life raft, Brasco watches the blackness envelop him in horror.

Suddenly, the skies become clear and sunny. Doyle stands on the deck of the ship, trying to keep calm, but the life raft and Brasco are nowhere to be seen.

Donner and Axon come up on top, and the team gathers by the railing, staring out at the now-calm ocean.

"How long?" Doyle asks.

"Inside the phenomenon for 56 minutes, 38 seconds," Axon says.

"Mainland Bravo team clocks us inside the phenomenon for 5 minutes, 38 seconds," Donner says, listening to his comlink.

"And Brasco?" Doyle asks.

"Gone."

Epilogue

After their return to shore, the O.S.I.R. investigators tested many theories in attempting to explain what they had witnessed. Perhaps they encountered geophysical anomalies or some unknown technology. If anything, their experience demonstrates that much more research must be undertaken. For now, the Bermuda Triangle's secrets remain locked within its mysterious waters and skies.

DAN AYKROYD

The rustle of the leaves in the wind, a bird's song, the voice of a loved one—our world is enveloped in an invisible and bountiful mantle of sound. When the O.S.I.R. investigated an inexplicable audio phenomenon in Cranbrook, Montana, the challenge was not only to trace its origins but to assist the Disease Control Center in ridding the town of a sudden and mysterious plague of rats.

DAN AYKROYD

The   B U Z Z

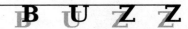 *After work, Ernest Hartley pulls into his driveway in Cranbrook, Montana, and trudges to the front door, coughing badly.*

In the kitchen, Randi Hartley makes dinner as Sally, 6, colors. "It's started again," Sally says, putting her hands to her ears.

Randi turns off the stove's timer, but Sally says the buzzing sound is still there. Randi turns as Ernest comes in. "You don't look good," Randi says, feeling his forehead.

"Daddy, make the noise stop!" Sally says.

"She's been complaining about a buzzing sound in her ears for two days now. I'm worried that maybe she's got an infection or something," Randi says.

As Ernest walks out, Randi looks down the hall and sees Ernest staggering. He grabs the handrail at the stairs and falls.

"Mommy!" Sally yells.

Just then, the baby, Andy, upstairs starts crying. Torn, Randi rushes upstairs but freezes in the doorway. The baby's room is teaming with hundreds of rats.

That evening, paramedics wheel Ernest through the hospital's emergency room, where Dr. Roger Ivers meets them.

" S T A R T   I V   S A L I N E , oxygen and an antipyretic," Ivers says.

The nurses wheel Ernest away. Randi hurries in, holding Sally's hand and carrying her baby. She accosts the head nurse.

"This might sound crazy but my house is overrun with rats. There were hundreds of them in Andy's room," Randi tells the nurse. "Could that have anything to do with this?"

"Let me take Andy and have him looked at," the nurse says, taking the baby from Randi and passing him to another nurse.

The head nurse returns to the desk to answer the phone. Randi is distracted by Mayor Winslow, who steps up behind her from the waiting area.

"Did you say hundreds of rats?" he asks. "My wife got quite sick this afternoon."

Dr. Ivers comes out.

"How's Ernest?" Randi asks.

"I'm not sure yet, Randi. How's everyone else in the family?"

"Sally's been complaining about a buzzing sound in her ears. I haven't heard it myself."

"I'll have a look."

The head nurse, still on the phone, interrupts. "Six more cases on the way. Same symptoms." The nurse hangs up the phone and nearly jumps out of her skin, screaming at the rat on the desk.

Suddenly Dr. Ivers hears a noise coming from the ventilation shaft. He climbs on the desk and pulls the shaft cover off. The shaft is full of rats.

"Good God!" he says, jamming the cover back on.

TIME & PLACE *The next day, an O.S.I.R. team in vans drives through the center of town where a monument stands.*

D O Y L E   R E C O R D S   A N initial log entry: "Case file #213127. Case manager Connor Doyle. We will be assisting with the investigation of an outbreak of a strain of deadly hantavirus. The Disease Control Center has been unable to explain the sightings of large groups of rats, as well as a mysterious intermittent buzzing sound that only certain residents seem to hear."

Investigators interview Dr. Roger Ivers. "The hantavirus is definitely coming from the rat feces," Ivers says. "It's not technically airborne but it can be carried on dust particles. If you sweep up an area where the droppings are, you can inhale the virus. We found rats in the air ducts. If enough of them do their business in there ..."

"I see," Doyle says. "How do you treat hantavirus?"

"You can't. Prevention is the only solution. Unfortunately, several lives were lost before the DCC could isolate the cause. The general population has now been warned," team member Davison says.

"What about the sound?" Doyle asks.

"There doesn't appear to be any explanation for it. Some people who hear it have the virus but others don't," Ivers says.

The next day, O.S.I.R. psycho-biologist Donner and pathologist Dr. Linda Davidson interview Sally in her living room.

" C A N   Y O U   M A K E a sound that sounds like what you hear?" Donner asks.

Sally makes a high-pitched sound that alternates between loud and quiet. Suddenly, Sally starts to frown. "It's started again!" she says.

Donner looks at Davison, who shakes her head. They don't hear it.

In the kitchen, O.S.I.R. physicist/statistician Peter Axon walks over to Doyle and Randi.

"Doesn't anyone else hear that?" Axon asks, in pain.

That afternoon, Doyle, Axon and Davison look at a map of the town in the mobile lab. Dots are marked on the map in a random-scattered pattern.

"There is no apparent link between those who have contracted the virus and those who claim to hear the sound," Davison says.

"Let's get full-range audio sensors on-line 24 hours," Doyle says.

"The dots on the map show where the experiencers live," Axon says. "There is no pattern or concentration. Loudness is somewhat subjective but, put through comparative audio tests, we, the experiencers, all identified a similar amplitude and pitch."

Donner enters. "The sound is back," she says. Doyle looks at Axon.

"I don't hear anything," Axon says.

"Where is the sound?" Doyle asks Donner.

"The library."

TIME & PLACE *Later, Doyle, Donner and Axon come down the library's stairs using sound-sensing and amplification devices. They hear a faint high-pitched sound resembling people screaming played back at high speed.*

" I T ' S   N O T   Q U I T E the same sound I heard before," Axon says as they walk into the basement.

Axon looks at the furnace and exposed pipe running up the wall. "It's coming from the pipes," he says.

"This tunnel system spans the entire town and connects it with other towns," Donner says.

The screaming sound grows louder. "The sound is getting closer," Axon says. "It's coming this way. Fast."

They are suddenly swarmed by hundreds of rats. "Hold your breath!" Doyle yells.

The horde of rats runs in and around their feet, streaming past them, illuminated by the beams from the flashlights. Their squeaking is making the sound.

The next day, investigators talk in the mobile lab.

Axon comes in carrying a tape recorder. "Listen to this," he says, pressing play. A high-pitched oscillating hum emanates from the recorder.

"While we were investigating the tunnels under the library, our sound-monitoring equipment picked this up," Axon says. "It's been amplified and lowered in frequency to make it audible to you. Roughly twenty-five percent of the general population have the range of hearing to pick up the original frequency."

"How long did it last?" Doyle asks.

"Fifteen minutes. The rats are migrating because they're being repelled by this sound," Axon says.

"Where is the sound coming from?" Doyle asks.

Axon hits a remote, and a map of the tunnel system under the town appears on the monitor. "You heard how the tunnel was distorting the sound the rats were making. My theory is that sound is being carried through the highly conductive tunnels. It's being resonated up into the town through the pipes."

"How are we going to find the source?" Donner asks.

"We're going to have to wait for the next time it starts," Doyle says.

A couple of hours later, Donner mans the control panel. An oscillating hum comes out of a speaker. Donner flips some switches, making it louder and clearer.

Meanwhile, that afternoon Doyle and Axon, dressed in hazmat suits, move through the tunnel with flashlights. Axon carries a portable audio sensor.

Donner monitors their movements from the mobile lab. "Take a right at the next junction," Donner says through the comlink. "It should be about 100 meters straight ahead."

Doyle and Axon approach the junction. They turn the corner, heading down the dark hallway.

The sound over the speaker in the mobile lab gets louder. Donner is confused. "It's right in front of you," she says.

Axon and Doyle approach a point where the tunnels converge. "There's nothing here," Doyle says.

"I'm picking up the waves but there's no visually apparent source," Axon says.

"But you're standing right on top of it," Donner says, shaking her head.

Doyle looks at Axon, and they look up simultaneously. "Or under it," Doyle says, asking Donner what's above them.

Donner calls up a surveillance camera's image of the town square. She pans the image remotely to the monument in the center of town.

TIME & PLACE *The next day, Doyle, Axon and Donner walk around the monument.*

"TESTS CONFIRM THAT the memorial is solid. It was erected by Stagmatta Steel in 1920. The company no longer exists," Donner says.

"Maybe the statue is just conducting the sound, acting like an antenna," Axon says.

Later that day, Doyle and Donner arrive in the hospital's emergency waiting area, and Doyle speaks into his recorder: "Case log update. The effects of the sound appear to be getting worse. Sally Hartley has been admitted to the hospital and is in serious condition."

"She's not doing well," Dr. Davison says. "She is in a semi-catatonic state. Any number of things could have caused it, but I'd guess that it's noise-induced stress. Sally just doesn't want to hear the sound anymore so she's shutting herself down."

Ernest and Randi walk up. "Good to see you up and around, Mr. Hartley," Doyle says.

"Unfortunately, we can't say as much for our daughter," Ernest says, as Randi goes down the hall.

Back in the mobile lab, Axon works on some notes. Doyle and Donner enter. Axon puts a map of the town on the big screen. Red circles are marked with numbers ascending from east to west.

"These are the rat sightings in chronological order," Axon says. "As you can see, they migrated through the town from east to west."

Axon hits a remote, and the screen becomes a map of the tunnel system. The red dots and numbers remain in the same places. Now there is a big blue dot in the center of the map at the junction point in the tunnels under the monument.

"The blue dot is the strongest sound we can find," Axon continues. "If the rats are repelled by the sound, then why are they moving across the city instead of outward from the center away from the sound?"

"Are you saying the rats aren't being repelled by the sound?" Donner asks.

"The rats came from the east. Whatever is repelling the rats has to be coming from here, the eastern end of the tunnel system," Axon says, explaining that the sound comes from interference.

"Basically, two sound waves collide and interfere with each other, causing the frequency to be altered. In this case, lowering it while increasing the amplitude," he explains.

"Why wasn't our equipment picking up the higher-frequency waves?" Donner asks.

"They were being overpowered by the lower frequency and higher amplitude of the combined wave," Axon says.

TIME & PLACE *The next day, Doyle and Axon in hazmat suits make their way down the dark tunnel while Donner mans the control panel in the mobile lab.*

AXON CARRIES AN audio sensor. "It's registering, 60,000 Hz," he says.

"That's extremely high, isn't it?" Doyle asks.

"Very few living things could hear it. Rats are one of them," Axon says.

Doyle and Axon continue, illuminating the tunnel with their flashlights. Two red lights glow in the dark distance.

They proceed cautiously. Slowly, the lights reveal a device, appearing to be a cross between a giant audio speaker and a satellite dish, at the dead end of the tunnel. An electrical cable snakes out from the back, leading under a steel door.

"The high-frequency wave is definitely coming from this device. It appears to be operational at the moment," Axon says.

Doyle tries to open the door but it's locked. "Donner, find out where this door leads," he says into his comlink.

"Unit two is reporting another device at the end of Tunnel B," Donner says. "Hey," she adds, "the sound under the monument just stopped. What happened?"

Doyle turns from the door to see Axon holding the cord, which he's yanked out of the device. Axon looks relieved.

TIME & PLACE *The next day, investigators meet at Digiknight Industries on the outskirts of town.*

DOYLE GIVES A case log update: "We are meeting with the v.p. of public affairs for Digiknight, a large computer company courted successfully by Mayor Winslow to locate its new microchip production plant in the Cranbrook Valley. It sparked the financial resurgence of the area but now may ultimately be responsible for the recent tragedies."

Jim Burns, a PR man, and a Digiknight lawyer meet with Doyle and Axon.

"We had no idea," Burns says. "The frequency they emit is not supposed to be able to be heard by people, just rats."

"Our analysis of the equipment revealed that the devices were operating slightly out of phase," Doyle says. "When the frequencies met at the convergence of the tunnels, they combined to form a new frequency."

"An unforeseeable accident," Burns answers. "The rats were significantly affecting production. Do you know how sensitive microchip production is? Either we solved the rat problem, or we would be forced to move the plant. I know the town wouldn't have wanted that."

"I doubt they wanted a deadly disease either. You drove the rats into the town," Doyle says.

Burns glances at the lawyer. "We've agreed to assist those affected by the unfortunate situation," he says, "but we are not accepting responsibility for the incident."

"I guess we're done then," Doyle says, glaring at Burns.

Back in the mobile lab, a tape recorder plays a sound resembling a fax machine.

"Sounds like a fax transmission or a computer modem," Davison says.

"This is the sound that was being radiated into town by the monument," Doyle says.

"The combined frequency of the two rodent-repelling devices?" Axon asks.

"Yes, but it's been amplified and slowed down by over a thousand times," Doyle says. "Digiknight denies that this is a transmission of any kind. They say the nature of the sound when slowed down is a coincidental phenomenon."

"What does our lab say?" Axon asks.

"It's a digitally ordered sequence, a message, but we don't know what it says yet," Doyle says.

"So it's possible that Digiknight said they were using the devices for repelling the rats as a cover-up for a secret high-tech transmission?"

"Makes sense considering the odds of the interference phenomenon occurring naturally or even by accident," Axon says.

That night, the O.S.I.R. vans leave town, and Doyle gives a final case log: "Sally Hartley and the rest of the town have recovered. We cannot proceed until we have proof that Digiknight was involved in something more sophisticated than high-tech rodent-repelling. But we will be watching Cranbrook, listening closely."

Epilogue

Ultrahigh-frequency sound. Unobtrusive and effective, a modern solution to an age-old problem—rats. And yet, because of the unanticipated interaction of the employed frequencies, the townspeople were subjected to a terrifying and deadly situation. These events are a vivid warning of what can happen when technology is employed without proper forethought. **DAN AYKROYD**

ŁU

As children we all brought home creatures that didn't belong in the house, like bugs, frogs, mice or even stray pets. Our parents were compelled then to inquire about the origins of these newfound treasures. Eight-year-old Kyle Hill's mother had to obtain the answer to such a question. But the last thing she imagined was that what began as a simple domestic matter would radically change her and her son's life forever. This case contains one of the most intriguing events I have ever seen documented in the files of the O.S.I.R.

DAN AYKROYD

UFO DUPLICATION

TIME & PLACE *Midnight. A piercing blue light illuminates the hamster cage in a farmhouse in Patterson County, Kansas on a cloudy summer night. The light emanates from outside the house, coming in through the open window.*

As Joan Hill, forty, sleeps, the blue light flickers through her room, waking her. Joan opens her eyes and looks around, calling to Kyle, her seven-year-old son. The light then sweeps out of the room, and the dog starts barking.

Joan groggily gets out of bed, picks up a robe, and, noticing that his bedroom door is open, goes into Kyle's room. His bed is empty.

Suddenly Joan hears two dogs barking and Kyle laughing. She walks through the kitchen, passing the hamster, the goldfish and Buddy's dish.

Joan steps out on the back porch in a robe. She looks out into the darkness at the barn. "Kyle? What're you doing?" she calls out.

Joan enters the barn, where a Frisbee abruptly plonks down at her feet. She looks down at it as Kyle jumps out at her.

"Kyle! I've told you not to do that," Joan warns him. It's after midnight and ... whose dog is that?"

"It's Buddy."

"No, the other dog."

"That's Buddy, too."

The two dogs come into the light, and Joan looks closely at them. They are identical.

"Kyle, we'll figure this out in the morning. Right now I want you to go back to bed," Joan says.

In the kitchen, two hamsters sit in the hamster cage, and two identical fish swim around in the fishbowl where previously there was only one.

TIME & PLACE *A couple of nights later, Joan tucks Kyle into bed, saying they'll try again tomorrow to find whose dog that is.*

THAT NIGHT JOAN tosses in her sleep. Finally she opens

her eyes, hearing garbled whispers and indistinguishable voices. She goes to the window and sees a light on in the barn. Joan goes to Kyle's room and glances inside. He's not there.

Annoyed, Joan comes out of the house. The twin dogs, Buddy and Buddy 2, sit on the stairs. Joan approaches the barn. As she goes inside, she sees Kyle naked and an odd glow brightening the room.

"Kyle? What in the name of God are you doing?" Joan asks.

Suddenly another naked boy, identical to Kyle, walks up to Kyle. Joan stares at the mirror images. She takes a step toward the light; then everything starts to dim.

TIME & PLACE *The O.S.I.R. mobile lab pulls up the next morning.*

O.S.I.R. CASE MANAGER Connor

Doyle, psychobiologist Lindsay Donner, psychiatrist Dr. Anton Hendricks and zoologist L. Q. Cooper get out of the lab as Doyle records an initial case log: "File #623119. We have arrived 80 miles outside of Wichita, Kansas, to investigate a reported case of life form replication. Preliminary interviews proceeding."

Investigators interview Joan Hill. "First it was the pets, and then my son," she says. "Kyle told me that his friends made them. Somebody out there is doing something to my family, and I'm terrified of what they might do next."

Kyle Hill, in a red T-shirt, speaks next. "Don't you guys get it? They only want to know us better, understand how we work," he says. "They're not like us. They're ..."

"... sorta like you guys," says Kyle 2 in a blue T-shirt. "They're scientists. I mean they don't force anything on anybody. It's not a bad thing they did. It's actually pretty incredible if you think about it."

Later that day in the mobile lab, Doyle, Hendricks, Donner, and Cooper look at photos of the two Kyles, their mother and the farm.

"My initial interviews with both boys didn't indicate any intentional deception," Hendricks says. "They appear to believe what they're saying. Same memories, same points of view. Aliens came and cloned them."

"Mrs. Hill seems extremely disturbed by the incident. I presume that whatever she saw triggered psychological trauma?" Doyle guesses.

Hendricks nods. "But I can't help thinking she's seen more than she's willing to tell us," he says.

TIME & PLACE *The next morning in the mobile lab, Joan lies in the hypno-chair, eyes closed.*

"TAKE YOURSELF BACK to the night of August 12th. What woke you up that night?" Hendricks asks.

"I don't know. Sounds," Joan says, flashing back. She watches herself checking Kyle's room and walking through the kitchen. "Kyle? What's going on?" she says.

"Joan, what is it?" Hendricks asks.

"No!" Joan yells, her body shaking.

Hendricks pulls her out of the hypnosis, and Joan relaxes.

A couple of hours later, Hendricks begins DEP test questioning with Kyle in the Hills' living room. Doyle walks into the den, where he looks in on Kyle 2, also hooked up to DEP, being interviewed by Donner. Both state their name as Kyle Aaron Hill.

"Where is your father?" Donner asks Kyle 2.

"He died."

Kyle answers the same question for Hendricks: "He was killed in a car accident three years ago."

"Do you remember your fifth birthday?" Hendricks asks.

"Yeah. My dad took me to a place where I could ride a ..." Kyle begins.

Kyle 2 tells Donner the same story. "... a horse. It smelled really bad. The horse was rust-colored and kind of wild. It threw me off and I broke my arm," he says, showing Donner his scar.

Kyle does the same for Hendricks.

Later that day, physicians put both boys under hypnosis in two separate rooms.

"... then they ask if I want another dog just like him," Kyle 2 says.

In the living room, Kyle answers Hendricks. "They want me to come outside," Kyle says. "They look like those kids who age really fast that I saw on the Science Channel."

"Did you want them to clone you?" Donner asks Kyle 2 in the next room.

"Yeah. It'd be cool. I can hang around with someone besides my mom," Kyle 2 says.

"Which one of you is the original Kyle, and which is the new Kyle?" Donner asks.

"I'm Kyle," Kyle 2 says.

In the living room, Kyle says the same thing. "I'm Kyle."

Later in the mobile lab, Donner feeds the fingerprint sheets from Kyle and Kyle 2 into a scanner.

"Voice-print analysis is not as widely used but more exact than fingerprint technology in identification," Cooper says. "Even identical twins show marked differences."

"Combined with fingerprinting and blood samples, the analysis should tell us whether or not they're twins," Donner says.

Donner looks at a video monitor, seeing that the boys' fingerprints are identical.

TIME & PLACE *After sundown, Doyle walks with Hendricks as Joan gets out of her car in front of her house.*

tests are the same within an extremely small margin of error," Hendricks says.

"The duplicated pets also showed uncharacteristically similar physiologies," Doyle says.

Donner approaches with a hard copy of the fingerprint results. Doyle takes the paper as Joan approaches."Oh my God, they *are* clones," Joan says, looking at the paper.

The next day, Kyle feeds his hamsters while Kyle 2 feeds the fish.

"Hey," Kyle 2 says. Kyle sees Kyle 2's concern and comes over. One of the fish is floating on top of the water, dead.

Doyle dictates a case log update: "With the death of one of the animals in the last 24 hours, we have shifted our investigation toward explaining the cause of death."

In the mobile lab, L. Q. Cooper examines the dead fish. "I have to admit, I haven't performed an autopsy on a goldfish before," Cooper tells Doyle.

"How about a hamster?" Donner asks, walking up with a dead hamster in a plastic evidence bag.

In the house, investigators perform environmental tests and search for hazardous materials or energy fields. Hendricks approaches Joan.

"I realize this feels very invasive, but it will allow us to keep close watch on your biological status," he says.

"Why are the animals dying?" Joan asks in fear. "Doctor, is it the clones that are dying, or is it...?"

"We just don't know," Hendricks says.

That afternoon in the mobile lab, Doyle and Hendricks study video footage of the two boys. Hendricks pauses the tape, and he and Doyle walk over to Cooper in the lab area.

"WITH THE DEATH OF ONE OF THE ANIMALS IN THE LAST 24 HOURS, WE HAVE SHIFTED OUR INVESTIGATION TOWARD EXPLAINING THE CAUSE OF DEATH."

"Anything from the autopsies on the animals?" Doyle asks Cooper.

"We were unable to determine the cause of death of the goldfish. The hamster, however, died of a viral infection. It's not an unusual cause of death in a rodent although it seems to have happened quite suddenly," Cooper says.

"Life span of a hamster is about two years?" Doyle asks.

"Yes, and a dog's about 15," Cooper says. "I thought of that. There may be a correlation between life span and the period it takes for the symptoms to show."

"Connor, I think we have something," Donner says, walking into the room. "We've been reviewing the physiological data we collected in the first exam of the two boys. Although we tested HLA antigens and B-cell antibodies for matches, we didn't test T-cell activity. It didn't seem relevant at the time."

"And now?" Doyle asks.

"One of each pair doesn't have T-cells in its system," Donner says.

"And T-cells fight viral infections," Cooper says.

"How common is a T-cell deficiency?" Doyle asks.

"In an otherwise healthy individual? Extremely uncommon," Hendricks says.

"But does the deficiency go with the clone or with Kyle?"

TIME & PLACE *Later, Joan and Kyle sit down in the house with one of the dogs.*

"**I THINK BUDDY'S** sick now too," Kyle says.

Joan pets the dog. "I'm sorry I've been so strange," Joan says, hugging Kyle. "How have you been feeling anyway?"

"I'm fine," says Kyle 2, who is standing in the doorway holding a Frisbee.

Doyle gives a case log update later in the mobile lab: "In an attempt to clarify what may have caused the phenomenon, I've requested Dr. Hendricks perform a second regressive hypnosis with Joan Hill."

KYLE WALKS OUT OF THE GROUP OF SMALL FIGURES. ANOTHER BOY, IDENTICAL TO KYLE, WALKS UP BEHIND HIM.

Joan is lying on the hypno-chair, eyes closed. "Take yourself back to that night again when you first saw Kyle and his twin," Hendricks says.

"Voices. I can hear them. They're all garbled, not making sense," Joan says, flashing back to when she approaches the barn. The voices get louder. Joan is bathed in the brightness of the light coming from one side of the barn.

"Kyle!" Joan yells. Her mouth opens and she reels in shock. Backlit by blinding white light from outside, the room is filled with tiny silhouetted figures milling about a slightly larger figure, making garbled whispering sounds.

Kyle walks out of the group of small figures, whose eyes follow him as he walks. Another boy, identical to Kyle, walks up beside the first.

"They're little aliens," Joan says. "Oh my God. What are they doing to my son?"

Hendricks snaps his fingers. Joan's eyes open and she looks at Hendricks in terror. She sits up, breathing hard.

In another part of the mobile lab, Cooper takes blood from the dog as Donner looks on. Doyle enters with Hendricks, who's done with the hypnosis.

"Her account of the extraterrestrials corroborates the boys' story," Hendricks tells Doyle.

"But there's just no physical evidence to back up their testimony. How's Mrs. Hill's psychological condition?" Doyle asks.

"Improved. Since she's realized that each boy believes he's the real Kyle and that, in effect, each

boy *is* the real Kyle, her attitude has changed ■ ■ ■ ■ ■ ■ **DUPLICATION**
altogether," Hendricks says.

"What have you found out?" Doyle asks, turning to Cooper.

"Mycobacterium tuberculosis," Cooper says. "Donner's hypothesis seems correct. The dog lacks immuno-competent T-cells. This animal is dying of pneumonia."

"What about the boys?" Doyle asks.

"Probably only a matter of time before one of them starts to show symptoms," Cooper says.

"Whoever or whatever did this must have used the original organism's base DNA as a source," Donner says.

"Then, using some sort of growth acceleration process, they developed the clone to the desired age," Hendricks says. "T-cells mature naturally in the thymus of children but by the age of puberty this process gradually slows down."

"By that time we have enough mature immuno-competent T-cells able to adapt and fight most infections," Cooper says.

"And in the rapid growth of a clone, this T-cell maturation process might have been unintentionally bypassed, which would mean it's the clones that are getting sick," Hendricks says.

"At this point, it's all conjecture. The important thing is to isolate the T-cell–deficient child immediately," Doyle says.

■ **TIME & PLACE** ■ *The next day in the Hills' living room, Hendricks and Doyle sit with Joan and Kyle and Kyle 2.*

"**WE'VE DECIDED THAT** this is Kyle Aaron," Joan says, touching Kyle. "And this is Aaron Kyle," she says, touching Kyle 2.

"Neither of them has said a word all day. They're worried about Buddy," Joan says, after the two boys go into the kitchen.

"I'm afraid it may be just a matter of time before one of the boys gets sick," Doyle says. "We have a course of action, but it requires complete cooperation from both of them."

Joan calls to Kyle and Aaron. They come in, Kyle 2 coughing.

"How're you feeling, Aaron?" Hendricks asks.

"Fine, I guess. I mean, I'm going to be fine, right?"

Later that night in a local hospital, two nurses wheel away Kyle 2, who is attached to an IV. Joan and Kyle walk beside them wearing surgical masks, and Doyle gives a case update.

"In an effort to supply T-cells to the deficient boy, we are proceeding with a bone marrow transplant, an operation normally complicated by tissue-and-blood matching," Doyle says into a recorder. "In this case, of course, the donor and the recipient are exact matches in every way."

The nurse takes Kyle 2 into a room. The second nurse takes Kyle into another room. Joan turns around and walks back to the waiting area where Doyle waits for her. Then Cooper enters and gets Doyle's attention.

"Excuse me," Doyle tells Joan.

"We couldn't save the dog," Cooper tells Doyle privately. "The infection was too advanced."

Weeks later, Joan and Kyle are alone in the house. Buddy, the dog, wanders over to sniff Kyle. Suddenly, a Frisbee flies by Kyle, who looks up, seeing Kyle 2 in the doorway.

"I said not in the house, mister," Joan says. Joan pauses in front of a mirror. She looks at her reflected image, considers. She hears strangely indistinct voices.

Doyle gives a final case log entry a couple of months later: "No further anomalous occurrences were recorded over the final observation period. Though we were not able to substantiate the subjects' claims of extraterrestrial experimentation, we are leaving satisfied that we have helped rectify the physical state of the deficient boy. The cause of the phenomenon will, for now, have to be left unexplained."

Epilogue

Officially, the O.S.I.R. has labeled this case unresolved. However, evidence seems to indicate the intervention of benevolent extraterrestrial beings who rewarded Kyle with a brother in return for providing source materials for this cloning experiment. And in doing so, they fulfilled his deepest wish. There's an old saying that goes, "Be careful what you wish for because you just might get it." While it may just sound like an ominous warning, surely it wasn't intended to stop us from wishing altogether.   **DAN AYKROYD**

AGRONOMY

The science of soil management and the production of field crops.

APPORTATION

Unexplained physical transference of objects from one place to the next without use of mechanical conveyances.

ASTROPHYSICS

The branch of astronomy that deals with the physical properties of celestial bodies and with the interaction between matter and radiation in the interior of celestial bodies and in interstellar space.

BIOPHYSICS

The branch of biology dealing with the study of biological structures and processes by means of the methods of physics.

CORPOREAL DUPLICATION

A form of reincarnation where a person, through subconscious compulsion, gains ethereal awareness of a past and synthesizes it into current life.

CRYPTOZOOLOGY

The study of the lore concerning legendary animals—such as Sasquatch, werewolves, Nessie—in order to verify the possibility of their existence.

ENERGETICS

The branch of physics that deals with energy; the physics of energy and its transformations.

EXTRATERRESTRIAL

Originating, existing or occurring outside the Earth and its atmosphere.

KINESIOLOGY

The study of muscles and their movements as applied to physical conditioning.

PARAPSYCHOLOGY

The branch of psychology that deals with the investigation of psychic phenomena—such as clairvoyance, extrasensory perception, telepathy—that are not immediately explained by known natural laws.

PHENOMENOLOGY

The study of all possible appearances in human experience, during which considerations of objective reality and of purely subjective response are temporarily left out of account; a philosophical movement based on phenomenology, originated around 1905 by Edmund Husserl.

PHONOLOGY

The science of speech sounds, including phonetics and phonemics.

PHOTOGRAMMETRY

The process of making surveys and maps through the use of photographs.

PLA

Portable linear accelerator. A last-resort use of technology employed by the military and the O.S.I.R. For use in measuring viability of nuclear warheads. A short-lived plume of radiation in an immediate area which sometimes eradicates paranormal activity.

PRECOGNITION

Clairvoyance relating to an event or state not yet experienced.

PSYCHOKINETIC

Abbreviation: PK. Movement of physical objects by the mind without use of physical means.

TELEKINESIS

Putting objects into motion without physical contact.

TELEMETRY

The science and technology of automatic measurements and transmission of data by wire, radio or other means from remote resources such as space vehicles to a receiving station for recording and analysis.

ULTRASONOGRAPHY

The diagnostic use of ultrasonic waves (acoustic frequencies above the range audible to the human ear) to visualize internal bodily structures and organs.